THE FILMS OF BUDDHADEB DASGUPTA

The Films of Buddhadeb Dasgupta

JOHN W. HOOD

Orient Longman

ORIENT LONGMAN PRIVATE LIMITED

Registered Office
3-6-752 Himayatnagar, Hyderabad 500 029 (A.P.), India
e-mail: hyd2_orlongco@sancharnet.in

Other Offices
Bangalore, Bhopal, Bhubaneshwar, Chandigarh, Chennai, Ernakulam, Guwahati, Hyderabad, Kolkata, Lucknow, Mumbai, New Delhi, Patna, Pune

First Published 2005

ISBN 81 250 2802 1

Typeset in 11/13 pt. Adobe Garamond

Typeset by
Scribe Consultants
New Delhi

Printed in India at
Chaman Enterprises
New Delhi

Published by
Orient Longman Private Limited
1/24 Asaf Ali Road
New Delhi 110 002
e-mail: olldel@del6.vsnl.net.in

Dedicated to
the memory of my mother,
who died while I was writing this book

Contents

Author's Note

I am very grateful to Orient Longman for bringing out this new edition of a book previously published under the title *Time and Dreams: The Films of Buddhadeb Dasgupta.* Much of the original text has been revised and two new chapters have been added.

The quotation that heads the final chapter comes from Buddhadeb Dasgupta in an interview with the author. The verses that head the other chapters are from translations of Dasgupta's poems, published in *Love and Other Forms of Death: Poems of Buddhadeb Dasgupta,* translated and edited by John W. Hood (Blackmuse, New Delhi, 1997).

Introduction

Buddhadeb Dasgupta is well known in Kolkata as a poet and somewhat less well known there as a novelist. He is eminently well known, throughout India and internationally, as a filmmaker. His films have won renown at most of the major film festivals of the world, and retrospectives of his work have been mounted in many cities throughout Asia, Europe, North America and South America.

Although it is easy to identify Dasgupta as an Indian filmmaker and, more specifically, a Bengali one, it is not such a simple matter to attach a defining label to his work. One can say that his films belong to Indian art cinema (or 'serious' or 'alternative' cinema as some would prefer to call it), as distinct from the popular or commercial cinema of what has come to be internationally known as Bollywood. Whereas similarity and even formula are basic to popular cinema, art cinema is not bound by the same kinds of commercial concerns, so allowing those who make it a freedom that has come to result in a wide diversity of artistic films (many of which have been commercially successful as well), but also militating against the emergence of any distinct Indian art film 'movement'.

Individual artistic freedom is something that the luminaries of serious cinema have jealously cherished. There has been no giant of the cinema to whom many or even some defer, nor has there been any 'school' whose particular ideals or values several or more might share. It can be said that Indian art cinema has a distinct regional basis, which has been in many cases a distinguishing factor, although such distinctions are usually little more than the obvious one of language, as well as, perhaps, the presentation of regional cultural features and customs; in some parts of India, landscape might also be a prominent distinctive feature. Yet, even within one region, the diversity among filmmakers tends to make such distinctions little more than cosmetic. The films of the late Aravindan and those of the contemporary Gopalakrishnan—two of the most accomplished of Indian filmmakers—are all set in Kerala, their language is Malayalam, the beauties of the Kerala landscape are prominent, and considerable deference is made to the history and culture, particularly the folk tradition, of that state. Yet it would be naive to suggest any real likeness between the films of Aravindan and those of Gopalakrishnan except for what, in the total perspective, are surface similarities.

The same is largely true of the art cinema in other regions of India, and certainly so in Bengal. Indeed, it might fairly be suggested that the best regional cinemas in India have been—and continue to be—those of Bengal and Kerala. The most internationally famous name in Indian cinema is Satyajit Ray, many of whose films are classics of Indian cinema; indeed, his *Apu* trilogy, *Charulata, Pratidwandi* and *Jana Aranya* would stand among the best in world cinema. However, whereas Ray was greatly admired by many younger filmmakers in Bengal, none of them deliberately set out to make films like his. A somewhat lesser filmmaker, though commanding a very strong cult following not only in Bengal but also in other parts of India as well as in Bangladesh, was Ritwick Ghatak. Prominent throughout his work—and one of the major reasons for his popularity—was a reverence for the idea of 'Bengal'—its land, its language and culture, its traditions. Yet while that reverence has been shared, perhaps just as passionately, by successive filmmakers, none has taken it up in his work to any significant extent. The other 'elder' of Bengali cinema is Mrinal Sen, clearly the most daringly experimental of the three, whose contribution to Indian cinema has been notable in a number of ways.

However, it is difficult to discern his influence—in ideology, in the use of cinema language, in narrative treatment—in the work of the younger generation of Bengali filmmakers.

Dasgupta owes an apparent debt to these important pioneers of Indian art cinema. His work very obviously avoids the sentiment of Ritwick Ghatak's films and is far better crafted, with a much more careful concern for perceptual precision and economy of expression. Dasgupta has never shared to the same extent Satyajit Ray's debt to literature, in the sense that Ray very much represented literature as cinema, nor has he experienced a similar need to give to narrative the detailed importance that it has in most of Ray's films. Also missing from his work is the provocative social 'relevance' and the intensity of drama that characterises much of the work of Mrinal Sen.

The most notable of the 'younger generation' of Bengali filmmakers, all of them now middle-aged, are Utpalendu Chakravarty, Nabyendu Chatterjee, Goutam Ghose, Aparna Sen and Buddhadeb Dasgupta. All of them, except Dasgupta, have a predilection for cinema in which deference is paid to traditional notions of narrative and dialogue, and in many ways their films are similar, but in many other ways—thematic interests and philosophical standpoints in particular—they pursue their own courses.

The importance given to the presentation of story is also prominent in the work of Dasgupta's contemporaries outside of Bengal. Two Mumbai-based directors, Shyam Benegal and Govind Nihalani, are established masters of narrative cinema. The filmmakers of Kerala have for many years been presenting films with a notably regional ambience and pace and in a style further removed from the more conventional style of Benegal and Nihalani, yet following their own lines in the metaphorical treatment of narrative.

Dasgupta is arguably one of the most strikingly individual filmmakers in India, if only for his distinctly minimalist approach. Dialogue in his films is very sparse, while the visual as an agent of communication is elevated much more than is the case with most other filmmakers, with the most probable exceptions being the Kerala directors, Jayaraj and Gopalakrishnan. But it is the poetic nature of his films—the cinematic use of such elements of poetry as metaphor and suggestion and the compression of images—along with the foregrounding (occasional in the early works, frequent in the later ones) of the seemingly extraneous, paradoxical or absurd, that give his films their distinction from those of any other Indian filmmaker.

As is common amongst the art directors of India, Buddhadeb Dasgupta writes the scripts of all his films; he has also written the music for some of them. The content of his films has been inspired by the rich fount of modern Bengali literature, which has offered a starting point for his screenplays, most of which are in the Bengali language, though two are in Hindi. However, it is important to stress that someone else's story is very often only the launching pad for one of Dasgupta's films, very few of which bear a close resemblance to their literary source.

It cannot be said that Dasgupta's films, nor those of any maker of art cinema, have been immensely popular in India; indeed, being widely appreciated is the province of Indian popular cinema, which breeds on its established and extensive marketing and distribution networks. Nevertheless, Dasgupta is held in exceptionally high regard by the many enthusiasts of good cinema in the major cities and towns of India. Moreover, his international reputation cannot be underestimated.

A criticism that has been levelled quite fairly at Indian cinema—and at cinema in many other parts of the world, for that matter—is that it too often keeps on coming up with more of the same. Year after year many films are made which would suggest that Indian cinema is stagnating, not knowing where to go. It is the works of filmmakers like Buddhadeb Dasgupta that give hope that there are, indeed, new directions to pursue, and that they may be pursued with artistic value and human significance.

ONE

Dreams for New Seasons

For so long you had done so much for your students,
prepared so many questions,
put so many problems before them, and
anxiously they would answer yes, and
anxiously they would answer no,
and the rubber road, gradually getting smaller,
goes into your pocket.
Then suddenly one day, with a determined grin and sealed lips,
you wipe away like magic from the shiny blackboard
curves, equations, numbers, statistics, names,
and overwhelmed by passion you fly from the classroom,
quickly pull on your boots and walk off alone,
on your shoulder that old camera of yours and the red filter.

(from *Cinema*)

The makers of independent India—men and women who had a vision of a nation free and equal among all the nations of the world—had their dream materialise (or start to materialise, as some would stress) when Buddhadeb Dasgupta was three years old. Though not exactly one of 'midnight's children', he was one of a generation who inherited early in their lives a country that was the fruit of a dream, a dream dreamed by their elders, many of whom were unable to relish the moment, given the categorical nature of the workings of the god of death, who makes the elderly fall asleep for ever as surely as he snuffs out the candles of those exuberant and zealous youths forced to mount the gallows of a foreign power. Dasgupta's generation did not inherit a nation fashioned by the Treaty of This or That, but claimed a birthright clothed in lofty philosophy and idealism illuminated by a mythology soaked in the blood of martyrs. They were unusual in that they had, for the most part, no actual experience of that from which this legacy had emanated. They took the dream of others in their stride, many of them utilising it to engender dreams of their own and make them proper.

It was in the maelstrom of international war, 'Quit India' passions and burgeoning communal tensions in Bengal that Buddhadeb Dasgupta, the third of nine children, was born in February 1944, in Anara near Puruliya. His father, Tarakanta, was employed as a doctor by the railways, a position that obliged him to move about from place to place, and so the family was never able to settle in any one town for more than three or four years. It was not until after Buddhadeb was sent to Calcutta at the age of twelve to attend the Dinabandhu School in Howrah that he was able to identify with a particular place, but although the city would be focal to the later artist's early films, it could hardly be said to have been indispensable to his creativity.

Although their rather peripatetic life was a handicap for the Dasgupta children in establishing a permanent and lasting circle of friends, it did give them the opportunity to develop a relatively broad vision of Bengal and to mix with a range of other children from a diversity of backgrounds. The Vaidya caste, to which the Dasguptas formally belonged, and the status of his profession counted for very little in the values of Tarakanta, a man who embraced with commitment the idealism of Mahatma Gandhi and his teachings on social justice, social responsibility and social equality. Most of his patients, wherever he was employed, were poor people from the lowest levels of society, and he quite deliberately encouraged his own children to mix and play with theirs, to invite them home and to accept their invitations and to share their food and sweets with them.

Dasgupta has an indelible memory of his father's coming home from the hospital on a sad January day in 1948 and informing the children of the assassination of the Father of the Nation. Tarakanta spoke movingly to them about Gandhi's dream for Indian independence which so much presupposed his ideals of self-sacrifice, ideals that directed the life of the railways doctor and the values which he sought to instil into his children. In the years immediately after independence, the family lived in Kharagpur, a railway junction town in southern Bengal, where a substantial part of the population were Telengi refugees from Andhra Pradesh. These people were extremely poor and lived in horribly overcrowded conditions in makeshift housing, which Buddhadeb and his brothers and sisters remember well, as they were playmates of the children of some of these deprived people. They remember too the intensity of the suffering of these people, including quite often the deaths of their children. Needless to say, the Telengis had very little if any money for such luxuries as medicine or medical treatment, yet Dr. Dasgupta often paid out of his own pocket for their medicines and his wife often made barley soup for those who had no food. Kharagpur was quite important as a railway town, so medical facilities there were relatively good. However, at Manindragarh in Madhya Pradesh, where Dr. Dasgupta was transferred for a time, facilities were less than basic, and Tarakanta had to be a medical Jack-of-all-trades, obliged to perform all manner of operations he had not been formally trained in and having, more often than not, to improvise techniques and procedures. At Kharagpur, he had had the professional support of some four or five other doctors, but in Manindragarh he was the only one. At least in a professional sense, his life was a perpetual struggle against adversity, and although they were comparatively well-off, the size of the family supported by a railway doctor's wage meant that they lived far from the lap of luxury. To their children, then, the Dasgupta parents were a constant example of self-sacrifice, educating them in the belief that everyone has the responsibility to do something for the good of their country. Eventually, there came a time when the dream had soured somewhat in the realisation that independence had not really brought about all that had been so enthusiastically promised, yet the family's idealism never abated in any way at all.

The era of the freedom movement in India gave to the young of the country a plethora of heroes, and for the young Buddhadeb—as for most of his generation in Bengal—Gandhi was but one, even second in importance to the leader of the Indian National Army, Subhas Chandra Bose. Bose, known reverentially by Bengalis as Netaji, was one with the rest of India's freedom fighters in his dream for an independent India and, like so many of them, he came to a violent and premature end. What set him off from the others, however, was his especially adventurous manner of resistance to colonial rule, providing in his militarist endeavour what many saw as the alternative to Gandhi's non-violent non-cooperation. To a large extent, the first generation of independent Indians inherited the tension between the lofty idealism of the Mahatma and the effectual activism of Netaji. While the adult Dasgupta would have no hesitation in describing himself as a man of non-violence, Buddhadeb the boy was greatly attracted to the swashbuckling image exuded by the man of adventure. In time the appeal wore thin, and despite the pervasive reality of violence in his world and the depressing realisation that total non-violence can never be more than a dream, the influence of his Gandhian father prevailed.

Buddhadeb's schooldays were exceptionally happy, and he is quick to recognise his teachers as the reason for this. He describes them as having been loving, devoted and self-sacrificing. The syllabus was rarely completed because, having succumbed to the universal schoolboy endeavour to side-track them, the teachers spent a lot of time talking about the ideals of the freedom movement, the men and women who had worked so selflessly for the country's independence, and the actualities of life in the new India. All this education off the beaten track was invaluable in inculcating in the young an idealistic awareness of what it was to be Indian in the modern world. But the teachers did not just talk. They served as an object lesson to their students when, after school was finished, they went off into the slums to give their services free of charge to the children of the poor.

Thus, from home and from school, Dasgupta imbibed a vital concern for social justice, service to the community, care for the welfare of others, and the value of self-sacrifice. Indeed, the family structure itself was a significant factor in the moral growth of the Dasgupta children. While their father earned a relatively generous salary, he also spent a lot—not only on the very poor among his patients, but also on his parents and the joint family set-up that he had inherited. His own father died when he was only seven, and he and his sister were brought up by an uncle along with his own thirteen children. He reared Tarakanta as his eldest son, and naturally, Tarakanta had to assume responsibility for a large family on the death of his uncle. Moreover, the fact that his own nuclear family was large meant that everything had to be rationed and shared, from sweets to books to outings. Yet this practical need too was morally educative in that it militated against self-seeking and demanded concern for others.

The practical lessons were given some reinforcement from religion, in so far as their mother would read to them stories from the Puranas and they would hear their father singing Brahmo hymns soon after he rose very early each morning. However, they were not a conventionally religious Hindu family. God was essential to the family's life, but in a strictly spiritual sense, not in any formalistic, ritual or sectarian way. Of course, important ceremonies such as marriage were practised according to traditional rites, while major festivals such as the popular Durga Puja were celebrated for their festive value and without recourse to ritual. Caste had no place in their lives either. Dr. Dasgupta treated people whose sole distinction was illness, and just as caste and communal distinctions were irrelevant to his profession, they were also irrelevant to the life of his family. Indeed, his children were never really aware of caste until later in secondary school. Tarakanta Dasgupta was a friend to his children, never an authoritarian *pater familias*, and the egalitarian attitude of his family was an essential basis for the democratic outlook with which Buddhadeb would grow up.

As children, Buddhadeb and his friends passionately embraced the new and independent democracy, being overtly proud to be Indian and wanting to show to the world that they and their country were of value. They had grand expectations, but these lasted little more than a decade, for by the early sixties it started to become apparent to them that things were not going according to promise. Having started out with great faith, they had to suffer the awareness of increasingly evident corruption and dishonesty; while so many had died for the freedom of the country, many others were beginning to exploit it for personal profit. This realisation was a particularly bitter one in the light of the memory of the imprisonment, torture and death that countless patriots had suffered under the British in the cause of India's freedom. As a student in the sixties, when the leftist trend in Bengal was becoming manifest, particularly amongst the younger generation, Dasgupta came to blame the country's political leaders for the decline that was setting in, a decline that was not merely political but one which he saw as threatening the cultural heritage of India. Quite in addition to things going wrong economically and socially, something of a cultural transition was to be discerned, as commercial entertainment grew to the detriment of the traditional performances that once had been so popular on the streets of Calcutta. In this realisation of decline is the well-spring of *Bagh Bahadur* (1989) and *Tahader Katha* (1992).

The leftist leaning that evolved quite readily out of the family's egalitarian values and its strong concern for social justice, along with its liberal religious ideas, found cultural company in the freedom of expression and intellectual exploration provided by the quite dominant role that literature and music played in Dasgupta's formative years. Readings from classical literature were offered to him from the Puranas and the Indian epics by his mother and his maternal grandmother, while his father would recite to him extensive passages from the Upanishads and the Bhagavadgita and translate them into

Bengali for him. Buddhadeb's mother was a pianist, and all of her children learned some piano and were encouraged to sing. Some of them developed a notable talent for music, especially Bishwadeb, who later composed the music for some of Buddhadeb's films.

Later in life, Dasgupta would acknowledge the value of this early musical training in inculcating in him an acute sense of rhythm, so important in developing a sense of balance and perspective in creative art. While some Western music was played, the family most enjoyed Rabindrasangeet, the songs of Tagore, which they often sang together even before the children could understand the meaning of many of the lyrics.

Of course, the influence of Tagore was almost universal in middle-class Bengali homes. The family had a select library, and while Buddhadeb studiously avoided Tagore's essays and lectures, he took immense delight in his poetry and prose fiction, and in time moved on to the works of Bankimchandra, Trailokyanath Bandyopadhyay, Upendra Kishore, Sukumar Ray and Saratchandra Chatterjee.

It was in the early sixties that Buddhadeb consciously confronted the ideas of the writers of the Kallol movement, which took its name from a literary journal of the same name (meaning 'wave' or 'billow'), committed to the publication of more 'modern', heterodox and non-establishment literature. His initial attraction away from the established masters, Tagore in particular, was largely due to his two maternal uncles who lived in the house of his grandmother. One of them, the noted poet Samarenda Sengupta, who became one of the editors of *Krittivas*, was the editor of the literary periodical *Kavipatra*, an eminent forum for poets. Whenever Dasgupta went to visit his grandmother, he was usually party to the discussions his uncles and their friends would be having about poetry. Thus, he came to think about Kallol ideas and, in time, started to develop a critical assessment of Tagore. It was also around this time that he started reading Buddhadeb Bose, Premendra Mitra, Achintya Kumar Sengupta, Tarashankar Bandyopadhyay and Manik Bandyopadhyay, coming to realise that Bengali literature was indeed much more than Tagore. Moreover, these writers were perceived to be 'modern' and therefore attractive to a young man in a way that Tagore could no longer be. (Although Tagore died as recently as 1941, he lived half his life in the nineteenth century and, the Kallol proponents might argue, carried through to his last days ideals and values that were essentially of a bygone era.) The alienation from Tagore was hastened by the fact that by his mid-teens, Dasgupta had started writing poetry of his own, and he was serious enough about it to realise that he would have to turn away from Tagore or else risk becoming a disciple, even a copier. The divorcement, in fact, was completed by the passion that he was developing for the contemporary master, Jibanananda Das (1899–1954).

Jibanananda's contribution to Bengali literature was in many ways as momentous as that of the new English poetry of imagists such as T.S. Eliot and Ezra Pound, in that they were committed to the view that the content of poetry has no limitation in human experience. As were Eliot and Pound, Jibanananda was remarkably original in his technique, challenging his reader with the depth and power of his images and writing verse that was germane to the times in which he lived. In a sense, he was a spokesman for an age and its sadness, writing of life in a world that had been fashioned by world wars and depression, and in a Bengal that had been marked by the Famine of 1943, the Partition that was the terrible cost of Independence, and the questionable directions that the newly independent nation was starting to take. Young readers of Buddhadeb's generation found his immediacy appealing and were at once profoundly moved and challenged by the notions of the inevitability of transience, the frequent helplessness of the individual against forces beyond his power, and the pervasive sadness of life.

Also of great importance to Buddhadeb were the three great novelists of the name Bandyopadhyay—Bibhutibhushan, Tarashankar and Manik. While in many ways their writings are quite distinct, their works bring the common man and woman into prominence, representing them in a realistic style that strongly appealed to Dasgupta. The attraction of these writers lay in the scope of their world and in the immediacy of its torments, its passions and its ordinariness. Like Jibanananda, they were products of a generation that had been shattered by the cataclysmic events of twentieth century history, conveying candidly to a younger generation the true nature of its inheritance.

Literature and music were the arts that dominated Buddhadeb's childhood, while a passion for painting came a little later. Modern Bengali painters such as Abanindranath and Ganganendranath Tagore, Nandalal Bose and Jamini Ray had a marked impression on him, but he was particularly moved by the paintings of Rabindranath Tagore. This may seem somewhat ironic after his conscious move away from the literary works of Rabindranath, except that it must be remembered that Tagore did not really take up painting until the last decades of his life, and in that medium his work was often marked by a stunning modernity and originality. Buddhadeb dabbled in the fine arts himself, first with water colours and then with collage, but he was sadly overwhelmed by his inability to do what he wanted to do. As consolation for this ineptitude, he spent a lot of time in the sixties and seventies indulging his love of the fine arts by visiting galleries, while he also benefited from the firm friendship of a number of young painters from whom he learned much about colour, light, composition, framing and perspective—knowledge that would have a significant transferability when he came to make films.

He never experienced a great attraction to dance, except, perhaps, for folk dance. As a boy in Kharagpur, he saw much of the tiger dance, which had its origins among the common people of Andhra, and which is the focus of *Bagh Bahadur*. He and his friends used to play at dancing in that style, acting out whatever they lacked the ability to dance. Folk dance is essentially secular and humanist, of the people and earthy, characteristics that would be significant in *Uttara* (2000).

So, after a boyhood saturated by Rabindrasangeet and the verse and prose fiction of Tagore, the significant cultural influences on Dasgupta as a burgeoning adult were, to some extent, folk or popular dance and, to a very large extent, fine art and literature that were vitally modern and which had the common people as a major focus. But although his education and family upbringing nurtured a social outlook that would naturally align itself with the left in any political expression, political activity was not a part of his life much before his undergraduate days at Calcutta University, where he eventually earned a Master's degree in economics. His embracing the general thrust of the ideology of the left met with no opposition from his parents who, like so many others, had become disillusioned and sceptical with the road the Congress was taking and had themselves come to see some hope in the Communist Party of India. Indeed, Dasgupta well remembers how bitterly upset his father was at the news of the first major schism in the CPI in 1964. His own political beliefs continued for some time to centre around Marxism, but from the mid-seventies he started to become alienated from politics, unable to cope in his maturity with the violence and corruption so often associated with it. *Duratwa* (1978) and *Grihayuddha* (1982) may be said to represent a somewhat mellow reassessment of the enthusiasms and excesses of youth—his own, perhaps, as much as anyone else's.

The Naxalbari agitation—a neo-Maoist revolutionary movement under the auspices of the Communist Party of India (Marxist-Leninist), formed in 1967—attracted Dasgupta from the outset, due largely to his daily encounters with radical passions and programmes in the university. It was very much a youth movement, with a philosophy that appealed because of its concentration on the pressing needs of the poor and marginalised, particularly in the rural sector. Naxalism started with great zest, trumpeting a lofty idealism, and Dasgupta was readily attracted to that which promised to deliver the poor and oppressed from corruption and exploitation and to punish the perpetrators of greed and inequity. Moreover, many of the younger generation of middle-class Bengalis had started to become impatient with the established Communist parties, the CPI and the CPI (Marxist), who had submitted to the democratic system and had been—as many judged—corrupted by it. The young radicals easily became irritable waiting for actual reform through the ballot-box. Thus, the provocative activism of the Naxalites was inviting and inspirational. However, as the more mature Dasgupta came to see, the ideology, aims and methods of the Naxalites were romanticised beyond all practicability. For one reason or another, many came to lose faith in the movement, while many others became fearful and ran away. The movement failed, as Dasgupta saw it, because it chose to burn bridges rather than build them. There were the predictable internecine squabbles that exacerbated the decline in the movement's effectiveness, but ultimately there was the simple impossibility of success when confronting a modern political system with its plentiful arms, trained forces and established infrastructures.

Nethertheless, the brutality of the establishment in crushing Naxalism could not have been ignored by any sensitive artist touched by those turbulent times, and Dasgupta's three films with their roots in the Naxalbari ferment, *Duratwa, Grihayuddha* and *Andhi Gali*, subtly yet significantly recollect some of the extremes of police thuggery. Numerous thousands of Naxalites were killed or tortured, and many of the victims of this official violence were merely sympathisers, or Naxalites' family members. There were secret killings; there were the killings of 'escapees' from the jails; there was poisoning of jail food; there were the shootings of Naxalite youths in front of their families; and there were the 'runaway' executions such as the one depicted in *Andhi Gali*. While similar brutality perpetrated by the British in earlier decades might have been shocking, it could be explained as part and parcel of imperialism. But what Dasgupta found perplexing was the savagery of Indian against Indian in a free and democratic state.

There are evident autobiographical echoes in this trio of films, such as the university context in *Duratwa*. Bijan, in *Grihayuddha*, is based on quite a pathetic character whom Dasgupta knew, a young man with excellent academic potential who was an extraordinarily effective mobiliser and leader, wielding tremendous influence over both the students and staff of the Commerce Department at Calcutta University, and who discontinued his studies in order to devote himself to the cause. He came from a very wealthy family, and so was able to escape a police round-up of many of his friends. In time, he was persuaded to sign for the police a statement of disavowal repudiating his involvement with the Naxalites and was sent overseas by his family. Some years later, he was met by Buddhadeb and some of their friends when he visited Calcutta as a dealer in gems, noticeably cowed and reserved. A potential revolutionary hero had become a trader in baubles—a quisling, but a pitiable one. Behind the making of these three films is Dasgupta's abiding repugnance at the fact that so many of the Naxalbari leadership were middle-class intellectuals who gave orders while at the same time keeping themselves out of physical danger.

Despite the extinguishing of the Naxalite flame, the initial ideological concern and compassion for the poor and dispossessed remained with many, including Dasgupta (and was a significant factor behind the making of *Neem Annapurna* in 1979). And in addition to Naxalism, there was also the marked and enthusiastic ideological commitment of Dasgupta and his peers to the emancipation of Bangladesh. Partition was less than a quarter of a century old, and many West Bengalis had roots in former East Bengal (Dasgupta's grandfathers had both been born there) and fostered the dream that one day the two lands would be reunited, a dream that is seen to fade in *Tahader Katha*. But in the Bangladesh struggle there was also a connection with Naxalite concerns, in that the war represented the perennial struggle for justice of the dispossessed and of the fight for freedom of the oppressed.

An independent Bangladesh was born, but not without the arbitrary murdering by government forces of Maoists in Dhaka; in India Naxalism was brutally crushed; and with the Emergency —'a heinous excuse for outrage that filled me with loathing'— Indira Gandhi gave India a taste of ruthless authoritarianism. Hopes for reform, for revewal, for re-strengthening had been dashed, categorically it would have seemed. Yet that intense and pervasive pessimism did not by any means militate against the artistic urge of Dasgupta, who continued to write poems and think seriously about cinema, and was 'just dying to make my own feature film.'

In one of his essays, Dasgupta writes of a heated discussion between his parents over the quality or otherwise of a Pramathesh Barua film they had just been to see. He was thus able to appreciate at an early age that cinema had the power to be controversial, at least in his own family. However, the attraction cinema had for Buddhadeb was more direct and was exerted a few years later when the family was living in Howrah and Buddhadeb was starting out as a secondary school student.

The local picture-house had a 10 a.m. to noon show every Sunday to which Buddhadeb and his brother, Jaydeb, were allowed to go, accompanied, once every month or two. Buddhadeb saw his first film here, a Tarzan movie. This treat was followed by *Treasure Island*, then a film about the Kurukshetra War in the *Mahabharata*, and then Chaplin's *Gold Rush*. Not surprisingly (and with due deference to Chaplin), cinema was not taken seriously in the Dasgupta family except by the boys, their elders seeing it as mere entertainment and somewhat frivolous at that. But Buddhadeb and Jaydeb had become votaries at this new temple, their worship even obliging them to lie to their parents in order to sneak off secretly on a Sunday when they were forbidden. As happens in all good films, however, they were eventually caught out and punished by their father.

Dasgupta's awakening to cinema was roughly concurrent with his formative years as a poet. He started writing poetry when he was fifteen, and after about a year he was encouraged by the appearance of some of his poems in print at the time when he was starting to think seriously about cinema.

In his senior high school years, his uncle started taking him to films shown by the Calcutta Film Society and, to counter the fare offered by the local movie house of past days, he now saw a Bergman retrospective. When he had become a university student and had joined the Society as well as all the other film societies of Calcutta, he saw a Chaplin retrospective, which he still remembers as masterly, and soon became aware of the works of Kurosawa and Mizoguchi, the latter of whom 'really had a great impact on me'.

He took his first step towards filmmaking in 1967 when he entered a competition for script-writing organised by the Federation of Film Societies. The panel of judges, which included Mrinal Sen and Satyajit Ray, recognised as the best script Buddhadeb Dasgupta's *Samayer Kacche* and, as part of the prize, the film was to be shot, but due to the predictable shortage of money, shooting lasted only two days before it was abandoned.

It may seem a little odd that a young man who was already a published poet and had won a prize that purported to recognise his potential as a filmmaker should become a teacher of economics, yet that was the career on which Dasgupta embarked in 1968. He lasted for four years at it. While lecturing threatened to dull his creativity, the urge to make a feature film of his own was becoming more and more intense, so in 1971 he took leave from the university to try himself out in the career of his dreams by making shorts and documentaries. Encouraged by what he saw as his potential, he resigned from the university in 1976.

While many, including Dasgupta himself, believe that he started making feature films some seven or eight years later than he might have, the importance of the years of self-trained apprenticeship between his first short film and *Duratwa* in 1978 cannot in any way be underestimated, for it was during this time that he learned and practised the invaluable technical lessons about filmmaking that would form the essential basis of the artist's stock-in-trade when he came to make features. His self-training started in the late sixties, when he would go to the film studios at Tollygunge and watch established directors at work. It was here that a veteran cameraman, Deoji Bhai, befriended him and got him started with an old camera, some lenses and some lengths of leftover film, and gave him the basic instructions on camera operation.

These Tollygunge sessions were also valuable in teaching him about the effective handling of actors. Buddhadeb remembers himself in those days as shy and painfully introverted, wondering how he could ever communicate orally as effectively as he apparently could in writing. He had to fight this perceived deficiency and learn the importance of approaching each actor independently and individually. He asserts quite strongly that he has never had any trouble with any actor. He has also had remarkable success with children, such as the seven-year-old little girl in *Neem Annapurna* who would often become self-conscious and frightened, obliging the director to take her on his knee, give her a cuddle or offer her some chocolate, and then get on with the job of shooting the film.

Away from Tollygunge and during his self-apprenticeship, Dasgupta learned early that the artist is not always a free agent. This is the focal idea in his *Seet Grismer Smriti*, (1982). Most of his short film and documentary work was sponsored, and it was the ideals of the sponsor rather than the creativity of the artist that were predominant. 'They used to feed us with ideas, and I was largely just a cameraman,' he remembers. Yet at the same time, he learned much about camera work, particularly in making newsreel footage, which often necessitated quick thinking and immediate action.

> All these films gave me much scope to learn about the technical aspects of filmmaking, such as framing and composition and, especially, training my eyes for the camera. It also taught me to know lenses and filters like my own fingers.

Dasgupta had no teacher or any formal training, nor did he ever serve as an assistant to any established director. It was while making short films that he taught himself the potential of the camera and a good deal about the art of editing. He has never really suffered from hesitancy. Once, when shooting a documentary on a remote island in the Ganges Delta, the cameraman got sick. If the film were not shot in time, the sponsor would lose a lot of money, so Buddhadeb did the shooting himself.

> There were circumstances that forced me to do many things—to edit, record the sound, shoot the film. Yet no filmmaker should ever work without mastery over all the technical aspects of film making.

Thus, he came to make *Duratwa* with a considerable degree of confidence and self-assurance. Needless to say, he had to cope with a marked paucity of funds, and to supplement his grant from the West Bengal government he had to importune his friends. He also learned to plan his films in such a way that their demands could be met by a small budget. There was obviously no scope for the spectacular, and there was no room in his casts for named actors: most of his players were newcomers and so commanded a considerably smaller fee.

Duratwa was a remarkably promising start to what continues to be a very successful career. Within the context of the grand dream of a new India, Buddhadeb, like millions of others, dreamed dreams, suffered the disappointment of their being broken from time to time, yet quite unlike millions of others he pursued the one dominant, overriding dream of saying the things he wanted to say through the medium he had resolved to master.

The endeavour to sketch something of the family background of Buddhadeb Dasgupta is not intended to speak at all of the man, but of some of the values and attitudes that might be seen to have influenced his films. Similarly, the historical developments in the India of his formative years are in no way recounted as the context of a personal engagement but rather as representing a challenge to which any responsible citizen, not just a creative artist, might be expected in some way to respond.

The self-sacrificing service to the poor and to the nation exemplified by his father and his teachers notwithstanding, it cannot be said that Buddhadeb Dasgupta's films beat the drum for the downtrodden or wave the flag for national integrity, nor can his films in any way at all be described as political or ideological. Nevertheless, the humble and the ordinary are very often focal, usually in tension with a world which in some way or another is seen to have gone wrong. Whereas innocence and simplicity are often characteristic of the protagonists, the antagonists might be seen to be simple abstracts such as corruption, self-interest, commercialisation of culture, state-inspired bigotry and individual freedom, to suggest a few examples, but a slight scratching of the surface will usually reveal an antagonism that has a profound and far-reaching complexity. Moreover, 'humble' and 'ordinary' are not necessarily determined by class. The struggling protagonist might be a well-off urban professional like Nabin in *Lal Darja* or a remnant of the rural aristocracy such as Shashanka in *Phera*. What is of interest is not class conflict but the struggles of individuals against forces seemingly beyond their control, as they endeavour to come to terms with an identity or a destiny or some kind of perception of reality. And in all his films, the poetic notion of dream has a prominence rarely if ever to be found in the 'political' or 'social' film.

TWO

The Frailty of Commitment

Eight-thirty at night: people come out of the cinemas,
leap onto trams and go off home.
A fire engine passes, the riot squad, a police car.
From the distance comes the sound
of pipe-gun and rifle fire. Just wait,
tomorrow morning
a number of nineteen to twenty-three-year-old corpses
will be lying on either side of the road.
Eleven-thirty: the last bulletin comes onto the radio.
Some piddling reader indifferently announces
a five-year plan
for worker and peasant self-sufficiency.
The hungry yawn yet again.

(*Night*)

Buddhadeb Dasgupta came to make his first feature film, *Duratwa*, in 1978. *Duratwa* along with *Grihayuddha* (1982) and *Andhi Gali* (1984) may be said to form a loose trilogy in that the three films deal centrally with the notion of the betrayal of idealism and the reassessment of values and redefinition of identity. The trilogy is loose because its parts are not sequential and are, as far as plot is concerned, entirely self-contained. *Duratwa* is about marriage, divorce and the hope of reconciliation; *Grihayuddha* has a detective-story focus; and *Andhi Gali* is a matrimonial tragedy. Common to all three films, however, is the fundamental concern with social identity and ideological commitment.

These notions had a notable contemporaneousnes at the time the films were made. The three are all set against the background of the Naxalite movement—the neo-Maoist agitation that rocked Bengal and then other parts of India following the schism in the Marxist wing of the Comunist Party of India in 1969. The protagonist of each film is a former Naxalite, one theoretically dedicated to the building of a better world and willing, if necessary, to lay down his life in the endeavour to bring it about, but who has been ideologically set adrift and returned, with neither deliberate design nor cathartic submission, to his middle-class moorings. The three films depict the dimming of the flame of idealism and, in its place, the kindling of the embers of respectability, fanned by the ardour of acquisitiveness.

The Naxalite background in each film is more convenient than vital, but as the notion of class consciousness was fundamental to the idealism of the Naxalites, it provides a ready basis on which to develop ideas about social conscience. There are, of course, obvious external elements indicating a certain period of time, but in general these are too peripheral to threaten to date the films at all. Particularity of time does not govern their core concern; hence, Naxalism is a springboard, not a context.

Duratwa ('Distance'), based on a story by Sirshendu Mukhopadhyay, was a promising start for the thirty-four-year-old Dasgupta, winning Film Forum's Dada Saheb Phalke Award for the best maiden feature film in 1978, the National 'Silver Lotus' Award for the best (Bengali) regional feature film in 1979, and in the same year, the Special Critics' Award at the Locarno Film Festival. It was also shown in 1979 at film festivals in Berlin, Chicago, Nantes and Mannheim.

On one level, *Duratwa* is a simple yet poignant tale of love. Anjali (played by Mamata Shankar) and Mandar (Pradip

Mukherjee) are introduced by a mutual friend, Amit (Bijon Bhattacharya). To start with, their liaison is academic—Mandar is a lecturer in political science and Anjali is a postgraduate student in the same college—but in time they grow fond of one another and eventually marry. Anjali might be seen as a victim of fate, however, for in an innocent yet transient relationship with Amit before meeting Mandar she had become pregnant. Amit had shown little care, apparently, for Anjali, and no desire at all for the child, suggesting abortion as the sensible solution. While Anjali is determined to bear the child, she is unable to stop herself from falling in love with Mandar. She is naive rather than deceitful in keeping her secret from him until after their marriage, frightened of her dream being shattered, but after intense mental suffering she confesses her condition to Mandar, insisting on the irrelevance of identifying the father. She makes her apology as selflessly as she can, giving Mandar total freedom to seek a divorce, and goes back to her father's house. Mandar has no trouble getting his divorce, and in time meets Nandini (Snigdha Banerjee) with whom he forms a regular relationship, although it is a relationship that brings him no genuine happiness. Early in the film, a chance meeting in the street with Anjali is enough to prod Mandar into the realisation that his persistent loneliness has really been an unconscious yearning for her, and so the film ends with the two of them seeming to embark on a new, wiser and more mature relationship.

The narrative's presentation is by no means as simple as its content. It would not have suited Dasgupta's purpose to have taken the conventionally chronological approach to the unfolding of the story, and instead he has cut, interchanged and spliced the present and the past to create an essentially holistic perspective of narrative time, making very effective use of the inevitable flashback and occasional repetition to enhance his purpose. Of course, *Duratwa* is considerably more than a simple love story, and it is through an exploration of the film's title that the intricacies and subtle perspectives of the film may be discerned. It is, indeed, the notion of 'distance', with its ramifications of detachment, alienation and remoteness, that gives to the narrative an integral significance governed by a poetic perspective.

There are several specific ways in which the notion of distance helps to create greater connotational relationships between the various elements of the film. Particularly, we might note the distance that exists between so many of the characters, the central one between Anjali and Mandar being fundamental. All the other emanations of distance—the distance between the ideal and the actual, the distance between the individual and the world in which he or she lives, the distances between the past, the present and the future—provide a poetic or symbolic context for the reinforcement of this central notion.

Basic to the film is the distance between Anjali and Mandar, a distance which the camera establishes quite early in the piece when Mandar steps out from a tea-house onto the street as an Anglo-Indian woman (incidentally representing a culture somewhat remote from Mandar's) passes by. His eyes follow her and, as she merges into the distance, Anjali appears and comes towards him. The distance is narrowed and dissolved as the two briefly exchange greetings, and then the camera, through Mandar's eyes, follows Anjali as she gradually moves into a long shot in the central background. Thus the separation between them is visually established. In fact, the Anjali-Mandar theme throughout the film is seen as a balanced perspective of their original coming together, in courtship and marriage, and their eventual estrangement. As the narrative unfolds, largely through the actions and perceptions of Mandar, we come to see how the resurgence of attraction reduces the distance between them.

Our awareness of their growing alienation is well enhanced by the camera, as in an early scene where Anjali brings tea to Mandar in their bedroom. The camera moves from the reclining Mandar to the standing Anjali, suggesting, albeit temporarily, a precarious and unreal dominance, yet even more clearly symbolising the gap between them and the two different planes that their psyches are currently inhabiting. Other bedroom scenes show a simple picture of Mandar asleep, with Anjali drawn and anxious. In the scene just before she makes her confession, her hand is shown reaching out to but not quite touching him. And then, when she ultimately leaves the house, the gap is fundamental to the camera's interest: in a high shot we look down on her packing; there is a level shot of the same and then she leaves, with Mandar, his back to her, looking over the balcony. As he turns to look at her once more, we are impressed by the eloquence of the camera as it shows, from above, her distressed descent of the staircase.

There is distance between Mandar and Nandini, too. She, it would seem, wants the formality of a husband while he, without appreciating the full significance of it, wants a replacement for Anjali. Nandini has a simplistic perception of the differences between them, observing that while he likes to write poetry, she likes only 'action and food', so suggesting that there is little chance of intimacy developing here. Then there is an emotive, pitiable distance between Nandini and her mother, a sad figure who appears to suffer from some mental or nervous debilitation. Wanting privacy with Mandar, Nandini resents an intrusion into the room by her mother and orders the old woman to go away, cruelly accentuating her desire for distance between them by throwing a tea cup at her.

Despite their brief physical intimacy that provides the source of the film's drama, there is also a gulf between Anjali and Amit, a pragmatist, who has no sympathy for Anjali's maternal desires. Their alienation from one another stems from Amit's suggestion of abortion. The alienation is aided, ironically, by the growing familiarity between Anjali and Mandar. And while Amit and Mandar apparently had once been friends, a gap has sprung up between them, for the film opens with Mandar trying to get in touch with one Nripati in order to find out where Amit is now living. By the time Mandar has visited Amit at his more than comfortable flat, with all the trappings of bourgeois acquisitiveness (and where an almost comically paradoxical reference is seriously made to the notion of a classless society), it is plain that the two men now move in worlds quite remote from one other.

It is clear, though unremarkable, that there are barriers to understanding between Anjali and her father and Mandar and his mother; in this there is nothing novel. Yet there is some interest in the distinction between Mandar and his brother, Shaibal. This distinction is pointed to early in the piece when Shaibal comes out onto the balcony with a cup of tea which he enjoys by himself. Jaya, their sister, remarks somewhat unkindly on his selfishness, before she fetches a cup for Mandar. Generally, whatever we see of Shaibal is of an independent, self-reliant young man, concerned for his sister's marriage, concerned for his former sister-in-law's welfare and, above all, concerned for his political work, as his late father had been and his brother, Mandar, used to be. Shaibal is not just a likeable character but one significant to the film's dynamics in the subtle yet direct contrast he provides to Mandar.

Throughout the film, we might also note the distance that distinguishes dream from reality, the ideal from the actual. For example, for Mandar there is a seemingly unbridgeable distance between his ideal Anjali and his actual Nandini. (Ironically, there is also something of a gap between his ideal and his actual Anjali). However, Dasgupta's interest in the distance between ideal and the actual is described on a broader, social level. Mandar dreams of a better world, of social change, while Nandini wonders that he cannot speak of anything else. There is a quaint irony in her naive observation:

> Looking at you one feels you have never faced any problem.

There is a gulf between the dreamer and the secretary, Nandini, and we can't help noting, too, that there is a seemingly infinite gap between Mandar's thought and action—he dreams and he talks, but he no longer does.

Closely related to this is the often evident alienation between the individual and the world; the individual is usually the dreamer—Mandar, but sometimes Anjali and occasionally Nandini, while the world is represented by the constant coming and going of people, the aggressive anonymity of Calcutta. Again, it is the camera rather than the script that points to this distance: there are shots from the balcony of Mandar's house distinguishing his private world from the public one below; a shot from the roof of Nandini's office building behind the imposing St. Andrew's Church shows Nandini and Mandar isolated against the panoramic sweep of Old Court House Street and Dalhousie Square; and numerous shots from a moving vehicle—bus, taxi, train—which focus on a particular character while the world is seen to be relentlessly passing by. Similarly, there are a number of shots *of* the distance. Particularly effective in its suggestive value is the picture of Anjali and Mandar on the banks of the Hooghly; as the couple happily warm to one another, the camera moves only slightly from them to reveal the river in its vastness, taking in Howrah on the opposite shore and encompassing all that can be seen of the river's distant, southward stretch to the sea. More mundane yet just as meaningful is the recurring picture of Mandar before his class: we see only him, never his students; he marks the roll mechanically, neither looking at them nor using their names (each student is registered as a number); indeed, his lectures might just as well be delivered to the back wall. Moreover, as he does not engage with his students, neither is he seen to engage with the city in which he lives—it is as though his life has been superimposed on a Calcutta travelogue, especially in those several shots which show him walking at night, walking in a crowd, running in the rain, all highlighting his insignificance by setting him against the mass but never really blending him with it.

Linking the notions of distance between the individual and the world and between the past, the present and the future is Mandar's repeated dream in which he is seen running urgently across the Calcutta maidan. At first he seems to be running *from* something—intimations of his activist past might be suggested —but then the figure of Anjali makes it apparent that he is running *to* her. Yet his movement does not culminate in her embrace, for just before that can happen he wakes from his dream to see a troubled Anjali looking over him, an anguished and pitiable woman agonising over her inevitable, imminent alienation from him.

This dream, which we see twice, with its suggestion of

Mandar's past, serves to indicate the political elements of the film and gives broader significance to an otherwise simple love story. Mandar's running is not that of a young man joyfully impatient to meet his beloved; it is obviously the haste of panic, of a man being chased, desperate to escape his pursuers. It is as though he would overleap a gulf in time, for indeed Mandar has tried to distance himself from his past; at various stages in the dialogue we learn that he has cut himself off from his former party associates, that he no longer mixes in the same circles as his politically active brother, Shaibal, and that he breaks a *quid pro quo* arrangement with Nripati by making no effort to find shelter for a young activist, pleading lamely that he has lost all his contacts. At the time of their marriage, Anjali fits well into Mandar's present; indeed, marriage with her offers Mandar an escape from his past. After their divorce, she comes to represent an idealised future in which there is promise of a consummation of that escape, a future to which his past, as he sees it, no longer bears relevance. On one level, then, Mandar's yearning for Anjali is also an urge to deny history. Moreover, in his lectures he talks about barbarism and civilisation as necessarily sequential stages, yet he apparently fails to apply such a theory of social progression to his modern circumstances. He also takes up a favourite talking-point of the Bengal Renaissance, the injustice of the subjugation of women, yet obviously misses the point of his own wish to deny Anjali freedom as an individual as she herself might determine it. Hence his lectures on Engels seem to be wooden and lacking in commitment.

This political aspect of the film warrants closer examination because of the broader assessment of the question of commitment that it offers. *Duratwa* was made in 1978 and is set more or less in that time, on the ebb-tide of the Naxalite Movement. The intensity and excesses of the movement had largely dissipated by then, although a passing demonstration while Mandar is in a café with Nandini serves as a reminder of the passions of that turmoil, in which Mandar had been directly involved until not long ago. His present connection with politics is, as has been noted, merely an academic one in his role as a teacher of political science. In introducing the film's political context, the Commentator assumes a slightly flippant tone in telling us that the political workers have been silenced by hooligans and that with the restoration of peace has come an urge to make Calcutta beautiful, so all political leaders have been removed along with the garbage, and Mandar has withdrawn from politics. The flippancy lies, obviously, in the juxtaposition of ideas that are not, at least immediately, congruous, no less than it does in the notion that Calcutta might ever become beautiful. Yet such an absurdity, along with the facetious association of garbage with political leadership, is not entirely off the beam in talking about the outcome of any movement of passionate ideology and endeavour that has set hearts and minds aflame yet has never been able to actually achieve anything at all momentous. Of course, Mandar has not been able to cut his ties with the Party altogether, as we see in the request from Nripati to arrange shelter for the young fugitive. A flashback to a secret meeting and flight from the police, as well as Mandar's recurring dream, reinforce the notion of the past still living in the present. This, then, is the background against which Mandar, and his love-life, must be understood.

The core of the film is actually caught somewhere between the two apparent alternative themes: love and politics. The closing words of the Commentator might suggest an explanation:

> Anjali's child and the shelter for Nripati's friend are not two different questions today.

But what is the connection between Anjali's child and the refuge for Nripati's friend? There are obvious similarities between them, such as the fact that both are rejected and both need shelter. The real connection, however, lies in what they tell us about Mandar, for he, in fact, has rejected them, the fugitive and the illegitimate. His excuse for rejecting the fugitive is a feeble one—that he has lost his former connections, although more to the point, perhaps, is the Narrator's observation:

> Mandar does not have the nerve for political work these days...

But his reason for rejecting Anjali's child, a reason clothed in middle-class respectability and one recognised implicitly in the divorce court, is essentially just as feeble. As Mandar is too selfish to put himself out for the activist, a young man who might well be himself a few years earlier, his own pride governs his love for Anjali enough to deter him from the acceptance of something not his but which is to her of immense importance. Simply, Mandar is too preoccupied with himself to truly love or genuinely care for someone else. Thus the real barrier between him and Anjali is not so much another man's son, but his own self-centredness, the same barrier that he places—on a somewhat less consequential scale—between himself and his friend, Nripati. However, not far from the end of the film we come to see that Mandar, through a dream of concern for the welfare of Anjali's little boy, is at last learning to care for the interests of others and that he may, indeed, be learning to love Anjali selflessly and out of respect for herself. Maybe he will even come to find some concern for Nripati's young friend, whose shoes Mandar, as it were, once ran in, a concern that might be a metaphor for the better society he had once worked for and the notion of which he had earlier articulated to Nandini. But the ending is an open one, and the 'maybe' elements remain just that—the Commentator's closing words offer us no certainty.

The Commentator fulfils an interesting function in this film. It could perhaps be argued that he is not at all necessary, as film is the art form that least needs such a device. The Commentator first appears in *Duratwa* doing what the opening titles might just as well serve to do: he actually introduces the two main characters in the drama, giving as well the names of the actors who portray them—something, of course, quite unnecessary given the potential of film as it has been conventionally employed. However, Dasgupta's purpose in this is not to provide the viewer with a programme but to establish a relationship between his characters and the audience, a relationship in which the Commentator will be a medium whose most important function will be to maintain an appropriate distance between the audience and the protagonists. Thus, in this introduction, he is establishing his familiarity with the two main characters, and through the early stages of the film he assumes a familiarity with the viewers, speaking to them directly as in conversation and all but giving them the opportunity to reply. His comments on garbage, civic pride and Calcutta's traffic nightmares establish a rapport with the audience, a kind of common ground, allowing him to gently advance the plot as is required from time to time. An important element in this rapport is a gentle humour which helps to restrain things from becoming too serious, for after all, despite whatever Mandar might think, there are indeed stories of considerably greater consequence than his. Perhaps, then, the Commentator's greatest value lies in keeping Mandar and Anjali in what the director sees as a proper perspective, one that will not allow the audience to get too close to either of them and in which, consequently, judgement of either character will be as impersonal as possible.

However effective the device of commentator is to *Duratwa*, Dasgupta has confined its value to that film and the next, *Neem Annapurna*, and dispensed with it in subsequent works. The absence of a commentator, however, is not the only difference between *Duratwa* and the next part of the triptych, *Grihayuddha* (1982), a colour film in which there is a greater emphasis on plot and a more conventional chronological development.

The word 'grihayuddha' means 'domestic or internal or civil dissension or strife', yet, oddly, *Grihayuddha* carries the English title 'The Crossroads', the sense of which seems obscure. Whereas the notions of civil conflict, domestic dissension and personal strife are clearly germane to the film, the significance of the idea of 'crossroads'—literal or metaphorical—is somewhat less evident. It might refer to the protagonist reaching a point in his life where he must decide whether to go straight on or take a turn. Nevertheless, this would seem a simplistic focus for the film, glossing over the complexities suggested by a literal interpretation of the Bengali title.

This is the only one of all Dasgupta's films to have an obvious reliance on conventional narrative structure. The plot is set in motion by two connected murders. The chief labour officer of a Barrackpur company, Steelwave, resigns after sensing corruption in management, and is soon after put to eternal silence. A young left-wing union secretary, Prabir (played by Prabir Guha), gets wind of the murder and he too is attacked and killed by hired thugs. With him is his friend, Bijan (Anjan Dutt), who escapes the attack and flees to Bombay. The thugs intimidate Prabir's family who, failing to get any police protection or even action in investigating the murder of Prabir, are forced to move house, while, ironically, the elder daughter, Nirupama (Mamata Shankar), is given work in the office of the same questionable company. Police apathy over Prabir's murder is countered by a young investigative journalist, Sandipan Ray (played with impressively slick efficiency by the eminent filmmaker, Goutam Ghosh), whose enquiries eventually lead him to a small-time football player, Sital Das, the thug who wielded the knife in the killing of Prabir. In the meantime Bijan has gained material prosperity and returned from Nasik, where he had found work after fleeing to Bombay, and soon becomes engaged to Nirupama. In a short time he acquires a comfortable flat in the fashionable south of Calcutta, and he and Nirupama set the date for their wedding. But Nirupama's apprehensiveness about the too-much-changed Bijan clouds the marriage plans and they are eventually abandoned. Sandipan dies in mysterious though ostensibly accidental circumstances, and Sital is anonymously liquidated. The film ends with a freeze focus on Nirupama, alone as one of the Calcutta crowd.

The narrative moves, at least in the first half of the film, through three spheres: the domestic sphere of Nirupama's family, the commercial sphere of the steel company, and the sphere of the sleuth-reporter, Sandipan Ray. The first two spheres are clearly integrated by the obvious fact of the employment of Prabir and, later, of Nirupama, as well as by the implication of the Company in the deaths of Prabir and the labour official, Ghosh. The sphere of Sandipan Ray brings this integration into sharp relief, putting into clear perspective the essential connecting elements of the scandal while unravelling others previously undiscovered or unsuspected.

Actually, Sandipan's investigations reveal little that is surprising. The corruption, duplicity and thuggery of the Company are concealed behind the armour of its pervasive omnipotence. Individuals are manipulated to its advantage according to its whims, and it remains accountable only to itself. In furthering its more dubious ends it uses little people like the crude and intellectually feeble Sital, and then employs similar pawns to eliminate them when its grubby purposes have been served. Maybe Sandipan might have gone on to show that the Company is not, in fact, invulnerable, but first he is taken off the case by his superiors, concerned at the potential loss of advertising revenue from companies such as Steelwave should justice be pursued too energetically, and then his premature death—by accident or design—puts paid to the possibility of exposing the truth. And so the detective-story element of the film is dulled by its inability to work itself through to a conclusion, fully uncovering corruption and so enjoying the characteristic tidiness of showing the guilty brought to justice. Rather, the guilty, and all their network of venality and bullying, remain unassailable.

Steelwave is perceived in this film as something of a character in itself, rather like an unseen villain in a mystery. This character is established at the beginning of the film when Ghosh, the labour officer, is summoned early one morning to the works. His car proceeds through as yet deserted streets, with the camera directed through the windscreen, looking well into the distance straight ahead. There is a feeling of inexorability in this movement, as Ghosh and the viewer are drawn directly into the domain of the Company. Once in the boardroom, Dasgupta stylises the situation by having Ghosh meet only with voices. (In fact, as far as we can tell, no Company personnel ever appear on screen.) Ironically, the only other face in the room is that of Mahatma Gandhi looking down from the customary and ubiquitous portrait on the wall. The director's intention is to show that Ghosh's confrontation is not with a man or men, but with power, and this is effectively conveyed by Dasgupta's stylisation; incarnation is only for the Company's pawns, its hired thugs and the like. Anonymity is essential to the character of Steelwave, for by it does the Company wield its corrupt power and behind it does the Company protect itself. Moreover, anonymity allows for a general understatement of the Company as a character, which in the total perspective serves to highlight the cancerous permeation of society by the forces of corruption, there being no faces or voices or human actions to dilute with even a semblance of reason the actions of a corporation ever ready to annihilate anyone likely to stand in the way of its particular interests.

Anonymity is also an aid to duplicity, allowing Steelwave to show paternalistic largesse by silencing Mrs. Ghosh, the labour official's wife, with a monthly pension, letting her keep the Company flat in which she lives, and giving her son a job. She is reluctant to help Sandipan Ray in his investigations, for having weighed her options, she has clearly come out better materially. Similarly and just as ironically patronised is Nirupama, who is successful in her application for a position with Steelwave. She is an unmarried adult in a family that is far from well off, and work is hard to find. She should indeed be grateful to the Company, her boss implies, informing her that Steelwave spends five million rupees a year on 'staff welfare'. One wonders if Sital Das and his fellow thugs are thought of as on the staff.

Giving substance to the insidiousness of the Company as a character is the reality of terror lurking never far from the surface of the film's atmosphere. The staid boardroom of the Company produces the order to kill Ghosh; the quiet, almost pleasant, region of the railway yards on a sunny afternoon provides the setting for the stabbing of Prabir; the domestic calm of the Datta family house is frighteningly violated by Sital and his thugs; Sandipan meets his death in the lovely parkland alongside the road near the Calcutta racecourse. Thus, Dasgupta makes the point that social terror has its origins and power bases far from the obvious back streets with their ominous lanes and alleyways. Moreover, the execution of violence lacks the style and efficiency that one might expect from the power points of commerce. The howl of excitement as Sital and his gang come up behind Prabir and Bijan that set the two political workers running and gives Bijan his chance to get away, and the clumsy, purposeless manner in which the thugs terrorise Prabir's family in fruitless search for Bijan, both reflect the crudely amateur status of these bully boys. The dirty work they do *for* the Company is done quite remote *from* the Company.

While at one extreme petty thugs work for Steelwave, there is also a strong suggestion that at the other extreme the police too are implicated in the Company's nefarious interests. There are police guards at the factory gates when Prabir is murdered, yet they do nothing. The police search the Datta house for Bijan, persistently questioning the father about his whereabouts, and it is quite clear that their interest in Bijan is not as a witness to a killing, for they dismiss the family's charge that Prabir was murdered as beyond their jurisdiction. Sandipan Ray asks Mrs. Ghosh if she really believes that her husband died as a result of an accident, and she informs him that she has not seen the post-mortem report and that the police have dismissed the case; what is there to gain in not believing that he died as the result of an accident? The murkiness of it all is indicated by the suspicion of Sandipan Ray:

> It could be that the deaths of an idealist labour officer and an unknown trade union leader are not all that significant. It could be that this is a big business conspiracy and that their growth is much more important than the survival of people, and that they will stop at nothing to achieve their ends.

There is, however, a fourth sphere to the narrative that gives the film a special focus that compensates for the truncation of its potential as a detective story. In the second half of the film, when Sandipan Ray, having identified Sital, might be thought to be getting somewhere, Bijan is brought back into the story, and the relationship between him and Nirupama is made central to the rest of the film, in connection, of course, with all that has preceded. Just before Bijan comes back, Nirupama is talking about him with her father and says, 'Everyone else has deserted us. Why shouldn't he?' And yet her assumption of his desertion is not entirely nullified by his return to Calcutta, for now we meet a new Bijan, indicated by the Western dress which he now prefers to the kurta that was his and Prabir's preferred style at the start of the film. And not only the kurta but the values he and Prabir had formerly championed together have now been abandoned by Bijan.

Bijan has not simply made money and become a business success. He has, in fact, been thoroughly 'bourgeoisified'; his former leftist ideals have lost their purpose for him and he has been redirected to a new, acquisitive self-interest. We may remind ourselves of the irony of his parting words to Nirupama when he fled from Calcutta: 'Don't give in.' However, like Mandar in *Duratwa* and Hemanta in *Andhi Gali*, his past has become unwanted by him; it is a handicap to what he wants his future to be and must, as far as possible, be expunged from his consciousness. Whereas Nirupama remains affectionate towards him and can admire his new-found ability, she cannot subdue a growing apprehension about the possible consequences of this change of character. His dramatic demand that they forget Prabir, made all the more heartless in the light of the father's undying admiration for his lost son, reflects not only a callous disregard for the memory of a one-time close friend but is also a gross betrayal—as Nirupama sees it—of the past, friends, Party, class and, ultimately, himself. We have been prepared for Bijan's turnaround, however. Just before the attack by Sital and his fellow thugs, Bijan had questioned Prabir somewhat sceptically about their planned protest. And before they set out, Bijan is shown playing the mouth organ, but on his return from Nasik, when he is asked if he still plays it, he replies with a simple, categorical 'no'.

Bijan would probably argue that he has betrayed nothing and no one, but rather that he has changed with the passing of time—matured, in fact. Whereas he once served 'the cause' with dedication, 'the cause' is no longer relevant to him. Indeed, it cost him his friend, Prabir, and nearly cost him his own life. And what has 'the cause' achieved? The film makes it clear that the Establishment, as symbolised by the Company, remains unshaken and that its power extends even to the unions that would seek to protect their members against it. Thus, there is a danger inherent in commitment to a cause, especially if that cause should in any way conflict with powerful vested interests. Whereas it might be easy to blame Bijan for being spineless, a traitor to his friends, Party and class, it is well to remind ourselves that, apart from all his intelligence, education and sensibility to social injustice, he is simply an average man (for whom it is so easy to feel sympathy as he walks, lonely, around his new flat), susceptible to the power—legal or otherwise—that big corporations wield. Perhaps he abandons his ideological commitment simply because he is frightened by his own vulnerability to the might and the commanding sway of the anonymous corporate machine. It is his tragedy, in fact, rather than his culpability, that he is made to side with the strong against his own people, and his efforts to justify that transition serve only to minimise him as a man, giving him, in his venality, much the same moral status as Sital Das. While the film's condemnation of the social thuggery of the ruling class is more than evident, there is also a point being made about the frailty and emasculation of the middle class. When Nirupama expresses her concern that the police are still after him, Bijan replies knowingly that they are not, allowing for his confession of total capitulation:

> Nothing matters any more. Nothing will be changed. Politics is not for ordinary people. Only Prabirs die.

Nirupama's marriage prospects with Bijan are, on the surface, promising. He is offering her a materially comfortable life, significantly better than anything she has been used to, while his own professional future seems assured. And as we are given no evidence at all that Nirupama is a serious political thinker, let alone a committed Party member, we might wonder why she should be at all concerned with the change in Bijan's political outlook. However, it would seem that Bijan's change of politics in itself is not the real cause of her concern. What worries her, rather, is Bijan's endeavour to deny and reject the past. What she admired in Prabir and Bijan was their total commitment—the cause itself was secondary. She was inspired and invigorated by their youthful idealism, their unwavering loyalty, their invulnerable belief in the absolute rightness of their mission. The Naxalite years were a time of acute and constant danger, and the courage of devotees such as Prabir and Bijan was unflagging. To turn around now and deny the value of all that was once so positive and so precious, to reject it as no longer significant, would be to root out something Nirupama had always cherished and which was to her a constant source of inspiration. Such memories are no mere entertainment for a daydreamer; they are an integral bulwark of her psyche, and a pillar to a family where loyalty and faithfulness to one another colour so touchingly the relations between her, the father, Aghornath, and Prabir. For Nirupama to go along with the new Bijan would be to diminish herself.

What emerges is the interesting realisation that all the social conflict that Sandipan Ray has been trying to untangle has been really a context for a more special conflict, the conflict between idealism and pragmatism that has grown between Nirupama and Bijan. The universally familiar macrocosmic focus has narrowed to concentrate on a human particular, the problem of how to deal with time and its passing. In *Duratwa*, Anjali is determined not to let time pass her by, while Mandar, preoccupied with introspection, wonders where it went. In *Grihayuddha*, Nirupama is comfortable as a product of her history, while Bijan seeks to manipulate time to reconstruct a history that he might use to give his life a significance which, it would appear, remains remote from him.

The notion of coming to terms with the past is fundamental, and much more dramatically so, to *Andhi Gali* ('Blind Alley', 1984), in which Hemanta (Kulbhushan Kharbanda), a former mathematics teacher, is a helpless prisoner of his past even though he is desperate in his efforts to use time as a medium for progress and, ultimately, escape. Ironically, an escape lies at the root of his plight, an escape from an 'encounter', the popular euphemism for an experience such as being driven in a police van with a number of other activists to a deserted space, on the pretext of being unofficially released, told to run off and then shot at. On that occasion death missed Hemanta but got several of his comrades, for whom he may well have been responsible. In acute fear for his life, he fled, like Bijan in *Grihayuddha*, to Bombay.

The film opens with a number of photographs of Calcutta, 1973, during the Naxalite disturbances, shown against the musical background of a revolutionary martial tune, a tune that becomes a theme for Hemanta's subsequent memories of this period in his life. The photographs are effectively arranged to convey the notions of violence, dissent and, especially, youth in something of a populist context. We are then shown Hemanta's capture by the police at his school, and his 'encounter'. We then see him with his mentor, Abhida (Satya Banerjee), to whom he has gone apparently to seek refuge and guidance about his immediate future. Abhida's counsel is something of a challenge:

> You must decide for yourself what you have to do. I can only speak for myself. Do you think I am safe here? I could be caught and killed any time. But I cannot run away. Time is against us at the moment, but it's our responsibility to turn it to our favour.

There is a cut to Hemanta running through a narrow alley, and then to a shot of him cutting off his beard. It is clear that, unlike his mentor, Hemanta *can* run away. Then the titles are shown against the major elements of the film to follow—boats and an aeroplane, high-rise residential buildings and city crowds, symbolising flight, consumerism and anonymity.

While he is physically safe on the other side of the country, Hemanta cannot subdue his uneasy conscience at having run from the struggle, nor can he shrug off the feeling of being a wanted man. During the course of the film it transpires that Hemanta did not just run away, that he had in fact been a traitor, compromising under police pressure the lives of one Suranjan and even Abhida, before his flight from Calcutta. In a voice-over dialogue with his conscience, he pleads that he left Calcutta because political activism had become meaningless (perhaps reminding us of Bijan and Mandar), but the reply is definite: 'You deserted because you were frightened for your life.' It is not until towards the end of the film, when our attitude toward Hemanta is becoming increasingly unsympathetic, that we are made fully aware of this. Even though it is under torture that he turned informer, we can't help feeling that he has acted characteristically, out of craven concern for himself. But in the early part of the film, when his blemishes are still to be fully drawn, he appears a pitiable character, a somewhat tragic figure facing a new life, alone, in a strange city, beset by deep psychological tensions; a man whose neurosis is constantly exacerbated by the fact that even in his new-found refuge there is still no end to running.

Like Bijan, Hemanta is running from his past, yet, unlike Bijan, he does not return to Calcutta to try to eradicate it and start again; rather, he is kept in Bombay by his ever urgent need to hide, always the fugitive clinging to the hope that the past will in time recede beyond the horizons of memory. He is on a treadmill, however, in that his neurosis is such that the past is kept never far from the forefront of his consciousness, causing him acute nervous tension and a psychological distress that are brought out very clearly, particularly in the first half of the film. Possessed by the demon of memory, he is beset by fear and suspicion, especially the phobia of being followed. The onset of a car's headlights, a man hurrying to catch up with a friend, even a shady character sidling up to him to sell dirty postcards, are enough to cause him severe distress, while his wife's innocent questions about his past or the clumsy verbal goading of his friend Rakesh (M.K. Raina) send him into a violent rage. A simple contrast is drawn between himself and Rakesh when Rakesh speaks warmly of his childhood days:

HEMANTA: You, too, prefer to live in your past.
RAKESH: Who doesn't?
HEMANTA (very definitely): I don't.

The fact that Hemanta is running without direction intensifies the film's pathos. In Bombay he is rootless. Although he has a job and a friend, and comes to marry Jaya, he never really seems to belong there. The character is marked by tension and unease, and even in his moments of happiness his laughter is laboured and his light-heartedness short-lived; indeed, the man is never relaxed. The only light that Hemanta can see at the end of his tunnel is the acquisition of property and the status and implied security that he believes go with it. Bombay is India's most expensive city, an observation made several times in the film. In a place where the values pertaining to consumerism and commercialism predominate, Hemanta deludes himself that he can buy an escape from a troubled conscience.

A logical step towards middle-class respectability is the acquisition of a wife. After his first meeting with Jaya, he is soon to return to her, and so begins a gentle, uneventful courtship, effectively condensed, cinematically, by minimal dialogue, appropriate instrumental music, and editing enhanced by simple costume changes. And yet he confesses to Rakesh his uncertainty about his feelings for Jaya. Why, then, does he want to marry her?

> There is one big problem in living alone. Every day one has to face thousands of unsolved questions. I don't want any more questions.

Perhaps at this point her father's words, uttered on his death-bed on the day Hemanta and Jaya first met, echo somewhat ominously:

> I am worried about Jaya. She won't protest. She just accepts everything.

The early days of the marriage are as gentle and uneventful as had been the courtship, but Hemanta's dream of a better house in a more desirable location, and Jaya's pregnancy, offer the promise of brighter days. We are not left deluded about this potential direction however, for soon after the joyous announcement, Jaya has a fall and is taken to hospital, where she loses the baby. The still-birth seems to be a metaphor for the marriage, for from now on their life will become increasingly joyless, with Hemanta's dream becoming a relentless obsession.

Hemanta quite reasonably protests that the three hours taken in commuting each day are an increasingly intolerable burden on him; if they had a flat in Bombay, this travel time would be cut considerably and their life together would be so much better. Yet it is hard to discern a genuine sincerity in this, for Hemanta has already emerged as the kind of materialist we noted in Bijan on his return to Calcutta from Nasik. In an early interview with his boss, Hemanta is reprimanded for his failure in a commercial deal in Ranchi. At first he actually toys with the idea of running to another job, but he swallows his pride without any evident difficulty, accepting the personal indifference and the arrogance of his superior along with the substance of the rebuke and, it would appear, comes to toe the Company line more assiduously, for soon we see him in a position of middle management, administering a similar rebuke—indeed, it is delivered almost word for word—to one of his subordinates. He has become, it would seem, a Company product; the former revolutionary has merged with the system he had once put his life on the line to oppose. He has now fulfilled, as it were, the political betrayals he made in Calcutta.

Again Rakesh throws Hemanta into relief. Rakesh earns a living by the acquisition and sale of human skeletons, and in a curiously effective piece of dialogue where he links the notions of corpses, whores and literature, he goes on, becoming obviously less facetious, to link Hemanta with the million or so beggars who have come to Bombay in pursuit of a cruelly naive dream. This gets him on to communism, which is his opening into Hemanta's past:

> Talk of revolution is all very well when you are hungry and naked. But put a few pennies in your pocket and you come to forget everything, remember nothing.

This is a simple truth that Hemanta cannot bear to hear uttered, and as he flies into a violent rage, the words of Rakesh are corroborated by another dialogue with his conscience, as more from his political past is unfolded to us.

Hemanta's quest for property is a simple outward manifestation of his transformation from a committed Marxist idealist to a self-interested middle-class consumer. (It is significant that Buddhadeb has Hemanta in the estate agent's office, indulging in talk about luxury living soon after Rakesh's trenchant remarks about beggars and rotting corpses. The irony of this is, naturally, lost on Hemanta.) Moreover, the quest for property is something that Jaya does not share. It is interesting that Hemanta, showing her the new flat, is similar to Bijan doing the same for Nirupama: in each case, the man is significantly more excited than the woman. Jaya's most significant reaction is an ominously significant wonder at the height of their balcony. Yet Jaya is loyal to her husband and gives him gentle encouragement in the pursuit of his dream. She is also more perceptive than he might think:

> I'll be happy with you wherever you are. But perhaps the same is not true for you.

In fact, Jaya has no urge to go beyond what she already has. The location of her father's house, far from the heart of the metropolis, is tranquil; a simple shot of a horse and cart moving through its serene and uncrowded streets provides a lovely contrast to the frantic come and go of Bombay. The house itself, draped in family memory, has a notable dignity and lofty charm, underlined by the classical religious song that accompanies Jaya's last visit there. Even if it were close to Hemanta's office, he would probably refuse to live in it, for in his frenetic desire to belong to the future, he is gripped by the need to put behind him even someone else's past.

But to Hemanta's future there is no primrose path. The acquisition of the flat is something of a shady deal from start to finish. At the outset it is a case of forty percent up front and the rest under the table, and before Hemanta is able to come up with the final amount and so take possession, the under-the-table sum increases several times, due to 'circumstances beyond anyone's control, etc.' Hemanta is discomfited by this, the financial strain weighing heavily upon him and his marriage as he becomes irate and, eventually, desperate. Clearly, the price is becoming too great, and not just in financial terms. However, he does not make alternative arrangements—he is too obsessed for that—nor does he take a stand on principle—in fact he can't, without losing his deposit; thus, he is trapped again. Yet there is adequate compensation in the end-result as he sees it. The flat signals for him a new order of existence, brightened by an attendant elevation in status, and its location on the sixth floor of a high-rise building promises the sense of a castle, as a man's home is traditionally said to be, offering Hemanta the fortress that will embrace his long sought ultimate escape.

The pursuit of his dream necessitates his ensnarement in the processes of organised debt, yet it is in contriving to honour his financial obligations that he demeans himself utterly in the exploitation of his wife. It starts off innocently enough after a chance introduction to a husband and wife team who run a lucrative advertising business; Jaya is persuaded to model for them. Jaya is by no means a simple, bashful village girl, but she has grown up outside Bombay and has inherited a value system that would be considered rather traditional in the fashion-setting circles of the progressive metropolis. Thus, she is reluctant to model, despite the fact that her natural charm makes her an instant success. She is uncomfortable with the simple causal sequence: modelling, generous salary, significant repayments on a flat—a flat for which her ever diminishing enthusiasm is in direct proportion to her distaste for her job. As she sees it, the material rewards are not commensurate with the work, yet with a sense of self-sacrifice and a desire to please her husband she is able to stick at it as long as she is advertising such things as a new brand of hair oil. At the same time she suffers increasing loneliness in her marriage, a condition that is exacerbated by both her husband's manic preoccupation with the flat and her discomfiture in her work. She can see that he is simply using her, obsessed as he is with his own particular interest. However, when a contract for a European firm comes her way, requiring her to be photographed, scantily clad, as a tribal woman, she will not compromise her principles. Jaya painfully looks at the preliminary shots and resolves to relinquish the job.

Jaya's increasing despondency is linked inextricably to the steady moral decline of her husband. Towards the end of the film, when we see Hamanta trying to be at ease at a swanky party given by the Alis, the wealthy and successful employers of Jaya, one cannot help imagining the impossibility of Abhida, for example, being seen at such a gathering. How far Hemanta has come from his roots! Yet at the same party he is, unwillingly, of course, reminded of those roots when he engages in casual conversation with another of the guests, a Mr. Khatri, who was forced by the Naxalite troubles, but more for reasons of business than politics, to leave Calcutta some years back. Hemanta goes home agitated, and again there is a conscience dialogue against the background of revolutionary music. Although nothing really new is learnt from this dialogue, it does foreshadow a chance meeting in the street with Abhida, a meeting that shows again, by contrast, the decline in Hemanta's character. Abhida's natural, warm civility is very difficult for Hemanta to deal with, for he expects instead Abhida's contempt and reviling. But the only hint of harshness comes when Abhida tells Hemanta that he can't give him his address as he is here on Party work. Nothing more is needed to state the alienation and loss of trust which are now Hemanta's lot. A flicker of the lamp (of revolution) that Hemanta would have extinguished comes from the steadfast older man: 'I have not lost hope yet, and there are others like me.' And obviously Hemanta cannot be reckoned as one of them.

The reprobate's treatment of his wife, who has already suffered greatly, is despicable. She had been married before meeting Hemanta, and was widowed before the birth of her child. Under pressure from her father, she agreed to an abortion. When her father became an invalid, she nursed him with devotion until his death. A couple of years into her marriage with Hemanta, their only child died at birth. To help Hemanta pay for the flat in Bombay she agreed to sell her jewellery and her father's house, and subjected herself to what was for her the indignity of a modelling job, even to the extent of posing for distasteful pictures. (Looking at the situation from Jaya's point of view, it is easy to see some broader significance in Hemanta's being accosted by a prostitute and by the man on the street trying to sell him dirty postcards early in the film.) It is against this background that Hemanta's rage at the loss of funds due to Jaya's withdrawal from the modelling job must be seen. The tragedy of the ending is set up by a sequence of shots that should, in ordinary circumstances, denote joy—a view across the bay to the luxury apartment buildings, the freshness of the interior of the new flat, the couple's return from a happy Sunday outing at a restaurant, all underscored by appropriately pleasant music. It is all, of course, preparation for just the opposite. Hemanta treats Jaya abominably, and then, under the delusion of a macho sex-can-put-it-all-right mentality, he submits to his physical urge and rapes her. It is a horrible scene in which the camera's focus on Hemanta shows him now in his true ugliness. The only words that Jaya can articulate do no more than state the obvious: 'You are not human.' She will be brought down no further, however. Her ultimate stand against the brute that Hemanta has become is to kill herself, thus denying him both wife and home.

The nobility of her principle is subtly underscored by the manner of his discovery of her death. He is far from the first to know, given as he is to heavy sleeping in the mornings. Continued knocking at last brings him bleary-eyed from his bed to the door, where he receives the awful news. As he looks down from his balcony, like many others from theirs, to the broken body of Jaya on the ground far below, he sees in an instant all his materialist and self-interested dreams shattered as well. From directly above his bed the camera looks down on him, highlighting his abjectness, while shots of an aeroplane soaring above indicate that for one such as this there can be no alternative to running.

> At the crossroads of life I didn't have the guts to choose the right path. And then it became impossible to return to Abhida.

The final shot of Hemanta running, with the high-rise apartment buildings of Bombay towering over him, makes the point that he can never be accommodated in his blind alley, nor does it seem that he will ever scale its walls. His only escape from this life of torment and debasement is death:

> I will escape…to a small island, through the clouds in the sky, in an aeroplane, to that lonely island where there are no human beings. No one will reach me there, not even Suranjan. There is a coffin for me there, and in it I will lie for thousands of years before I am dug up and put in a museum where people will look at me in wonder.

For all his running, for all his stress, for all his work, Hemanta has got nowhere. As he stepped over even his own wife in his struggle to climb the ladder of social advancement, he might have done well to give thought to the truism of Rakesh: 'The skeleton of a Brahman and the skeleton of an untouchable both fetch the same price.'

In the long run, then, what are all our efforts worth? Here are three films in each of which a man fails to find true meaning or happiness in his life. Obviously, Hemanta's failure is the most devastating. Not only is he condemned to continued torment by his indomitable conscience, but he has lost his wife, her earning power, and all the peace of mind they were supposed to bring him. Much less dramatic is the fate of Bijan. He does not have the agonies of conscience that might make his plight similar to Hemanta's, and he has already realised and enjoyed the fruits of a materialistic lifestyle. While he has lost Nirupama and, in the losing, been delivered a moral lesson that he would rather not have had—but one which he will probably soon forget or rationalise out of his conscience—a safe, middle-class, suburban existence is promised to him. The case is similar with Mandar, with the bonus of the possible hope that he and Anjali might even start up together again. Of the three men, Mandar is the only one who comes out of it at all chastened and in any way respectable. While the good that Nripati, Prabir, Sandipan and Abhida, for example, have done may well live after them, it might be said of Hemanta and Bijan, and possibly even of Mandar, that all that their lives will probably be good for is the legacy of bones they might bequeath to someone like Rakesh.

On the other hand, the women teach us a more positive lesson. Anjali, Nirupama and Jaya all remain steadfast and true to their principles; in fact, they demonstrate moral growth. Anjali does not crawl away in shame with her illegitimate son to try to lead a life of contrived respectability. Having been truthful, whatever the cost, to Amit, to Mandar and to her father, she devotes herself to the upbringing of her little boy and at the same time pursues her own education, by which she might hope to strengthen her independence, her self-reliance and her self-sufficiency. At the outset of the film Nirupama is politically uncommitted and uninvolved, but this neutrality rapidly dissolves as she responds intellectually and emotionally to the murder of her brother, the mission of Sandipan Ray, and the fecklessness of Bijan. Jaya has to suffer the experience of seeing traditional virtues such as loyalty and self-sacrifice, characteristic of her, being perverted in the cause of greed. Corresponding to Anjali's quest for education and the politicisation of Nirupama, Jaya's moral development is most obvious in her defiant repudiation of her lucrative modelling job. However, circumstances as she perceives them are not such that she may seek a future similar to that of Anjali or Nirupama. Contrary to the popularly alleged cowardliness of suicide, it can be said that Jaya takes the firmest possible stand on the assertion of moral principle and in defiance of shameless greed and callous bullying.

The three leading women, then, are all unwavering in their resolve, while their male counterparts are deficient in character and remarkably easily lured and led. Given the strength, too, of the wife in *Neem Annapurna*, Dasgupta's second film, some critics were tempted to hail Dasgupta, early in his career, as a notable feminist director. Perhaps they spoke too soon, for some rather admirable men and some less than respectable women were to appear in subsequent films. While equality of the sexes is a stalwart plank in Dasgupta's philosophy of life, he can hardly be described as a feminist on the basis of these four films, nor can it be claimed that he even went through a feminist phase early in his career. It would be quite simplistic to be beguiled by the feminist trumpet in recognising the moral superiority of Anjali, Nirupama and Jaya over Mandar, Bijan and Hemanta, when one is also obliged to recognise the moral superiority of Nripati, Prabir, Sandipan and Abhida over such women as, for example, Nandini, Mrs. Ghosh and Sheila Ali. In the world as Dasgupta sees it, there are admirable and despicable people of both sexes.

It would seem, however, that Dasgupta is notably more categorical in his opinion of the personal calibre of the men of management in the commercial world. Throughout the trilogy, the bosses of business are represented variously as asinine, conniving, morally malleable, pragmatic, without principles, and bullying, so much so that their depiction often borders on caricature. There is Nandini's boss in *Duratwa*, mildly hypochondriac, preoccupied with secretaries, whose wit extends to the coinage of words such as 'sexperience', and whose fatuousness is visually highlighted by a silly twitch. In similar vein is Sandipan Ray's boss in *Grihayuddha*, absorbed, behind his three different-coloured telephones, in an adult picture book, *The History of Striptease*, which he describes as fascinating. There is the boss who is inordinately amused at the absence of a ladies' lavatory and the intimidating boss of Nirupama's father. In *Andhi Gali* we note the aggressively patronising manner of Hemanta's boss, a manner Hemanta faithfully adopts when he has subordinates of his own, and there are also the cunningly manipulative estate agent and the ruthlessly demanding Alis. The captains of commerce are, of course, the helmsmen of the middle class, the leaders looked up to in various ways by Mandar, whose values are largely moulded by them and their minions; by Bijan, who is offered security and job prospects by them; and by Hemanta, who is more than willing to submit and grovel to them in the hope of even becoming one of them. As we may deplore the dilution and evanescence of the former activists' idealist convictions, it is natural that Dasgupta should not allow us to be in any way enamoured of the beacons to whose light they are drawn.

The three films are obviously closely connected in substance, but they vary greatly in style and demonstrate a degree of imbalance in quality. There are the evident surface distinctions: *Duratwa* is in black and white, its language is Bengali, and it runs for ninety-eight minutes; *Grihayuddha* is in colour and it too is in Bengali and runs for ninety-eight minutes; *Andhi Gali* is in colour, it is Dasgupta's first film in Hindi, and it runs for one hundred and forty minutes. The most filmic of the three is *Duratwa*, with its great reliance on the skills of the cameraman in creating the images that give the content its significance. *Grihayuddha* was quite a box office success, probably because of its more conventional narrative structure, a form that Dasgupta was to move away from in subsequent works. The poetic devices of metaphor and symbolism play a much greater part in *Duratwa* than is required of them in *Grihayuddha*. And while the narrative aspect of *Andhi Gali* makes it closer to *Grihayuddha* than to *Duratwa*, it lacks anything of the impact of *Grihayuddha* during its drawn out and uncomfortably laboured two hours and twenty minutes. Of the first, third and fifth of Dasgupta's films discussed in this chapter, it is the first that bears most resemblance in form and style to the more mature films to be heralded by *Phera*.

THREE

In Pursuit of Defilement

When I look at this shirt,
the seventh shirt I possess,
I am filled with contempt
for those who wear worn-out old clothes
and talk of troubles and troubles and
troubles without end.
Dear shirt number seven,
you must never change.
Stay just as you are,
smooth and shining.

(*Stay Just As You Are*)

Once upon a time Calcutta, with its Georgian buildings, wide streets and broad green *maidan*, lying comfortably on the banks of the lower stretch of the Ganges known as the Hooghly, was known to the world as the Second City of the British Empire. The town was young, hardly struggling out of infancy at the advent of a century which would be coloured by the reign of a foreign queen who, early in the twentieth century, would be commemorated at the southern end of the *maidan*, close to the racecourse and the zoo, in Calcutta's most visually striking building. The Victoria Memorial is something of an architectural enigma, derivative in form and style, functionless except to house examples of the weapons that won the Empire, portraits of English notables closely connected with imperial triumphs, and portraits—somewhat less grand, for the most part—of loyal Indians who played some significant role in the service of the British crown. Part of the enigma, too, is the fact that this huge white marble monument attracts crowds of Calcuttans each day and hordes of them at weekends and on public holidays, to inspect what is essentially foreign in their heritage, while, more understandably, the surrounding lawns provide an appropriate ambience for young couples to plot their dreams and groups of young men to plot their minor mischiefs in spite of the signs beseeching one and all to 'Commit no Nuisance'. But one does not have to go very far from this reminder of the splendour of British India to be stunned into an awareness that the grand dream of empire has become the nightmare of post-colonial realities and that the Victoria Memorial seems a thousand miles away.

Yet, in the days when the East Indiamen sailed up and down the Hooghly, Calcutta was a thriving port dealing in the exotic wares of the east and the mundane necessities of the west, its prosperous commerce providing a lucrative living for its developing class of entrepreneurs and giving reason for existence to its growing civil service, government officials and those who played with the lives of millions, ensconced in the cantonment of Fort William, for this was the seat of the British Raj, the capital of India, the Jewel of the Empire.

Eventually the glory was to wane, and as time went by notions of liberalism and human advancement—of political independence, even—would gain currency and bring, paradoxically, a vague hope to many and a clear discomfort to a few. Riots were enacted on the pleasant streets and terrorism and secret societies prospered in the lanes and alleys. Friendships, public and private, became strained and broken, a new capital was proclaimed far to the northwest, civil strife found easy accommodation, war and the massacres of a horrendous famine came and went and scarred the town, partition uprooted and destroyed millions, and.... In short, the Georgian buildings fell into decay, the broad streets became pot-holed and were made narrow by myriad hawkers' stalls, even the *maidan* experienced a degree of encroachment by the bazaar phenomenon, and all around the splendid white lady the city's population grew and grew, taking in refugees from this famine and from that civil war, giving rise to dense slums and unserviced shanty colonies. Not very far at all from the Victoria Memorial, around the boutiques of Theatre Road and the nightclubs of Park Street, and among the middle-class comfort of the southern suburbs, wealth and squalor exist side by side.

In Dasgupta's second film, *Neem Annapurna*, it is a less obvious city, the Calcutta of the alleys-off-the-backstreets, the bowels of the ghettos of the deprived, that is the *mise-en-scène*, so ruthlessly exposed by the camera, so imposing, so indispensably fundamental to the film's logic and so inextricably involved in every detail of its action and its dialogue that it emerges also as the film's major character. In *Duratwa*, Calcutta also played an intricate role (though with considerably less dominance than in *Neem Annapurna*), but this was middle-class Calcutta—the homes of the relatively comfortable and the streets of the city. In *Neem Annapurna*, the Calcutta of nightmare poverty, whose inhabitants were amongst those for whom the young prophets of a better tomorrow took up their cudgels, suggests, incidentally, a degree of hopelessness in the Naxalite idealism, for it is slum-Calcutta alone that emerges victorious from the film. *Neem Annapurna*—perversely or realistically—is a song of triumph for poverty, a fanfare for despair, an anthem of callous indifference to the plight of the destitute.

Neem Annapurna's English title is 'Bitter Morsel', which is appropriate to what the film is about but hardly a translation of the Bengali title, the significance of which is worth considering. *Annapurna* means literally 'replete with food', and it is also an appellation of the Mother Goddess, Durga, recalling particularly the legend of the goddess serving many from only one grain of rice, thus giving a suggested spiritual association to the physical interpretation of the word. The real point is given by the word *neem* which means 'almost' or 'nearly'. Thus, the negative effect of the title is important, denoting that which is *not* gained or realised, albeit *nearly*. And, as will be seen, the title has a wider application than to just full stomachs.

The villain of the piece, the agent of disappointment and discomfiture, is presented cinematically as a *mise-en-scène*—a Calcutta slum locality with its sights and sounds and suggested smells, even the fetid closeness of steamy humidity, the smoke from coal-fires and the vapours of open drains that make the tubercular condition of two of the characters an unremarkable fact of life in an over-crowded, unsanitary slum. The character of the villain is presented without any nicety of modesty, yet with sufficient control and architectural authenticity to make it credible. The film is an experience in oppression, not shock. The apparent paradox in the coupling of vastness with meagreness is established quite early in the piece. In one shot the camera looks down on the rooftops, broken and makeshift, here and there taking in enough of the locality to quell any hope in the viewer that something lovely lies not far beyond. In another shot the camera is at eye-level, taking in the suffocating narrowness of the lanes. Many of the shots are from above, and while not taking in vistas of rooftops, they do accentuate the notion of entrapment in a world steeped in meanness. Whatever the height or angle of the camera, Dasgupta's characteristic interest in doorways and windows is so often used to establish a qualitative distinction between here and there—a 'here' that is open and free and, through an effectively positioned and framed doorway, for example, a 'there' that is enclosed and stultifying. A frequent and telling shot is from outside looking in on the wife, Pritilata, squatting inside her cell-like tenement room, or a close-up of her in the same position with an open window and a splash of sky framed tantalisingly in the near background.

The general visual impression of squalor is initially created by the black and white film, which does not allow a splash of blue in the sky or a yellow sari to permit any degree of brightness to detract from the pervasive bleakness. Thus, the black and greys of film stock take on an important metaphorical significance. As well, evidence of disrepair is abundant in the physical environment. Nothing new or well put-together comes before our eyes to offer some slight suggestion of optimism. Disorder is emphasised by the ramshackle buildings and walls whose veneer has broken away, leaving exposed the rough brickwork. The interior shots reveal no mats on floors, no curtains on windows, not a vase of flowers nor a coat of bright paint anywhere; the only decoration is provided by three or four tatty calendars with iconic pictures. Nothing is there that might alleviate the gloom and oppression. And there is an easy, merciless logic in this: such niceties cost money and are therefore out of the question for people who cannot even afford food.

The picture of poverty is enhanced by numerous visual details. The shabby clothing of the children, especially the dress without buttons of the younger girl, Lati, is an obvious sign of deprivation, while the small children defecating in one of the open drains that run down the sides of the alleys suggests something about the level of public health in such a neighbourhood.

There are, however, moments for the audience of seeming respite from this visual misery. We note a degree of comparative ease in the house where the little girl, Lati, steals some bird-seed, and a brief scene in Aunt Malati's house reveals some basic comforts, such as a bed with cushions, a chair, and a dressing table bearing a woman's luxury items; there are the rooftop gatherings of Prabhat-da and his friends; there is the hustle and bustle of the traffic and the crowds along Chowringhee; there is the open space along the railway tracks where the children go to gather scraps of coal. Yet rather than provide relief, these glimpses of a life removed from misery serve only to highlight the squalor that is the core of the film.

The soundtrack also is important in enhancing the atmosphere of poverty. The film has very little plot to speak of, and what there is is advanced by minimal dialogue. While the message of this film is a visual rather than a narrative one, that message is given emphasis by a range of appropriate aural effects. There is only a little background music, which befits the context and advances the mood quite powerfully. In addition, there is the barking of pariah dogs, traffic noise, popular radio music, snatches of indistinct conversation, the spells of heavy rain (which make life even more difficult by wetting the coal), a classical song, trains, the beating of drums, children at play, a wedding band, the plaintive wail of the old beggar's singing and, almost as a leitmotif, his sickening cough with its suggestion of impending death. As well there are connoted smells—the open drains, the smoke of the coalfires, goats, the staleness of a cramped environment, and, tantalising to Braja and his family, the characteristic aroma of rice being cooked.

Neem Annapurna is, then, an intensely atmospheric film, and it is in the opening seconds that this atmosphere is given its distinct edge. Before the opening credits there is a close shot of Pritilata rushing from the house to vomit. The picture then freezes with a close-up of her face, the eyes revealing an almost demonic blaze of apprehensiveness, over which the credits are superimposed. The accompanying music, a vocal ensemble singing without words against a relentless rhythm, is disturbingly ominous. The film, in fact, begins at the end, and does so with remarkable effect. It is a disturbing opening to what is to be a disturbing piece of cinema.

The device of a Narrator, used previously in *Duratwa*, is used again here, but to a notably lesser extent and without the Narrator becoming as much of an engaging character. He simply provides the essential background to the coming to Calcutta of a particular family, while at the end he makes brief mention of what became of them, not to complete the story so much as to give significance to an implied universality of their condition as yet another, similar family on a similar train make the journey to Calcutta, presumably to duplicate the experience of Braja and his wife and daughters. He provides, along with the vomiting of Pritilata, a logically cyclic structure for the film.

As we watch the family of four travelling by train to Calcutta, we learn that they are of middle-class origin. Braja, 'who read the morning papers every day,' had been educated right through primary school and had then become a teacher, but his village school had closed down and, in need of work, he took a position as a factory worker in the industrial town of Asansol. Again he became unemployed (we learn later of trumped up charges of theft in order to effect cheap retrenchments). And so, like so many deluded hundreds of thousands before him, he gathers his wife and two daughters and their few possessions and sets off for Calcutta, goaded by the belief that there is money there, there are jobs there, there is opportunity there. So far his life has been a constant process of decay and dispossession, and his real tragedy, at the outset of the film, lies in his inability to see that his migration to Calcutta is surely an advancement of that process. The opening segment of narration gives no cause for optimism, however, and is immediately followed by shots of the family settled in their new neighbourhood of unmitigated gloom.

The plot is extraordinarily thin and it is a mark of Dasgupta's poetic genius that the film should have such a powerful impact with the support of such meagre narrative content. What happens in the film? Braja looks for work, unsuccessfully; Pritilata sits at home worrying about their immediate future; the two girls gather pieces of coal from the railway track and the elder, Juthi, pursues—apparently—a discreet liaison with the proprietor of a tea stall, Bishu, from which she occasionally gets something to eat. All of this, of course, is not to mention the climactic event of the film, which will be discussed a little later.

Neem Annapurna finds its integrity not in its plot but in its characters, particularly Pritilata (Monidipa Roy), who is focal to the film. Dasgupta's skill in drawing characters abundantly with a strict economy of material is nowhere more cogent and convincing than in his creation of Pritilata. For most of the film she is passive. In theory she is a housewife, a woman who is occupied by the chores of cleaning and cooking—but with no income, what is there to cook? She is a victim of a particular kind of economy and must endure what is done to her, for she has no real agency in life. She sits, seemingly for hours, in the corner of a squalid room, a prisoner of her own worst thoughts. The onus of bringing her daughters up decently weighs heavily upon her, and fundamental to that responsibility is the need to feed them. While she willingly goes hungry herself on some pretext or other, their hunger is always an intensification of her own suffering. For much of her day, then, she must sit and wait, clutching the ever-fading hope that Braja will find work and come home with rice. If he does not, they will have to continue to try to survive on whatever handouts he might scrounge and whatever might be borrowed from Malati. Making Pritilata's plight even more miserable is her consciousness of their status, as distinct from their economic reality, and her nostalgia for 'twelve years spent happily in our own home'. They are Brahmans, traditionally a status of some social seniority but not necessarily of economic advantage. Yet notions of caste have a strong hold over Pritilata. She chides Lati for the way in which she refers to their neighbour: 'Don't say "old beggar!" That's the way vulgar people talk.' When Malati thinks she might be able to arrange a job for Juthi, cleaning, washing dishes and looking after a little girl in return for her keep and a small wage—an offer of salvation, given their circumstances—Pritilata states her opposition to the idea on the grounds that it would be demeaning work for one of their caste. Indeed, had Braja not been out of work, she would have sent the two girls to school. 'Don't think us low-born—it's only poverty that keeps us here.'

Mention of the flour that she owes Malati brings Pritilata back to earth. But given her pride, how degrading it must have been for her to have her little Lati, having been caught stealing birdseed in an endeavour to ease her hunger, dragged home in disgrace by a neighbour. And so she dreams unrealistic dreams of escaping her lot—finding her uncle 'who lives near the Kali Temple' (but what could he do for them?) or simply leaving this place and going somewhere else (but where?). Three months rent is owing, and how much longer can she keep on borrowing flour from Malati? She has no control over her own life, and is trapped in her degradation. Yet, while her husband's acceptance of their plight might be realistic—though some might say is it submissive—Pritilata will always struggle against it, no matter how unrealistic the fight might be.

Whereas Pritilata emanates distress bordering on despair, her daughters are the film's most salient source of pity. There is quite a gap in their ages—Juthi wears a sari and, despite her obvious adolescence, is very much the young woman, while Lati, in her tattered little girl's dress, is still at the age of innocence. Pity for the lack of youthfulness in Juthi's life comes readily, while so much of the poignancy of the film comes from Lati's make-believe born out of a naggingly empty belly.

> Do you know how the cloud is formed? The smoke from a thousand kitchens rises and forms the cloud. The cloud brings rain. and there you see the cloud of lentils and there the cloud of fish curry.

Earlier she observes to Juthi that the neighbouring beggar, to whom they have offered water, is a fool for swallowing it straight down, telling her that she always chews water to make it seem like food. Before that, again famished, she tries to steal seeds from a bird-cage. Towards the end of the film she sings a children's song in which rice figures prominently. There is a charm in her wondering about where the birds go, and about the moon and the people who live there, a charm made wistful by the sombre background music with its pronounced drum beat. There is also a degree of pride—as well as a note of significance—in her 'Don't call me a beggar!' when she is castigated for stealing seeds from the pet bird. It is the essentially childlike innocence of all of this in the context of cruel deprivation that sharpens so intensely the edge of pity that Dasgupta develops in these two hapless sufferers.

The one on whom the mother and girls depend is Braja, the film's meekest character, played by Sunil Mukhopadhyay. It is easy to feel sorry for him; he is a pathetic victim of economic forces and the often inhumane people who wield power, and it would seem that his condition will only deteriorate. Even before the film starts, he lost any hope of a modest inheritance when his father sold his small landholding to pay for the wedding of Braja's sister. Subsequently, this woman's husband drives her out, and with her parents now dead she becomes a victim of alcohol and unscrupulous men and is presently 'who knows where?' We have noted the dramatic decline in Braja's employment fortunes, and we learn that he also suffers from tuberculosis. Given his chronic under-nourishment, his daily trudge through the streets of the city in search of work is a veritable ordeal. One of the most depressing moments in the film is when Pritilata, in genuine desperation, says to him as he sets out on his daily pilgrimage of hopelessness, 'You must bring something back tonight, otherwise we'll starve.' The reality is that hunger is more than a physical pain—it is also an agent of degradation and mortification; hence, the shot of Braja's face frighteningly reveals an immediate understanding of the implications of his wife's simple statement.

Despite his grim plight Braja remains optimistic. He never complains, he is even cheerful at times, and he accepts stoically his condition. When Pritilata voices her indignation about having a beggar for a neighbour and suggests that Braja ask the landlord to find him somewhere else to live, Braja's reply is simply realistic: 'We owe him three months' rent. Thank your lucky stars he hasn't thrown us out.'

Having once read the newspapers daily, he still keeps up with the news, somewhat later, from the papers that the family, engaged in some piece-work, make into paper bags. He reads with obvious amusement an article about the Abominable Snowman; he goes on to read about the Foreign Minister being in the United States and the Prime Minister being in the Soviet Union. There is an element of the absurd in this, for what could be more remote from Braja's world than international affairs of state? And then, on hearing the report of a Soviet promise of 5,000 tons of rice, there is an implied cynicism in Pritilata's. 'That's a lot of rice. I wonder who will get it.' Obviously, they won't have much of a share in it. But it is the implicit faith that they will be fed that somehow keeps them going. Braja's philosophy is simple: 'If you have enough food to eat, everything is fine—your village, your Asansol, even this Calcutta.

But before he can aspire to such contentment, Braja must endure not only the strain of extreme destitution but also the thousand humiliations innate to that condition. The very fact of looking for work, knowing that the quest is hopeless, is humiliating; knowing he cannot feed his wife and children is humiliating; having to try to cadge a little from people such as Prabhat-da is humiliating. It is on Prabhat's rooftop, where he is entertaining his friends to a meal, that Dasgupta shows us a callous attitude to the poor in the notion that poverty is the fault of the have-nots, a view which comforts the conscience of the haves. Braja intrudes into a gathering of men who can afford to espouse fascism, in other words, men who are not bothered by moral scruples nor burdened by any sense of social justice or compassion for the downtrodden. As the men talk of the Lord Krishna's approval of violence, Hitler, and the potential of the late fascist sympathiser, Subhas Chandra Bose, we hear that such heroes would have 'put the bastards in their place'. And then, 'The country is full of Brajas. But where are they leading the country?' In this context Prabhat quite unwittingly offers a truism: 'Borrowing has become a habit with you. So many people are working to survive. Why can't you?' Then, after a formal enquiry after his wife and daughters, he dismisses Braja empty-handed. His callousness is a reminder of an apparently inconsequential scene earlier in the film where a confectioner is throwing his scraps to the birds, boasting that he does not offer stale food to people, and keeping a vigilant watch in the process to see that none of the beggar boys get any of what he is throwing away.

We know quite plainly how willing Braja is to work, and at one stage it would even seem that a light has shown up on the horizon. Hope is offered, but in his desperation Braja has strayed into the realm of industrial politics, and for his trouble he is beaten by a group of unionists. So the scoundrel is given a thrashing and the callousness of Prabhat's friends has been subtly emphasised. Another political angle is given to poverty by Braja's friend, the harmonium mender:

> It was the great famine when we came out to this city to beg, my father and I. The freedom fighters drew me into the Party. I set

> their songs to music and sang them. They told me things wouldn't remain the same forever. Then came independence and all the dreams burst.

But as we are never given anything more than similar passing opinions, the film remains characteristically non-political.

Braja's neighbour, the elderly and chronically ill beggar, is the remaining character worth discussing. Buddhadeb's purpose with this old man is to provide the catalyst for the dramatic event that brings the film to its conclusion, as well as to highlight the condition of Braja and Pritilata through the nature of the relationship he bears to them. There is an ominous similarity between Braja and the beggar, in that both men are suffering from tuberculosis, but there are also some ironic differences. We do not see the fat, well-fed landlord calling on the beggar for overdue rent as he does, threateningly, on Braja; presumably the beggar pays his dues. The old man indulges himself in some elementary pride in appearance: he shaves, whereas a razor would be a luxury item for Braja. We have noted the awful stress under which Braja survives from one day to the next; his elderly neighbour, on the other hand, seems quite at peace with himself, despite his ghastly ill-health. Whereas he is self- reliant, Braja and Pritilata are totally dependent. The old man begs without shame; Braja cadges, cap in hand, from people like Prabhat, Pritilata is in debt for flour to Malati, and both husband and wife are conscious of a status categorically superior to that of any beggar. It would seem that the old beggar represents an advanced stage in the decline in which Braja is inexorably caught up, while at the same time being notably more content; the beggar is reconciled to his lot, while Braja and Pritilata still defer to notions of respectability determined by a class-society that has long ceased to be relevant to what their lives have become.

More obvious is the physical relationship between the beggar and Braja's family, for all there is to separate them is a wall with an open window cut into it. The old man's singing can be heard as plainly as if he were in Braja's room, as can his coughing, a sickening sound which is a constant, mordant signal of his doom (and, by suggestion, of Braja's). Of even greater concern to Pritilata than this vexing and nauseating aural proximity is the constant worry that she or one of her family might actually touch him. It is this fear of ritual pollution, integral to centuries-old caste superstition, that provokes Pritilata's warning to the girls to be careful not to touch him when they offer him water, and which makes almost palpable her own horror when he interrupts her preparation for prayer with a simple request for matches.

Pritilata's profound, innate disgust at the thought of physical contact with one so lowborn is absolutely fundamental to an appreciation of the film's conclusion. In her desperation to feed her family, she sneaks into his room after he has gone out one day, to steal the rice he has hoarded in a sack. This in itself is a remarkable indication of her hopelessness, for the notion of accepting food touched by one of such low degree should be appalling to someone of high caste. But the sin becomes greater, for the beggar returns for some reason or another, and catches Pritilata in the act of trying to steal his rice. She struggles with him, for she has been driven beyond the threshold of discretion, and, in the process, he drops dead. Not only is Pritilata responsible for the old man's death, but she has come into contact with his corpse. After the body has been removed with due ceremony to the cremation place, there is a superb shot, accompanied by sinister drum-beating, of Pritilata coming out of the alley, emerging gradually out of an obscuring shadow; the camera then follows her at a respectful distance to the river where she will wash away her sins.

And so the film draws to an end with the dead man's rice ready to eat. The family sit down together and eat as they have not eaten for so long—all, that is, except Pritilata, whose sins have not been completely washed away. In the awful and continuing realisation of what she has done, she rushes out to vomit. There is an almost sardonic humour in Lati's understatement, 'Mother is upset by the death of the old man.' And what a superb touch of irony it is that on this evening, Braja has been successful in obtaining some rice to bring home to feed his family.

The shot of Pritilata vomiting has brought the film full circle and, as was the case at the opening, there follows a shot of railway tracks and then, inside a train, a family coming to Calcutta to seek a better life. As the Narrator tells us that little Lati has been killed in a road accident, that Juthi has gone off with Bishu, and that Braja and Pritilata 'are lost amongst the millions of homeless and hungry,' an awful cloud of pessimism descends over the young family coming to the vast city of great hope, a cloud that thickens with the biting understatement:

There was no glory surrounding the lives of Braja and Pritilata.

Neem Annapurna gets nowhere, and that is its purpose. Transcending the pathetic hopelessness of the petty lives of Braja and Pritilata and Juthi and Lati, it is an affirmation of the actuality of the *status quo*, and therein lies the story's tragedy. The circular structure in which Dasgupta has conceived his film is, in itself, a statement: that on the treadmill of poverty the Brajas and Pritilatas are continually being replaced, and the only way out for all of them is death.

Neem Annapurna is indeed a depressing film, whose affective harshness derives simply from the cruelty of the reality it portrays rather than from any artifice or cleverness—philosophical, political or aesthetic—articulated by the director. Yet its simple story could so easily have been sensationalised, sentimentalised or even glorified, making its major characters heroic, battling survivors, thereby assuaging the popular conscience. Simplicity is vital to the film's cogency, as is the fact that the characters are ordinary and their plight is naturalistically portrayed. The film's power lies in its intensity, created by remarkably taut editing and careful presentation of the visual image, appropriately enhanced by an exceptional soundtrack. The work maintains conviction and credibility by minimisation of the narrative and magnification of the poetic, thus facilitating the optimum empathy of its audience. There are various images that fit together so subtly and with such care for balance, perspective and coherence that much of the film's effect, on first viewing, at least, is quite subliminal. The dragging of a group of goats into the alley might immediately suggest the narrowness of the lane, yet the point should not be lost that the animals provide milk and food for those who have money. We note the relative comfort of the life of the bird from whom Lati steals, while a thought-provoking sequence of shots of pigeons, at first scurrying around pecking for food amongst the rubbish on the road and then in the full freedom of the sky, serves to underline the circumscription in the miserable lives of so many thousands of people. Juthi and Lati watch in wonder a seemingly never-ending parade of ants; Lati says, 'If we were ants…' and the point is made, so gently and yet so cruelly, that they, indeed, count for less. Pritilata reminisces about their life in Asansol, how she and Braja were married in August, and that now it is again August. But it is a bitter nostalgia, as the audience realises that whatever happy times she may recall are gone forever. As she continues to reminisce, she is interrupted by the singing of the old beggar in the next room. Her initial indignation subsides when she recognises his song as one she used to sing, suggesting a hitherto unthought-of connection between Pritilata and the lowborn old man. This appalling connection is strengthened by a shot of the beggar peeing by the roadside, vomiting blood—both the imminence of his death and the defilement of Pritilata are indicated here. The sudden and apparently inconsequential shot of a boy lying dead on the road might indicate the cheapness of life in such a world as this, but it also foreshadows the fate of Lati, who is so keen to get away from the scene. The use of a chorus singing without words throughout the film suggests that Braja and Pritilata are not alone in their destitution, while the singing without words might imply an inability to fully articulate their pain or communicate their cries. And there are also indications of another world, if we need reminding, to serve to underline the deprivation of the world of Braja and his family: mention of money for the race-course, close-ups of photographic equipment, a sign advertising cold beer, and a board on which a café's menu is displayed.

There are several moments in the film where one is prompted to think, albeit fleetingly, of Satyajit Ray's classic, *Pather*

Panchali. There are two children in each film, one a virtual young woman and the other still a child. Like Ray's Durga, Lati is accused of stealing, and in both cases the mother, humiliated, delivers the girl a ruthless beating. Harihar's family and Braja's family each has an unwanted, elderly attachment (in one, a star boarder; in the other, a neighbour) who dies as part of the story. Hunger drives both Lati and Durga to fantasise over food. Both pairs of children feature in scenes by the railway line. In both films the mother is forced to endure the humiliation of debt. Pritilata's refusal to let Juthi take on the job suggested by Malati is reminiscent of Harihar's demurring about taking on work that promises wealth to the family. Yet in each one of these apparent similarities there is an essential difference. Ray's two children are a girl and her younger brother; the beating of Lati almost consciously refuses to emulate the detail of the beating of Durga; Indir Thakrun dies of old age and perhaps a degree of neglect, while the old beggar meets an unexpected and violent end; and notwithstanding her poverty, Durga does not know the actual pain of hunger as acutely as Lati does. There is something exotic about the railway line in Ray's film; there is nothing exotic about electric trains crammed full with commuters. And while Harihar's demur is out of concern primarily for himself, Pritilata's is for Juthi. The associations, then, are not quite similar, while the differences are not quite strong enough to prevent their being suggested. It would seem that Dasgupta is affirming a divorcement between his cinema and the traditionally revered cinema of Bengal. Ultimately, of course, there is no similarity between Ray's film and Dasgupta's film; *Pather Panchali*, like the novel on which it is based, is a romantic idealisation of the village life, even with all its attendant ill; *Neem Annapurna* depicts faithfully a world where lyricism of any kind would be perversely out of place.

The film offers no entertaining story; it has no political message with which to stir its audience to some stance of outrage; it does not idealise ordinary people as heroes rising spiritually and morally above privation. It is simply a starkly honest depiction of life as it really is for millions of people in

India and other developing countries. It is probably enough to say that because Braja and his family are typical of millions whose plight is appalling, and the economic disparities and social injustices under which they suffer are real and universal, there is reason enough to make a film on them. If an artist feels the need to respond to his world, he can hardly ignore Braja and Pritilata.

FOUR

Troupers, Tigers and Transistors

I never listened to
the songs you sang.
You never listened to
the songs I sang.
But I certainly heard the
the poison
in your voice,
and you certainly heard
the poison
in my voice.

Today, after a long time,
Clouds are gathering in the distance.
Today, after a long time,
Rain is falling in the distance,
filling the house with its fragrance
and smashing down
the distant walls of darkness.

Are you still singing?
Am I singing?

(*Song*)

Few if any in the Bohemian circles of Calcutta would deny that a Bengali without a passion for poetry is probably, in fact, a foreigner. Published poets are indeed legion in Bengal and while many of them go out of print and are soon forgotten, their art shows no evidence of a declining popularity. Bengalis love language, particularly their own, and they are inveterate conversationalists and story-tellers. However, it is not just the literary arts that prosper in Bengal, for Bengalis pride themselves on the breadth of their rich cultural heritage and its continuing tradition. So while the region pays homage to its literary giants, its painters, filmmakers, dancers and musicians also have been famous throughout India and much of the rest of the world. Yet these representatives of the higher arts of universal acclaim might with the luminosity of their exceptional talents obscure the fact that Bengal, like so much of the rest of India, is also rich in the arts of popular regional traditions. Popular culture in Bengal would be unthinkable without clay idol modellers, acrobats, conjurers, contortionists, animal tamers, Bauls, Patuas and the Jatra.

Of course, as long as there are the numerous Hindu religious festivals there will be work for the modellers of the countless images that are central to those celebrations. Throughout the country, in towns, cities and villages, peripatetic performers entertain for a pittance with their gymnastic skill or sleight of hand, or with their animals. The ones who are good attract the biggest crowds and make the healthiest livelihoods, the lesser ones at best just get by. It is not an over-crowded profession, one might assume, dependent as it is on rather uncommon talents, nor does it seem to be greatly threatened by the technological revolution. Commerce and technology have encroached, however, on some of the purest of the popular art forms of Bengal. The Bauls—wandering minstrels, joyously self-exiled from society—have seen some of their number cutting records, living in California and even singing songs about the twentieth century, its technology and its materialism. The Patuas have suffered a decline in the numbers actively engaged in their traditional art of hand-painting scrolls, for, given simple technical resources, imitations are easy to produce and the clever players of the market can make a great commercial success out of just what the foreigner would like. And the traditional itinerant repertory theatre, the Jatra, must compete to some extent with television and, to a much greater extent, with the extraordinarily popular Hindi cinema.

The survival of tradition and the threat to its integrity thrown up by an increasingly commercial world are central concerns in three of Buddhadeb Dasgupta's films: *Seet Grismer Smriti* ('Season's Memoirs', 1982), *Phera* ('The Return', 1986) and *Bagh Bahadur* ('Tiger Man', 1989).

Seet Grismer Smriti is Dasgupta's least accomplished film. It was produced for Doordarshan (Indian government-owned television), and the restrictions of the medium on the characteristic artistry of the director are evident throughout. The film is set almost entirely within four walls, and the narrow scope and confined space made their obvious limitations on what the camera is able to do and on how interesting the visual quality of the *mise-en-scène* is able to be. Moreover, the progression of time throughout the film is never clear, although apparent time lapses here and there suggest a plot time significantly greater than the running time of the film. The limited scope allows for little by way of character depth or development; the main characters appear as stereotypes while the rest are irritatingly silly in their playing at theatre. The end of its fifty-eight minutes comes as something of a relief from a thickening claustrophobia. Nevertheless, despite the aesthetic and technical limitations and its flimsy script, *Seet Grismer Smriti* does have some important things to say and should not be cast aside peremptorily.

The film is about Shaibal, the director of a semi-professional theatre group. He has written a play (whose title is that of the film) and is seeking funds for the production of it by his small company. The play, from what little we see of it, seems to have two lines of interest: the human interest story of a poor clerk and his wife, each of whom secretly wants to save up and buy something special for the other; and a political interest story about notions of trade unionism arising out of a retrenchment and subsequent suicide. It would also seem to have an element of commercial satire. Shaibal has no trouble in getting generous production sponsorship from the kind of stereotypical businessman, prone to flattery and hyperbole, whom we have already seen in *Duratwa* and *Grihayuddha*, and goes about preparing his play for production.

The rehearsals do not run smoothly. Some of the cast of amateur actors have difficulty in combining their labour of love with their paid employment. There are dissensions amongst the cast, based on perceptions of uneven degrees of commitment. There is criticism of the script. The sensibilities of some become bruised when conflicts arise between their personal responsibilities and their involvement in the play. As the idealism of his company wanes under these various pressures, Shaibal is seen by some as a petty tyrant. The big hurdles have been crossed, yet minor ones are now proving to be stumbling blocks:

> Amazing! Only a few days ago we had all raised the money to meet the expenses of the production. We went into rehearsal in that dingy little room in Surya Sen St., sweating our way through load-shedding. Uttam sold his watch to pay for the lights. Our only worry was getting the money to put on the show with. Yet today there are no such concerns, only personal worries have become so great. Amazing!

Complementing the quibbles and developing dissensions (which, nevertheless, do not prevent the play from getting to the dress-rehearsal stage) are several examples of failure in communication and unwillingness to understand. Shaibal is wholly dedicated to his art. After all, his involvement in the production has put his office job in jeopardy and is threatening the comfort of his family. Because he is willing to endure such stress, he will not sympathise with Arun, who wants to take his nine-months pregnant wife to the doctor, nor with Sumita who wants to spend some time with her husband. While he demands dedication from them, they demand understanding from him. Although the director wins, the victory is at the cost of loyalty and friendship. The play within the play has its communication problems too, such as the mix-up between Reba and Hemanta over the coat that each wants to buy for the other, and the tragic lack of understanding by his workmates that allows for the suicide of Prabir Tarit.

But the cataclysmic breakdown in communication, as far as Shaibal is concerned, is the withdrawal of sponsorship during the dress rehearsal on the grounds that the play is political and, therefore, offensive. The origin of this problem lies in the opening scene, in which the sponsor is enjoying himself as a munificent patron of the arts. While Shaibal is explaining the play to him, he listens only to what he wants to hear and pompously cuts off Shaibal when he tries to make mention of the play's political elements. In the play within the play, Hemanta is seen as one who is perennially afraid of the unknown, a fear that is mirrored by the sponsor. But whereas Hemanta's fear simply underlines his feebleness as a humble clerk, the sponsor's fear underlines his worthiness as a prudent businessman.

For the sponsor, then, the business of art is not to serve its own ends, but to serve the ends of business. The value of Dasgupta's film, however, lies in the questioning of this commercial value. The question is immensely important, for without money little more than the most simple folk art can get very far. The filmmaker knows only too well the commercial vicissitudes to which his art is so often subject. The history of patronage of the arts since as long ago as the Medicis has been marked by the inevitability of a demand for *quid pro quo*—while the patron may give, he will invariably want to receive in return. Hence, the desire of sponsors to get something for their money has so often resulted in the compromise of art in the interests of patrons. And here, in brief, is the dilemma of the serious filmmaker in contemporary India: be a box office success at the cost of one's artistic principles, or defend one's integrity and live on spinach. *Seet Grismer Smriti* ends with Shaibal on the horns of this dilemma, a man of integrity confronted by the temptation to compromise. We do not become privy to his resolution: in this sense the film is open-ended, idealistically leaving to the viewer the question of Shaibal's predicament, one which every serious filmmaker in India knows only too well.

This issue of the vulnerability of art to business interests is taken up in *Phera* ('The Return'). Apart from this similarity in substance with *Seet Grismer Smriti*, however, the two films have really nothing in common. Although the conflict between art and commercialism is basic to *Phera's* simple plot, the film also has a very significant human and moral dimension in its quest to seek such virtues as responsibility, steadfastness, faith and hope, while exposing vices such as bitterness, revenge and exploitation. Dasgupta is not partial, judgemental or moralistic. His characters are depicted warts and all, and are allowed to unravel in their own ways the entanglements they have made of their lives.

Phera is a visually beautiful film, exquisitely crafted with an intense concern for perspective in the manifestation of its visual richness. But it also shows a careful balance between its visual and intellectual elements. The film's easy, at times languid, pace might give a false sense of simplicity, for substantially it is a very complex film. Moreover, whereas the film is remarkable for its visual elegance, the camera work is never an indulgence as an end in itself, but is splendidly employed to prevent the complexity from becoming difficult.

Much of the poetic effect of *Phera* derives from contradistinctive juxtapositions which are, for the most part, quite subtly presented, and the contrasts that emerge often suggest a harmony or a balance rather than a conflict. There is conflict, of course, in the confrontation of artistic integrity and commercialism, brought into focus by the ideological differences between the traditionalist Shashanka and the timber merchant, Mantu, who has taken over Shashanka's Jatra company. Yet this is a conflict that is softened by the sensitive presentation of Saral, the young actor who would love to spend his life as a disciple of Shashanka but who is burdened with that most common of all necessities, the need to make a living. The somewhat more obvious contrast, that between violence and quietude, is played out on the environment by passing incidents involving woodcutters and later would-be horse thieves, and against the tranquil background by wrestlers. Yet there is also an element of harmony in the presentation of the wrestlers, in that their ongoing duel has its rules which they respect, and that they fight without malice in simple athletic endeavour. And then there is the broader juxtaposition of profanity and gentility, suggested in several ways, but most notably by the combination of literary erudition, represented by the cultivated Shashanka, and simple rusticity, represented by his crude drinking companion and manservant, Rashu. This connection might appear anomalous, yet it is more than credible in showing Shashanka in a raw, earthy perspective. Significant too is the contrast between the intellectual and idealist Shashanka and his sensual and frivolous wife, a juxtaposition that can be seen as a metaphor for the tension between the finer arts and the phenomenon of popular appeal. Simmering throughout the film are the emotional tempests of people and their irrational cruelties, set against the extraordinary beauty of the natural environment. And an ingenious integrity is given to this web of contradistinctions by Shashanka himself, who contains many of them in his own character.

The plot, however, is by no means complex. Shashanka, a gentleman of Bengal's decaying landed aristocracy, and the director of the Chandra Theatre Company (which he inherited from his father along with the estate on which he lives), has submitted to a take-over bid for his company. Determined to have nothing to do with a commercially viable company indulging in vulgarity in its appeal to populism, he is now forced to reassess his future. He agrees to a request from his widowed sister-in-law, struggling to keep herself and her young son, to come and live with him. The initial stages of the sojourn are coloured by Shashanka's bitterness at losing his company and the lingering rancour which he continues to harbour over the adulterous desertion of his former wife, the sister of his present house guest. It is the little boy, Kanu, who provides the catalyst for the regeneration of Shashanka and the positive, optimistic conclusion to the film. The story, then, is hardly significant in itself, but serves rather as an arena for the emotional interaction of the characters and as a vehicle for the transmission of ideas about art and human relations.

The central character of Shashanka is played by Subrata Nandi with exquisite technical polish and an emotional depth that is sometimes even disturbing. Shashanka is portrayed as credible yet quite unpredictable, a complex personality with the potential to unsettle the viewer by unexpected, disquieting traits of character that are revealed with forensic precision. Shashanka is intelligent, cultivated and kind, yet it is, quited credibly, also part of his character to be irrational, vulgar and cruel to the point of utter swinishness. The tensions between creativity and destructiveness that might torment a society are played out here in a single character, logically and powerfully.

The counter to this complexity of Shashanka is the innocence of Kanu, a simplicity that is required to be just as logical and even more powerful than the tensions in Shashanka, for it is the power of youthful innocence that must hold sway over the perverseness of the older man, drawing him out of the darkness of acrimony into the light of hope. The role is played beautifully by Aniket Sengupta, whose strength here is an exceptional candour that brings the character to wield a power of regeneration of which he himself is unaware. Vital to his credibility is his appearance. His refined though boyish handsomeness reflects intelligence and sensitivity, while his movements suggest the eager curiosity and spur-of-the-moment arbitrariness characteristic of childhood. Kanu's is a wonderfully filmic role, in that the character has little dialogue, much of which is delightfully inconsequential or disarmingly pointed and artless.

The pair work extremely well together. The freshness and naiveté of the one plays almost inexorably against the twisted and confused sophistication of the other, making the boy, indeed, more than a match for the man. The relationship is developed very gently. Initially, Kanu might as well not even be there as far as the cold and aloof Shashanka is concerned. Then the man becomes overtly irritated at the boy's trespass into his Jatra room, but when he finds him there again, his attitude turns, for he sees in the sleeping boy—holding a prop and wearing a snatch of costume—the burgeoning of a soul mate. Kanu's innocent friendliness is stunted, naturally, by Shashanka's irritation, causing the boy to keep his distance and to maintain a degree of suspicion of the older man. The malleability of Kanu is suggested in a piece of dialogue late in the film that brings the two another step closer together. Kanu, without a trace of malice or insolence, candidly accuses Shashanka of being a bad man, an excessive drinker who is cruel to Kanu's mother. Only seconds later he is declaring that he wants to grow up to be like Shashanka, to act and write plays for the Jatra. Shashanka woos the boy with his ideas about life and the theatre and with impromptu performances from his own writings, the background Jatra music confirming the communion which they now share. He even suggests to Kanu the notion of his 'becoming' his father, which the boy, with the literalness of youth, simply snorts at. The pursuit of Kanu by Shashanka to conclude the film, where they run towards the dawning of the new day, is a moving physical presentation of a man and a boy in pursuit of a dream together.

However, it is not possible to isolate the Shashanka-Kanu relationship, for the boy's mother, Saraju, is entwined in it as well. Saraju, played with excellent restraint by Alokananda Dutta, is a helpless victim of circumstances. Her widowhood has both enhanced her responsibility to her son as well as severely limited her means of fulfilling it. Other members of the family have rejected her pleas for help, and she has no choice but to approach, cap in hand, Shashanka, fully aware of his lecherousness and remembering that he once had a flirtatious interest in her. As far as Shashanka is concerned, she comes to him knowing exactly what she is letting herself in for, and he has no qualms about his unrestrained sexual exploitation of her. Significantly, she puts up little resistance. Whether this is due to defeatism born of her economic plight or because of a degree of attraction she might have for him is not immediately made clear. As is the case with the relationship between Kanu and

Shashanka, the relationship between Saraju and Shashanka will be worked out gradually.

Saraju comes to Shashanka's house in the first place under a cloud of deceit. Responding to her request for help, he writes to her that she might stay with him and take care of his aged aunt. Of course, there is no aunt; Shashanka's ploy is to conceal with an element of mock respectability his perverse delight at the prospect of Saraju staying in his house. While receiving her graciously, yet at a distance, he goes through all the formalities of hospitality, which only serve, ironically, to make her feel uncomfortable. First of all, he puts her in Jamuna's old room and then, in answer to her question, informs her he has no aunt.

> SARAJU: You haven't changed at all.
> SHASHANKA (*giving a slight smile*): Only my wife and my youth I have been unable to keep. Everything else remains—acting, wrestling, wine.

At this point Kanu sings a snatch of a devotional song which provides an unwitting, innocent contrast to the intemperate Shashanka, yet also faintly suggesting that he is, after all, redeemable.

Then he puts in Saraju's room all of Jamuna's saris, which are quite inappropriate for a Bengali widow who, according to convention, wears only white. She challenges him for an explanations:

> SARAJU: …Was this some sort of a joke?
> SHASHANKA: Maybe it was.

Perhaps provocatively, she raises the prospect of his remarriage. Shashanka's response is to offer her another wifely present, Jamuna's jewellery, insisting when she demurs. He then tries to embrace her, but she struggles and breaks free of him. His look of anger at the end of this scene is not due to his advances being frustrated but rather to Saraju's perceptiveness:

> SARAJU: You are angry with Jamuna. Why do you want to take revenge on me? What have I done to you?

There is a logical cut to early next morning, as Saraju and Kanu quietly leave Shashanka's house. But at the station she hesitates; clearly, her will to leave is not strong enough. While concern for Kanu's well-being must be paramount, one cannot help thinking that maybe Shashanka is not such a monster in her mind after all. She returns to his house, and a series of lovely shots reveal a Saraju quite at home there and by no means uncomfortable in bringing to the still sleeping Shashanka his early cup of tea. Most significantly, she has changed her widow's sari for one of Jamuna's that he had given her.

Pertinent to both relationships is the indispensable third. Saraju is obviously uncomfortable in her affair with Shashanka, knowing that Kanu is aware of it. Constrained in her ability to relate to others, she tries to compartmentalise her relationship with Shashanka, on the one hand, and her maternal love for Kanu, on the other. Yet the maternal relationship is dependent, materially, on Shashanka, and the connection between material dependence and the granting of sexual favours is obvious. The attempted partition, then, is rendered ineffectual, and the major factor militating against it is the burgeoning friendship between Shashanka and Kanu. Shashanka's growing fondness for Kanu and his keeping company with him more and more is disturbing to Saraju, whose concern for propriety, initially, makes her resolved to maintain the trappings of widowhood; she rejects Shashanka's present of Jamuna's jewellery, and she chides Shashanka for using her name in front of Kanu. Given this deference to accepted decency, it is indeed discomfiting for her to see the man whose bed she goes to developing a closeness with her only child. She tries at first to simply forbid them, and Kanu—in boyish innocence, not impudence—merely laughs at her and runs off with Shashanka. Her more sophisticated stratagem proves even more futile; in a clumsy endeavour to make herself more attractive to Shashanka, she over-dresses and adorns herself, cutting a pathetic figure from whom Kanu runs and Shashanka turns silently in an attitude of both pity and mild contempt. She is not really needed any more, not by Shashanka nor by Kanu.

In the background to the working out of these relationships there is the quite different liaison between Rashu and Kalyani (Sunil Mukherjee and Chanda Dutta). Rashu is the servant of Shashanka, uneducated and unsophisticated, good-hearted and happy-go-lucky, and Kalyani is his rustic sweetheart, humble, physically unattractive, also good-hearted, and mute. This is a relationship totally free of artifice, where neither party would dream of taking advantage of the other. In clear and pointed contrast to Shashanka's marriage with Jamuna and his affair with Saraju, the love between Rashu and Kalyani is undemanding, total and constant. And yet, as though to tell us that the world takes most from those who have the least, their simple and joyous wedding day is destroyed by the gang rape and murder of Kalyani and the suicide of the consequently maddened Rashu.

This episode is particularly distressing, set as it is against something that might have been idyllic, and in its awfulness it goes infnitely beyond any of the sordid aspects acted out on the major plane of the narrative. And yet, ironically perhaps, the tragic episode serves, in its enormity, to rescue the main story from becoming a sentimental romantic drama, in that it gives a strong and perceptible fillip to the regeneration of Shashanka, being effected less perceptibly, yet more surely, by the magic of youth. While we might draw a parallel between Kalyani and Saraju in that both are exploited sexually, cast off without any care for their consequent plight, the main purpose in this disturbing episode is the effect that it has on Shashanka.

The immediate indication of Shashanka's being emotionally moved is a simple visual one. Earlier in the film, when Shashanka and Rashu get drunk together, the scene ends with Rashu squatting on the floor, the camera at his level, looking up to Shashanka, who is standing; the status of one and the submissiveness of the other is quite simply established. Now, maddened by the death of Kalyani, Rashu takes refuge at the top of a tree and resists all efforts to persuade him to come down. At night, Shashanka goes out alone to try again, and for much of their dialogue the camera is at ground level with Shashanka looking up to Rashu. Previously Rashu had been merely talked at by Shashanka; now Rashu points out to him the mute Kalyani's ability to communicate and the failure of the articulate Shashanka:

> RASHU: Babu, Kalyani was dumb. She was born dumb. She was never able to speak a word. There was great sorrow in her heart. So I too would not speak with anyone. She would move her lips, babu, signalling to me that she wanted to talk. She made signs to me that she wanted to talk. I understood that, babu.
> SHASHANKA: You used to talk with me, Rashu.
> RASHU: That was not talk, babu, that was habit. I never had any real talk with you. You would speak and I would just answer.
> SHASHANKA: Not real talk? What do you mean, Rashu, not real talk?

Rashu does not answer; the scene ends in silence. Then there is a cut to early the next morning with a medium long shot of Rashu's body at the foot of the tree. The condensing of these moments of dialogue and the discovery of the body, with Shashanka central to both, clearly suggests an enlightening effect on Shashanka, which is first made clear by his Jatra character:

> Through the window of death, life can be seen, Your Majesty. That realm of faith and love that was gradually taken far from me now seems to have returned and surrounded me. I am being made new, Your Majesty. Death is not the last word—it is life that is the last word.

A little later, this enlightenment is underlined in a short scene with Kanu:

> SHASHANKA: I was looking for someone, sitting here.
> KANU: Who?
> SHASHANKA: Someone. He went missing from me some time ago.
> KANU: Did you find him?
> SHASHANKA: I found him. Eventually.

The idea is further strengthened when, in reply to Kanu's asking why Rashu died, Shashanka says nothing but simply looks at Kanu, slowly turns away to the door and opens it to reveal a long wide shot of the beauty of the scene outside. It is clear that now Shashanka has come to appreciate, through Kanu and enhanced by Rashu and Kalyani, a vaster, richer world beyond the bounds of bitterness. It is, of course, significant that much of the Shashanka-Kanu relationship is played outside in the natural world, vast in its possibilities, free from the confines of the house and its unhappy associations, and close to the remnants of a splendid past.

Buddhadeb has given us in Shashanka a man easily knowable on one level, yet one who is remarkably deep and complex. The primary interest is in Shashanka the artist. The film opens with a series of close shots focusing on his face being made up for a role in a Jatra performance, followed by the opening titles appearing over a still of Shashanka as the eighteenth century ruler of Bengal, Aliwardi Khan. Here the director has established the dominance of theatre in Shashanka's life—we soon learn that he is the star of his troupe, a playwright and, until now, the owner-manager of the Chandra Theatre Company—and suggests Shashanka's status as the last generation in an old Bengali rural aristocratic family. The effectiveness of Shashanka's appearance as the Nawab Aliwardi Khan is somewhat more subtle, in that it provides a historical image suggesting notions of betrayal and desertion, notions that will be seen to be basic to Shashanka's negative view of life and the bitterness that sours his attitude to others. With the titles out of the way, the film opens with Shashanka in performance as Aliwardi, declaiming, significantly, against Mir Jafar Khan for his treachery; but only a short way into the oratory the temporary theatre catches fire—how easily all one's hard work can amount to nothing—causing the audience to flee, leaving Shashanka alone. Thus is foreshadowed the essence of his discontent.

Perhaps Shashanka, merely by belonging to the twentieth century and given his unwavering commitment to principle, is doomed to discontent. The dedicated idealist is rarely in tune with popular taste or opinion, and as long as he belongs to an age in which popular taste and opinion are resolutely manipulated by powerful commercial interests with efficient technological and communication resources, he is going to find it very difficult to make his voice heard. Shashanka is a talented writer and actor, admired greatly by his fellow troupers. He could probably make a lucrative career for himself on the stage, were it not for his resolute stand for art over commerce. However, in the performing arts, especially, most find it expedient to bend with the wind, as does Shashanka's colleague in the Chandra troupe, Saral. An actor must have a means of livelihood, and if this can be provided by a timber merchant or any other man with money, performing his tasteless plays for a regular wage would be preferable to being rich in artistic integrity and unemployed. Shashanka, however, demonstrates a disdain for money. In a dispute over a small tract of land, he asserts that the affair is a question of status and breeding, not of money, and later, in a confrontation with Mantu, he accuses the new owner of having ruined the company merely for reasons of money. While not wealthy, Shashanka has inherited means and can afford with considerably less difficulty than Saral to remain committed to his principles.

The strength of Shashanka's principles lies to some extent in their antiquity. He has inherited the once splendid estate on which he lives; he has inherited the Chandra Theatre Company; but most significantly, he continues to be heir to a rich cultural tradition. The stateliness of his gait and posture suggests a sense of nobility, while in the scene showing the arrival of Saraju and Kanu his lordliness of manner is displayed as the camera looks up and diagonally across to him, striding elegantly along the upper cloisters while his guests wait on the ground floor. His sense of wonder is animated by the past, and the awe in which he holds the great names of history is the primary inspiration for the plays which he writes and performs.

> Galileo, Copernicus, Sophocles, Shakespeare—so many! Siraj-ud-Daulla, Sher Afghani—such lives! Those lives direct me, they call to me. I write plays about them. Each life has a direction, a purpose.

A delightful contrast is incidentally provided when Rashu refers to the inglorious death by snake-bite of his father, who rued the fact that he had given his son no direction in life. Yet it would seem that it is with the direction of greatness that Shashanka identifies, even though he is, in fact, no more than a self-appointed apostle for the greatness of others. He is not deterred from setting high standards for himself, and he makes uncompromising demands on those with whom he lives and works. Drama inspired by anything less he contemptuously and categorically dismisses as smut. He has very definite views of decency and of beauty, views which flow over into everyday life, such as when he chases away the woodcutters and, with obvious pain and sorrow, looks at the wound they have made on a tree and lovingly caresses and tries to heal it. However, from this shot of tenderness the film cuts to a shot of the wrestlers in energetic bout, subtly implying the violent side of Shashanka.

One of a dwindling aristocracy, Shashanka has his roots in antiquity, identifying with a world long gone and communing with the ghosts of the past.

> KANU: Have you ever seen a ghost?
> SHASHANKA: Yes. They chat with me. Then they start to talk in other voices—these bricks, the door, these windows.

The importance of tradition and cultural inheritance is brought into sharp relief in a later scene in which Shashanka and Kanu are walking by the tombs of Shashanka's ancestors. This is an experience of great delight for the man, for in Kanu's curiosity about Shashanka's forebears there is another indication that the tradition need not end with himself but might be carried on by the young. Coming to see Kanu as a cultural legatee is an important part of the regeneration being worked in him.

So far it would seem that our hero is a typical romantic. Actually, he is more of an anti-hero and his portrayal is often notably unromantic; indeed, his imperfections are essential to Dasgupta's interest in him. He is dissolute, self-indulgent and opinionated; he is aloof, a trifle arrogant and sometimes pompous. On occasion, he appears judgemental, a moralist, yet he is also baldly revealed as lecherous and given to drink and immoderate and abusive language. While all of these faults might be easily forgivable—some of them, perhaps, might even be seen as endearing—they are, in fact, underscored by his inability to forgive and the malevolence that emanate from that.

Notably human is Shashanka's loneliness, which the director is at pains to establish early in the film. There are shots of Shashanka playing chess against himself, resting and sleeping, writing, and tinkering about in his Jatra room. There are also some excellent shots taken, significantly, at a distance and with particularly effective angularity of Shashanka juxtaposed alone wth the timeworn architecture. Most movingly underlining Shashanka's loneliness and alienation from his times is the shot of him watching helplessly as Jamuna runs off with her lover, followed by a cut to a close-up of a glass of brandy, with the sound of Rashu's drunken singing in the background.

Shashanka might find it theatrically attractive to stand alone against the world; in actuality, it is something he finds great difficulty in doing. A devoted wife, loyal collaborators, staunch supporters and true friends would all have made Shashanka's life perfect, but sadly they have all deserted him. His wife has left him for a man manifestly inferior to himself; his collaborators and supporters have either pledged their allegiance to Mantu, the new proprietor of the Chandra Theatre Company, or gone off to Calcutta to seek fame and fortune; and his one true friend is his illiterate manservant, Rashu, whose companionship consists in no more than sharing his brandy and listening to him talk. While this relationship might appear anomalous, it quite credibly establishes a crude, earthy perspective to Shashanka. Moreover, he is only too well aware that the public, from whom his audiences might come, remains fickle and ever-attracted to the 'smut' that merchants like Mantu will offer them for money. Hence his insular pride, his purely physical interest in Saraju, and his initial aloofness from Kanu.

Shashanka also has an acute sense of having been exploited. He has worked diligently and with immense dedication in building up the Chandra Theatre Company, only to see it taken over by a timber merchant. He was generous to Jamuna, yet she ran off with another man. He is also concerned that Saraju is taking advantage of his generosity (a concern which he might well rationalise as an entitlement to take advantage of her). The exploitation of Shashanka is underlined more obviously by external forces, such as the woodcutters who try to steal his timber, and the thieves who try to steal his horses. Shashanka makes an ostensibly simple observation on the passing of time when he tells Kanu that the white horse they see running by now pulls a cart, but he also gives focus to his own situation: 'Your mother and your aunt used to load me up just like that old horse.' A reference to the ruins of the debtors' dungeon on Shashanka's estate is a reinforcement of this notion of social injustice, giving it, too, the strength of antiquity. There is also significance in Shashanka's having written a play about this dungeon which Mantu refused to produce, for Shashanka's quotation from it to Kanu, despite its exaggerated rhetoric, is indicative of his life as he sees it:

> O king! How any years more? One hundred, two hundred, three hundred? Thousand more years? Do you not hear our groans? Our lamentations of agony? The sounds of the beating of our breasts? It is amazing, your majestry, truly amazing, that our world should be bound within this dungeon. How many more thousands of years will be spent here? This world will fill many, many dungeons. What will you do when your entire kingdom has gradually turned into one vast prison for all your people?

While Shashanka might well consider himself an innocent victim of betrayal, he can hardly blame those who desert him. We are not told why all his relatives have gone to Calcutta, but one might fairly guess that there were good economic reasons for the move. Saral and the others of the Chandra troupe are portrayed on the bus as ordinary everyday men who do theatre for a living, more because they are good at it than as a result of a burning idealism; thus they too have pressing economic reasons for moving on. When Saral comes to say goodbye to Shashanka (his Western dress contrasts significantly with Shashanka's traditional garb) the master plays on sentiment as he reminds Saral of all the things they did together. While Saral is moved, he is moved more by financial need. Shashanka's inability to understand this is evident in the coldness of the farewell he gives to Saral.

As for Jamuna, it is perfectly clear that theirs was never a sensible match. She wants to live, he wants to write; she is sensual, he is intellectual; she is active, he is reflective; she is modern ('Take me to the cinema'), he is traditional. She is bored, lonely and restive, and it is no surprise that she submits to what is for her a more exciting, promising match.

However, it is for Mantu, the new proprietor of the Chandra Theatre Company, that Shashanka saves a particularly intense disdain. His indignation reaches a pinnacle when he calls in on his old company and finds that work on a new play has started without his having been informed, a play whose title perhaps says it all: *The Wife Became a Dancing Girl*. He demands that Mantu be sent to him and treats him, when they meet, with marked contempt: Shashanka remains seated on the only chair, and stands Mantu before him like an errant schoolboy. He does not respond to Mantu's fawning, and makes no bones about his disgust at Mantu's commercialist 'destruction of the company'. Mantu means to have the last word, declaring that Shashanka's plays are irrelevant and commercially non-viable. Aiming to play the winning card, he says: 'Shashanka-babu, I have bought the company from you, for money.' Yet it is Shashanka, in fact, who has the last word: 'But you have not bought me.'

However, blaming others ultimately becomes irrelevant, as his feelings of bitterness and yearnings for revenge dissolve in the process of the rehabilitation wrought unwittingly by Kanu. The Shashanka who runs towards the rising sun in pursuit of youth and innocence is a rejuvenated, resolute and optimistic Shashanka. Kanu helps establish this:

KANU: Do the trees talk to you?
SHASHANKA: They do.
KANU: What do they tell you?
SHASHANKA: They say, 'Shashanka-babu, be like us. Stand firm with the sun, the storm, the rain.'

And the earth tells him that from a small seed one can make a great tree, so he announces his resolution to Kanu:

> Kanu, I am going to write another play, form a new company, and no one will see Mantu-babu's plays. Everyone will come to my company and yours.

A burst of Jatra music signifies the new inspiration of Shashanka and his determination not just to outdo Mantu, but to fully live again.

Phera is a splendidly visual film, a quality that is intricately germane to its dramatic development. After the colourful make-believe opening, we are taken gradually into the world of Shashanka, arriving in what was once a gaily painted horse-drawn cart along narrow lanes flanked by lush vegetation and the ruins of ancient buildings still suggestive of an erstwhile grandeur, where the tranquillity of the environment allows for a sense of isolation. The pervasive quietude provides an effective contrast to the spiritual turmoil of Shashanka, while the remoteness from the world of hustle and bustle is essential in framing the singular realm of Shashanka and focusing on his perceptions, his troubles and his dreams.

The pace is unhurried, even languid, and appropriately determined by the film's vicissitudes of mood. This is well illustrated by the arrival of Saraju's letter. Its importance is heralded by a shot of the postman cycling up the road to Shashanka's house. He is seen to get off his bicycle, walk up to the front door and put the letter in the letter box. He then walks back to his bicycle, not having noticed that the letter box has no bottom and that the letter has dropped through it to the ground. Only then comes the close-up on the letter revealing, quite inconsequentially, Shashanka's name and address. And for the time being, that is that. From the close-up of the letter there is a cut to a shot of Shashanka sleeping, and then there is a scene of Shashanka and Rashu drinking together, at the end of which Rashu casually remarks that a letter had come for Shashanka that day, and then the sender and the contents are made known. This allows for a simple compression of time, facilitated by one or two still shots connecting the letter—or its writer—with Shashanka's unhappy marriage, economically detailed in flashback, merging past wounds with imminent events. The arrival of Saraju and her son is the single most important event of the film, an event which Dasgupta is in no hurry at all to bring about. And this lack of urgency is exactly what underlines the event's importance.

Punctuating the film's languid pace and lending strength to its metaphorical aspect are the wrestlers who, save for a brief exchange of greetings with Shashanka at the beginning, say and do nothing throughout the film other than wrestle with one another. The easiness of the pace is brought into relief from time to time by shots of their vigorous bouts; their aggressive grappling complements the emotional hostility being acted out by other characters, and their total detachment from the plot helps to frame the drama with definition. Like Shashanka the actor, they take particular pleasure in being watched, and they symbolise the raw, physical and aggressive aspects of Shashanka's character. Moreover, they provide Shashanka with the opportunity to vicariously work out his revenge on his enemies. 'Watching them wrestle gets rid of my anger with others.'

More poetic than the films preceding it, *Phera* represents something of a turning-point towards a new phase in which plot is minimised, allowing for an increasing interest in the power of suggestion, the richness of imagery and the deployment of metaphor. Hence, *Bagh Bahadur* ('The Tiger Man', 1990) follows on from *Phera* in many ways. Again, plot is minimised in order to evoke interest in that which in fact *is*, rather than that which is shaped by elements of narrative. In other words, semiotics, imagery and metaphor are deployed to make statements about what is already known as distinct from what might be discovered from the interplay of dialogue, while the dramatic impact lies in the unfolding of crises and tensions and the working out of consequences. As for substance, both *Phera* and *Bagh Bahadur* make statements on the nature of contemporary arts and artists, using village-based folk art as their context. In both films the focus is distinctly rural and the atmosphere rich and colourful.

However, there are significant differences. Shashanka is an upper-class intellectual whose associates are, for the most part, educated, whereas Ghunuram, the Tiger Man, and Sibal, Radha and the villagers of Nonpura are unlettered and notably unsophisticated. A rural setting is common to both films, but the rusticity of *Bagh Bahadur* is considerably more pronounced than that of *Phera*. Such meagre hints of the modern world as are to be found in *Phera*—bus, post office, railway station and references to Calcutta—are missing from *Bagh Bahadur*; indeed, Samba's radio, the hunters' jeep and the reference to Patna serve only to intensify the isolation and pre-modernity of Nonpura. Shashanka's once grand stately home contrasts quite obviously with Sibal's earthen cottage with its simple folk designs painted on the outside wall. While most of *Phera* takes place in or around Shashanka's home, the action of *Bagh Bahadur* commands a more diverse setting; the interior of Sibal's house and its courtyard, the jungle, the open fields, the vast river, and the village lanes, temple and bathing ghats all have their moments of prominence. Finally, the moral dimension of *Bagh Bahadur* is simpler, though perhaps starker, than that of *Phera*, given the absence of the complexities of character and personal relationships germane to the earlier film.

The simple story is about Ghunuram (played by Pavan Malhotra), a quarry labourer who, for one month in every year, visits the village of Nonpura, where he is able to experience fulfilment in the artistic tradition of his forebears as the Tiger Man, dancing to the beat of a drum the dance handed down from father to son over many generations past. His artistic joy is complemented by the close friendship he shares with the elderly virtuoso drummer, Sibal (Vasudev Rao) and the affection he nurtures for Radha, Sibal's daughter (played by Archana), whom he intends to marry one day. His credentials as a suitor are his talent as the tiger dancer and the admiration and esteem which his art earns him for him from the villagers of Nonpura. But his talent is brought into question when a small-time travelling animal act, involving a live leopard, comes from Patna to Nonpura, bringing before the villagers a confrontation between artistic creativity and 'real-life' appeal. The conflict is resolved in tragedy when the Tiger Man enters the cage of the leopard to challenge his rival in the defence of his honour.

Simple as the plot is and innocent and naive as are the victims—and, indeed, the perpetrators—of its tragedy, the story, nevertheless, is constructed on a number of intricately connected counterpoints and complements. The first few minutes of the film establish the fundamental contrast in Ghunuram's life, that between his work as an oppressed and bullied labourer at the quarry and his one month a year as an acclaimed and valued artist at Nonpura. The opening shots focus on the dominance of the rocks, complemented by the harsh and callous manner of Ghunuram's boss. As he moves away from where he is, in effect, a prisoner, we see him gradually blossom on his journey to Nonpura, as his imminent freedom is reflected more and more in his easy relationship with the lovely rusticity of green and lush jungle, friendly labourers and playful village girls. He has a considerable distance to walk to Nonpura, and his joy in anticipation of his arrival there becomes more and more apparent as in his mind he hears the song of Radha and the beating of Sibal's drum, sees himself in his tiger costume and make-up, and is heartened by his anticipation of the adulation of the crowd. As we see for the first time Ghunuram dancing his tiger dance, we can appreciate the radical transformation of the rock-breaker: against the counterpoint of the erstwhile humble labourer stands the lofty idealist as creative artist. Ghunuram has emerged as his true self.

But such self-fulfilment is rarely achieved independently. Ghunuram's artistic reality is complemented by that of the drummer, Sibal, whose talent depends, in turn, on Ghunuram for its fruition. The essential intimacy of one artist with another is matched by the closeness of the friendship between the two men, while the artistic consummation of dance and drum parallels the elementary harmony of man with woman and is a simple metaphor for the growing consonance between

Ghunuram and Radha. However, the consummation of this basic human relationship is closely connected with another artistic counterpoint—the artist and his audience. No art can meaningfully exist in a vacuum: the writer must be read, the musician must be heard and the dancer must be seen. Of course, this implies more than mere witnesses, for an artist must also be appreciated if his endeavours are to have any significance at all. Ghunuram's talent has been attested to over the years by his drawing of audiences that not only value his work but pay generously as a mark of their admiration. This is the objective and palpable indication of his worth, the basis of the pride on which he can legitimately build his dream to settle in Nonpura with Radha as his wife. This particular relationship of artist and audience is, indeed, both vital and delicate, for to remove one part of it is to render worthless Ghunuram's dream.

A hint at what might be an agent in the exploitation of the potential fickleness of every audience comes early in the film when Ghunuram is still on his way to Nonpura. He wakes in the dawn light on the last day of his journey to see a small circus troupe on the road, the focal interest of which is a large cage containing a live leopard. Ghunuram approaches them and asks where they are going, and the arrogance and flippancy of their manner in answering him contrasts notably with the friendliness of the other people Ghunuram has met up with on his journey. They tell him that they are going to Nonpura, and rudely go on by. Thus, the basic dramatic counterpoint—protagonist and antagonist—is established.

Pertinent to Nonpura's particular accommodation of this confrontation is the coupling of the notion of isolation with that of intrusion. Nonpura is typical of most of the villages of India—certainly in the early sixties—in that it is remote not only from industrialised, urban civilisation, but also from the technological and commercial expressions of that civilisation. Most of its inhabitants who have travelled at all have probably done so by boat, by bullock dray or on foot, and over a relatively short distance. The village is not generally electrified, probably has few if any telephones, and its people have, for the most part, enjoyed at best an elementary education. They are simple folk, unsophisticated and easily impressed. Thus, when a troupe from the city comes into their isolation with a desire to make money by the appeal of a live leopard, their dress, their promotion techniques, their snatches of popular movie songs blaring from an amplifier on a pole against the lovely background of the natural landscape, and even the trainer-manager's transistor radio, make their visit an intrusion. And while the intrusion has a significant effect on the values and the collective life of the village, no one comes to feel it more profoundly and more painfully than Ghunuram.

On the artistic level, the intrusion brings into conflict the dance of a man made up as a tiger and the derring-do of a man who subdues a live leopard. It is an encounter between the aesthetic and the spectacular, the artistic and the showy, and the simple villagers of Nonpura are cast in the role of cultural arbiters in a conflict in which the relative refinement of the one and the crass vulgarity of the other cannot be discerned by the same villagers who have for years extended their acclaim to the Tiger Man. Bedazzled by the dramatic immediacy of realism, they are unable to see its innate limitations, for inexperienced as they are, they have no conception of the distinction between art and reality and the inherent capacity of the latter to lose its novelty and inspire boredom. However, no matter how shallow the slick, realistic act from the city may be, it does make the audience gasp; the most the Tiger Man could ever do was please them. And so the folk tradition is popularly, uncritically and naively rejected in favour of the modern and the new. What is sad about the villagers' expressed preference is their unawareness of realism's essential indifference to humanity, a quality they have always taken for granted and which they now somewhat contemptuously reject.

Here, then, is the core of the drama and the focus of Dasgupta's interest: the conflict between traditional culture and popular, commercial entertainment. This broad, overriding theme is complemented by the breakdown of the relationship between Ghunuram and Radha, for as the once loyal and appreciative audience of the Tiger Man gradually abandons him for Sambalal and his leopard, so does the once faithful and admiring Radha allow herself to be lured by the attraction of what she perceives to be 'a real man'.

The closeness of the relationship between Ghunuram and Radha is first established through Sibal. As Ghunu nears the village, Sibal is waiting for him, and their initial greeting is one of drum and dance: Sibal beats his energetic welcome, signalling his joy at the return of the Tiger Man, and Ghunuram responds by entering Nonpura in immense pride and majesty. Thus, the spiritual communion of the two artists is established, and out of this the elements of their more personal association emanate. Sibal lives only for his daughter and his drum, and for him the natural complement of both is Ghunuram. A sublime moment for Ghunu is Radha's singing to Sibal's drum while he is making up as the Tiger Man. The dream that drives his simple life is merely to dance so well as to make enough money to buy a small house in Nonpura where he can live with Radha. It would seem to be an innocent dream, and yet there is something slightly disquieting about Radha's response to it.

> RADHA: You like dreaming, don't you?
> GHUNU: Who doesn't like dreaming? But remember, my dream will come true.

We might well suspect that the dream won't come true, for during this sequence the camera reveals a suggestion of dissonance between the two characters: Ghunu is presented in facial close-up, appropriate for a dreamer, while Radha, emerging as the pragmatist, is in medium shot, trying on the bangles Ghunuram has brought for her, so starting to reveal herself as attracted to tangible values, too realistic to support someone else's dream, too selfish to share it. The point is underlined all too clearly as the sequence is interrupted by children's voices referring to a tiger, followed by the sound of an animal's growl.

Naturally, Radha joins the other village girls in going off to see the visiting show and its wild beast. In the evening she goes back for another look and meets up with the great Sambalal himself. Naively she praises his courage, while he teases her by inquiring after the Lord Krishna (whose beloved's name is Radha). She runs off giggling, already enticed into his web of simple seduction. Ghunuram discovers this indirectly:

> GHUNU: You didn't use the make-up I gave you.
> RADHA: I did when I went out last night. The leopard is handsome, and so is his trainer.... He's a real man. All men should be like him.

Ghunuram is crushed, unable to reply.

Later, Radha has a close-up look at Samba's transistor radio and hears its strange voice speaking in a foreign language about events and places she would never know about even if she could understand the language. She does not even know of Patna, and she finds Samba's talk of cars, aeroplanes, big shops, electricity, cinemas and theatres utterly entrancing. When he asks her, 'Will you go with me?' new thoughts are set off in her mind, and again she runs off, giggling in delighted embarrassment.

Ghunuram is understandably angry and forbids Radha to go again to the leopard show. This provokes more defiance and further estrangement, forcing Ghunu to consider either abject submission or radical action. Hence a change is being wrought in the relationship. What was once a harmonious trio is now three distinct parts: an overhead shot shows Ghunuram lying on his bed, preoccupied with his troubles; Sibal moves to speak with him, but decides against it; and Radha continues to make up in preparation for Sambalal's show. The dialogue strengthens the poetic indication that the three-part harmony will not be heard again. When Sibal puts the idea of marriage with Ghunu to Radha, she rejects it without demur. 'What has he got?' is her simple justification, a heartless one in that it totally overlooks Ghunu's once famous talent. But it is also an indication that she has been bedazzled by the glitz of Sambalal, which has eclipsed the artistry of the Tiger Man. (Not prominent, but worth noting, is a parallel conflict of affections in the troupers' camp. When Rat thinks that Champa is his, and tells her so, he merely gives her the opportunity to put him down with a scornful comparison of himself with Samba, reminiscent of Radha's definition of a 'real man'.)

The abandoning of the true and the worthy in favour of glamour and excitement in the film's personal relationships underlines the essential philosophical focus of the film: the superseding of genuine artistic values with the plastic values of a commercial culture. In the early 1960s, where the film is set, the energetic urge to industrialise set in motion profound changes in society and, in particular, in popular culture. Technology came to play a more and more prominent role in the cultural realm, bringing about mass production of canned entertainment in the form of transistor radios and audio-cassettes, for example, and encouraging the extension of popular cinema into the rural regions of India. Television would follow, and the now ubiquitous video-cassette, proffering glitter and glamour at the press of a button, would even further suppress the need for live entertainment in the long established folk traditions. In this context Ghunuram and, of course, Shashanka, are symbols of a kind of artistic purity, but such symbols, ultimately, are destined to lose in the confrontation with the overwhelming power of the modern media that has come to manipulate the cultural needs of the masses. At the heart of the media are urban values that are characteristically violent in their assertiveness, transient and lacking in sensitivity and causing art, artists and audiences alike to be desensitised, rendered uncritical and vulgarised.

The Sambalal circus is appealing in a number of ways. It is something new and therefore pleasing to those like the young man who scornfully shouts to Ghunuram, 'Show us a new dance!' It is modern, in that it has amplification that can blare out over a distance the simple film music that the media makes so popular in India. Rat with his megaphone and cheeky advertising spiel and Champa exaggeratedly wiggling her prominent and shapely bum in imitation of Hindi film fare easily entice the villagers away from the Tiger Man they have all known for so long. Kamal the dwarf lends a touch of the exotic and Samba might well be on the covers of a dozen glossy movie magazines. And the leopard itself is *real*, underlining the gentle scorn of Gopi: 'You don't become a real tiger by painting your body.' Realism will always appeal to the young mind too impatient and uncreative to imagine. There is an echo here of the village girls whom Ghunuram meets on his way to Nonpura at the beginning of the film. When he introduces himself as Ghunuram, the Tiger Man, they reply, 'Real or pretend?'

There is a vulgar collousness about the itinerants. Slick and brash and fresh from the big city, they laugh superciliously at the awe and timidity of the unsophisticated villagers. When Ghunuram dances to the temple and through the village to the clearing where he starts his performance, the crass publicity machine of Rat and Champa destroys the sublime with vulgarity as they intrude themselves into the act, making scornful fun of Sibal and Ghunuram, and, with snatches of cheap pop songs as as their lure, they entice Ghunu's small audience away to take in the excitement of the real beast.

The question of realism is fundamental. While Ghunuram looks threatened on hearing the news of the leopard, the ever-optimistic Sibal accepts it as a challenge, and is not at all naive in his assurance that a real tiger cannot dance as Ghunuram can. The old artist is clearly of the view that art can only be diluted and ultimately dissipated by reality, and so he trusts—and here he is, indeed, naive—in the discernment of the villagers in preferring the dance to the beast. Reality is everyday, and even the novelty of a live leopard will soon become ordinary. So, of course, in terms of quality there can be no comparison between Ghunuram's act and Sambalal's, and yet, on hearing Rat and Champa boast of the great and heroic deeds of Samba, the credulous villagers literally flock to the inferior show. The realism of popular entertainment consists in its dimension of immediacy—the switch is flicked and the effect is achieved—and its popularity is due to there being no call for concentration, imagination or mental effort of any kind at all.

Dasgupta seeks the audience's sympathy for Ghunuram on two levels. On one we are led to feel pity for him as he bewails the serious downturn in his material circumstances: 'I won't last a week at this rate. What I earned in a month kept me going for three.' And, of course, he no longer has his job at the quarry, where he endured so much just for the joy of his one month a year at Nonpura: 'I feel alive only during this month.' But his real sadness lies in his perception that the villagers' attitude towards him has changed and that they no longer respect him or value his work, for that esteem was something that he regarded as 'worth more than food and clothing.' Here there is an echo of the age-old truism that art does not pay, and there is also a very clear declaration of the idealism of the artist and his justification of art for art's sake. This is at the root of Ghunuram's simple philosophy of life. His greatest joy would be to stay in Nonpura; Sibal wants him to stay; should he stay they could drum and dance to their hearts' content. Certainly, it would be easy for Ghunuram to settle in Nonpura, at least on the material level. But life, to the artist, depends on being appreciated for his art; as long as he is no longer respected as the Tiger Man, the thought of settling in Nonpura is utterly out of the question.

On the other level the director seeks to establish a basis for why an audience might respect the traditional artist. There is, of course, the total dedication of life to art, as reflected in Ghunuram's 'I feel alive only during this month,' and in Sibal's 'I practise playing the drum throughout the year so that I can accompany you when you dance. My hands itch to play the drum to your dance. Playing the drum gives me all my pleasure.' But there is also the melding of the art itself with Indian tradition and some of its heroes, men whose deeds quite obviously eclipse the braggadocio of Sambalal. As Ghunuram says, 'When our soldiers were fighting the British, my ancestors performed this dance for them.' Then he remarks poignantly that when the time comes he will not teach the dance to his son. Sibal is taken aback:

SIBAL: What, will this beautiful dance simply die out?
GHUNU: My time has passed, Dada.

The pity of this reality is brought into focus by a shot of Samba in his caravan counting his money; hence, belief in tradition and in the beauty of the dance is superseded by the commercial reality of entertainment.

Enhancing our respect for Ghunuram and all that he stands for is his reneging on a scheme, made with Sibal when the two of them were drunk, to poison the leopard. Ghunuram's morality is simple: 'A warrior fights in the open.' To emphasise the honour of Ghunu, there is a cut to the village centre where the Tiger Man is in performance, a performance that is interrupted by calls to see a man fight a *real* leopard and blighted by the cynicism of the young man, Gopi, mentioned earlier. Gopi's father gives heart to Ghunu: 'Ghunuram is an artist, not an animal.' But the restoration of the Tiger Man's pride is only temporary. He walks with head held high past the painted temple; we hear folk music on the river bank and we see the floating lamps on the water; and all of this serves to remind us of the rich tradition of which Ghunuram's art is a part. However, as he strides through the jungle, he is accosted by three amateur hunters, obviously 'on safari' from the city and ludicrously dressed for their excursion, who force Ghunuram to the ground and have themselves photographed on him as trophy. The Tiger Man's humiliation is now complete. It only remains for him to put away his tiger costume and make-up, retire from his dreams and leave Nonpura to find a job as a labourer somewhere.

To Dasgupta, this would mean the submission of art to commerce, and so he elects to make Ghunuram's demise a truly heroic one. After the failure of an inspired burst of drumming to arouse the Tiger Man, Sibal challenges Ghunu on the honour of his ancestors to perform his hereditary dance. There is a shot of the door shutting, seemingly on the past, and then the Tiger Man appears, proud and majestic. As he strides through the jungle like a king, there is a cut to a shot of the leopard: the denouement is clearly imminent.

There is little call for dialogue now. To the sound of amplified film music we watch the crowds arriving at the circus in droves and the warm-up act of Champa and Rat, the purpose of which is to squeeze as much money as possible from the gullible spectators ('the leopard won't move until they pay'). After this brief, effective reminder of the crassness of the Samba circus, the Tiger Man appears and makes his final statement:

> Your leopard is fake. You are a fraud and a thief... All of you are snubbing me for that dead leopard. Can it dance like me? No. Can it talk to you as I do? Can it portray happiness and sorrow in its show? No, it can't. That man will just rob you of your money and then he'll leave.

And so we are left with the thought that, unlike art, realism, by definition, is limited.

Although Sibal and Radha plead with Ghunuram not to accept Sambalal's invitation to enter the cage, the Tiger Man approaches his fate saying, 'A man must live with pride. I intend to do just that.' Ghunuram's resolution is immutable, and Sibal stands in solidarity with him in the only way he knows, passionately drumming the Tiger Man to the end of his last performance. The crowd flees in fear, Radha screams and pleads, and the entertainers sit stunned as the blood of Ghunuram pours onto the ground.

In one sense the ending is a tragic one, depicting a horrible suffering that arises out of apparently simple circumstances. The beast has won, yet the animal is only a metaphor for the real adversary. Does Dasgupta's film proclaim the victory of commercial culture? The answer lies in the proud, frenzied and defiant drumming of Sibal that continues as the tragic scene telescopes into extreme long shot and at last the haunting theme music heralds the closing titles.

Bagh Bahadur is essentially a metaphorical film, the intense effect of which is enhanced by its exceptionally tight economy of expression. It is true that it lacks the depth and complexity of *Phera*, but given its more pronounced rusticity and its concentration on the folk element in Indian tradition, any intellectualisation of its theme would be inappropriate to its characters and obscure what is, in fact a penetrating statement about cultural integrity. *Phera* takes one view of a problem, *Bagh Bahadur* another. Like most of Dasgupta's work, *Bagh Bahadur* is a restrained, somewhat understated film, powerful in its lack of polemic and intellectual demands.

The three 'artistic integrity' films—by no means to be thought of as a trilogy, not even in the loose sense of the three 'commitment' films—together make a particularly strong point about cultural values and the pride of the artist in contemporary society. While *Seet Grismer Smriti* is an eminently forgettable film in most respects, the other two mark Dasgupta's candid embrace of cinema as a medium for a more poetic expression of ideas, minimising dialogue, simplifying plot, and maximising the significance of the visual experience, not merely of *mise-en-scène*, but, more especially, of the juxtapositions and relationships that seek to be interpreted through it.

FIVE

But Nothing Stays the Same

Give back to me the embryo of that earlier birth;
it was intended for a different purpose.
In it there formed a cruel human arrogance
and the malice of the misbegotten
as well as the sorrow of the darkness.
Give back that aborted embryo;
that aborted embryo is mine.
Let me take it to the emaciated mother
and throw it at her tender feet
to seek to know if it was ever in her womb.

(*Give Me Back*)

Mahatma Gandhi often stressed that India's independence would not be an end in itself, but could be the means to a greater end. For the vast many, however, who had their eyes wide open on that fateful midnight hour in August 1947, light and freedom were manifestly visible; the paramount achievement had been won. Long years of civil strife, violence, deprivation and imprisonment—to say nothing of the myriad injustices of colonial rule—had at last come to an end, and India might walk into tomorrow as its own master, serving its own interests according to its own values and aspirations. Of course, the achievement had come at a great price. Apart from the lives lost by so many in fighting for it, there was the great and awesome responsibility inherent in democratic self-government, especially of a country as large, populous and poor as India. Yet the enormous blight that would keep coming back to haunt the revellers of that first Independence Night was the reality that, in order to become independent, India had also been partitioned into two countries: India, a secular state with an obvious territorial integrity, and Pakistan, a Muslim state made up of two wings hundreds of miles apart. None could deny that partition was an act of political expediency, yet at the time there were few who had any real inkling of the very worst in human behaviour that the uprooting of millions of people on apparently sectarian grounds would give rise to. This, perhaps, was the greatest component in the cost of Indian independence, and the most palpable evidence of the truth in Gandhi's warning that Independence would not be an end in itself.

Buddhadeb Dasgupta's *Tahader Katha* ('Their Story'), made in 1992, is founded on the realities of the last eight years of colonialism and the first three years of independence in a partitioned India, or, more precisely, a partitioned Bengal, for the former East Bengal had become East Pakistan. Shibnath Mukherjee (played with intense insight and sensitivity by Mithun Chakraborty) had been typical of so many Bengalis of his generation—high caste, an intellectual and a terrorist. He had graduated with an M.A. and had dedicated himself to the freedom movement which, in Bengal, particularly, was considerably more violent (or at least less Gandhian) than in most other parts of India. For the killing of a policeman—the nightmare reality of which continues to haunt his consciousness throughout his remaining years—he was sent to the infamous Andaman Islands penal colony. After eight years of his sentence, however, India became independent, and while many political prisoners were set free, Shibnath was transferred to a mental asylum for three years. The film opens after his release from that institution as he travels, after eleven years of alienation from history, back to his home and family.

The plot couldn't be more simple: Shibnath fails to adapt to life on the outside, becomes alienated from his wife and former friends and associates, kills a travelling conjurer and is returned to custody. But this is the plot of a superb film, so, obviously, the story has to be told more slowly.

Fundamental to Dasgupta's screenplay, based on a short story by Kamal Kumar Majumdar, is the characters' radical misunderstanding of their roles in history. Shibnath, albeit apprehensive and suffering quite consciously the emotional and intellectual wounds—and, to a lesser extent, the physical ones—inflicted on him during his eleven years of incarceration, hopes that things are much the same as they had been when he was taken away. On the other hand, his wife and friends hope that he will simply fit into the changed lives that they have come to take for granted. The kernel of the tragedy lies in the fact that neither side anticipates the effect of an eleven-year absence, especially one as cruel as that endured by Shibnath, on an attempt at rehabilitation. Often throughout the film, it is as though Shibnath and his wife, for instance, are looking at one another across a gulf palpably eleven years in breadth. One of the film's main aims is to examine this gulf.

We first see Shibnath's wife, Hemangini (Anasuya Majumdar) buying some trinkets from a travelling vendor of gewgaws. This image serves to stress the essentially feminine in her, and when the children rush up to break the news they have heard from the postman that their father is on his way home, her eyes gleam at the prospect of being a complete woman once again. When Shibnath arrives she is almost as bashful as a young bride, but it is soon clear that she is not the subject of her husband's evident preoccupation. Nevertheless, she does not relax in her desire to pick up exactly where they left off, as though eleven years is nothing more than a short break in time. She wants him to plan, to become active. She is anxious to make a new start, reminding him that he had been a school teacher and could teach again, that he was educated and that people admired and respected him. It does not occur to her that he is quite without bearings, cut adrift without a compass, one whom the unthinking easily describe as mad as they laugh at the intensity of his eyes and the clumsiness of his movements. While Shibnath remains the idealistic dreamer who was imprisoned for his lofty passions, Hemangini's values have become worldly. She tries to inspire Shibnath with challenging references to his former friends and associates, like Bipin, who has bought property and owns a big house and a rice mill, and those others who are 'now big people in Calcutta.' For her, the past is gone; now, for the sake of their children, they should concern themselves with the future.

Nevertheless, one must not be too critical of Hemangini's pragmatism—the last eleven years have been particularly difficult for her. Thanks to Bipin, she was able to get fifty rupees a month, and surviving on that has been by no means easy. She is unhappy that their daughter, Purni, has to go to the Deputy's house to work each day and is worried at the prospects for Jyoti, their son. Shibnath, however, cannot respond to this, other than introspectively: 'Fifty rupees. The price for all my pains!'

There are attempts to resume intimate marital relations, but they are blighted by uncertainty and apprehensiveness. There is the time that Shibnath goes to Hemangini's room, but is unwilling to wake her. On another occasion she gently rejects him with: 'Not now. I feel afraid,' and he turns, humbly, back into his loneliness. Later in the film she asks, bravely, 'Do you need me?' but this time it is he who does not respond. The sadness of it all is sharpened by the continuity here. As we watch Shibnath staring fixedly ahead, a prisoner of his past, the film cuts to a shot of Abdullah the magician and his dwarf, crossing a stream. The juxtaposition of profound melancholy with trivial artifice is extraordinarily poignant.

Much closer to Shibnath are his two children. Purni was just a little girl when he went to jail, while Jyoti was yet to be born. Between them they have less than minimal memory of their father and therefore their expectations of him are few. After all, the natural affection and simple loyalty which children so easily bear towards a parent are not tainted by thoughts of his supposed failure to live up to preconceived standards. Thus, when

Shibnath is lampooned and taunted by the village children, Purni and Jyoti are hurt and filled with pity and compassion for their apparently helpless father. Purni argues with her mother in trying to prevent her wages from being used to buy a chain with which to restrain Shibnath. Indeed, the distress she suffers on his behalf is sincerely due to her affection for him. Jyoti, too, is protective. He attacks the other children for their teasing and stone-throwing, he anxiously and earnestly looks for his father when he goes missing, and he wakes Shibnath just in time to foil the nefarious chain scheme. In a beautifully tender scene on the river bank, Jyoti shows himself eager to share in his father's past, both the triumphs and the sufferings. When asked about his dreams, Jyoti tells Shibnath that his dream is to take him by the hand and go on a long walk with him. The eleven-year-old boy has a perception of his father's qualities acute enough to render insignificant the failings and shortcomings that Hemangini and Bipin emphasise.

Of course, Hemangini is very embarrassed by the image Shibnath puts before the public, and indeed he does present a ready object of ridicule. Years of confinement have given his face an introspection marked by beautiful yet profoundly worried eyes. He is unshaven and his hair is unkempt. Gross indignities inflicted on him by warders' batons have left him with virtually no control over his bowels, so submitting him to further indignities whenever and wherever he may be taken. He also walks with an absurd, ungainly gait. So while his children are mortified by the jibes and stones thrown by the village children, Shibnath looms before his wife as a source of irritation that grows into despair.

To a large extent it is the reputation that precedes him that makes him all the more pitiful. The news of his release and imminent return home is first given to Purni and Jyoti by the postman, who refers to their father as one of the great freedom fighters. Soon after Shibnath's arrival at the house, this reputation is reinforced by an old man:

I saw him so often back in Taherpur. I heard his speeches. He inspired many to fight the British and join the Freedom Movement. He was well known and people respected him.

If reality were true to popular literature, Shibnath would be akin to a victorious warrior, coming home in triumph to a land fit for heroes. As we are to realise, the land is not fit for heroes, triumph is inappropriate, and the warrior's victories are becoming irrelevant as they start to fade beyond memory. Such is the stuff of the prevailing sadness of this immensely moving film.

The major indication that the dream has turned sour is Shibnath's friend from eleven years back, Bipin Gupta. It is Bipin who brings the East Bengali Shibnath to the home in West Bengal that he has never seen, and it was Bipin, as we have learned, who offered assistance to his family while Shibnath was in jail. It is also Bipin who will try to do everything possible to get Shibnath back on his feet again. And yet Bipin is by no means a simple, good-natured man whose wish is nothing more than the welfare of his friend. We may sympathise with his endeavour to restore Shibnath to social acceptability, but we also wonder how realistic such an endeavour is; indeed, the naiveté of it becomes gradually clearer as we get to know Shibnath better. Bipin wants to entice Shibnath back into teaching, and tries to whet his appetite for that profession by talk of land that is being set aside for Shibnath's own school. Shibnath's refusal angers Bipin:

SHIBNATH: What will become of my dreams? The people of Taherpur are still waiting for me.
BIPIN: No one is waiting for anybody, Shibnath.

But no one takes the trouble to ask Shibnath what his dreams actually are, and the gap between him and Bipin is made evident by Bipin's impatience:

SHIBNATH: Don't you have any dreams, Bipin?
BIPIN (*angrily*): Stop talking nonsense, Shibnath!

Such impatience at one so psychologically scarred and who has suffered so profoundly in the name of patriotism would seem more than odd in an old friend, but the sad fact is that Bipin is no real friend. Bipin has political ambitions—essentially personal ones, for he is no idealist as Shibnath is—and his scheme is to advance those ambitions by exploiting Shibnath's reputation as a freedom fighter, for Shibnath will surely involve himself energetically in Bipin's campaign, resurrecting the skills of oratory with which he impressed so many people years ago. At least, that is Bipin's vision, but Shibnath sees that campaigning for him can hardly be likened to fighting for the freedom of India, and his reaction to Bipin's scheme is quite perceptive:

> Eleven years is a very long time. One forgets almost everything. But you were released after only two months.

And later he reminds Bipin:

> They let you out of jail because you confessed, while Mohitosh and I rotted there for so many years.

Nevertheless, Bipin's resolve is not dampened. He is determined to take Shibnath to the Deputy in order to get a certificate to make up for the now lost papers of his academic record, and he will strengthen his efforts to convince Shibnath that he can provide a career for him. There is a hint of how all this might eventuate as the two of them set off to the Deputy's house, Bipin full of words of practical wisdom about elections, money for the school and the Deputy himself, when their path is crossed by the bizarre trio of Abdullah, the dwarf and their horse, Jahanara. This simple intrusion of one image into another provides both a cogent comment as well as an indication of the direction the plot is to take. Bipin's intentions for Shibnath are as fake as the magic of Abdullah. Shibnath might be 'mad', but he is no fool, and as they approach the Deputy's house, he starts to see things clearly when Bipin expresses impatience with his particular weakness:

> BIPIN: Do you have to shit?
> SHIBNATH: Yes. On your face! On your father's face! On the Deputy's face!

Predictably, perhaps, the visit to the Deputy turns out disastrously. The Deputy is a fatuous man, reminiscent of the bosses in *Duratwa* and *Grihayuddha*. He trivialises Shibnath's reputation and humiliates him, provoking Shibnath to abuse him and run enraged from the house. (This is a hint of the film's final dramatic act, a signification that is reinforced by Shibnath's reaction to Bipin's desire to control him: 'If you tell me to be a goat, will I be a goat?') Bipin gets angry, not out of despair for Shibnath, but merely on account of concern for his own political skin.

The counter to Bipin might have been provided by Mohitosh, but he, for reasons of altruism, is absent for the most part of Shibnath's limited homecoming. His importance to Shibnath is established early in the film, when Shibnath is on the train; one of the first things he asks Bipin is, 'Where is Mohitosh?', a question that is to be repeated several times, both to Bipin and Hemangini, before the two men actually meet up with one another for the first time after the three years that Shibnath spent in the asylum. When Shibnath finally gets an answer to his enquiry about Mohitosh, the question is asked of Bipin and, given its timing, clearly implies an unfavourable comparison of him with Mohitosh. Bipin informs Shibnath as disinterestedly as he can that Mohitosh wouldn't fit into the new India, and has gone—to no one's disappointment—to teach literacy to tribal children in a nearby village. Mohitosh is one, apparently, who believed with Gandhi that Independence was to be a medium by which greater things might be done for the benefit of all, especially the least advanced of the newly emancipated. Clearly, he was of no use to Bipin and his like, and could be easily forgotten.

Shibnath's eventual meeting with Mohitosh is, cinematically, a most impressive one. The composition is arranged vertically, with the class of small children, their backs to the camera, in the foreground, Mohitosh on a veranda step in the centre, and Shibnath calling to him through a barred window beyond the veranda's open doorway on the other side of the tiny schoolhouse. The unexpectedness of Shibnath's voice, more tangible at first than his visual aspect, gives enough of a shock to Mohitosh to urge him to run. It is but an impulse, not a genuine endeavour, given force by the eleven years of hellishness that the association brings so suddenly to his mind. When the two men do sit down with one another, Mohitosh quietly, rationally and extraordinarily graphically spells out his cynicism of the newly won freedom.

> Gradually the country is filling up with caterpillars. We did not realise it. The English are gone, but now what? We have a worse raj, a caterpillar raj, crawling all over and under the throne, and for just a little gain they will eat each other's vomit.

To Mohitosh, the battle has not yet been won, so the fight must continue. In his work, humble and with minimal material reward, he makes sense of this notion of the ongoing battle with the caterpillar raj led by the Bipins of Bengal.

The recently proclaimed free India is not the only India that is represented in Dasgupta's film. There is the India of the tribal people, for example, whose distant singing we hear at night and to whose children Mohitosh has dedicated himself. But there is also a hint of an exotic India, a land far from the twentieth century, yet all too easily accommodated in the modern era just the same. This India is suggested by the anonymous, faceless hawker of trinkets and, to a much greater extent, by the itinerant magician, Abdullah, and his dwarf. Essential to their livelihood are the rustic people who provide them with an admiring crowd and a handful of coins wherever they perform. An intelligent viewer might think twice about Shibnath's alleged mental disability when Abdullah announces himself to a gathering of villagers:

> I am Abdullah the Magician with magic medicine. I can give life to the dead and take it away. Ghosts and demons dance at my call.

Central to his act is to call on a member of the audience, whom he 'turns into' a goat, which he then 'marries' to the dwarf (already declared to be a she-goat), who produces from her costume 'their' kid, as the audience applaud with rapt enthusiasm. Dasgupta is careful to put this particular aspect of the exotic into proper perspective by showing the slipping of a coin a little later to the volunteer from the audience. The illusion is finally destroyed when, before bathing in the river, the dwarf takes off his dress and false bosom and the great Abdullah removes his colourful, flamboyant robes and wades into the water in his underpants, clearly nothing more than an ordinary man. The show business fake is a parallel to the social and political fakes that Shibnath sees in Bipin and the Deputy, frauds that Mohitosh has long been aware of.

However, if the dissemblers and the charlatans are applauded and advanced, where does that leave Shibnath? Like anyone who cannot fit into a given society, he is declared 'mad', and the reasoning for declaring Shibnath to be mad is no stronger than that which Shakespeare gives to Polonius to use against Hamlet:

> Your noble son is mad:
> Mad call I it; for, to define true madness,
> What is't but to be nothing else but mad?

Tahader Katha should not be viewed as a film which seeks to define true madness, for it is in no way a psychological polemic. Whether Shibnath is clinically sane or otherwise is not the film's point. The point is that Shibnath is an intense idealist, a dreamer and a stickler for truth and sincerity, who does not fit into a society which has started to establish itself before his coming to it. Undoubtedly, there is a great gap in Shibnath's empirical understanding of the new order, a gap that might lend circumstantial credibility to thoughts of his mental deficiency. He needs to be told by Bipin that there is no such thing as East Bengal any more and that his native village of Taherpur is now in a foreign country. He also needs to be told that he has a son. Hemangini talls him of the riots that accompanied partition, of the burning of houses and the forced dislocation of millions. She talks frankly of their midnight escape during a storm, the drowning of first his father and then his brother trying to save him. She talks of his mother's disappearance in search of her son. Shibnath listens to all of this dispassionately, his stoicism perhaps disproving that he is unable to comprehend it. But one thing that Shibnath can understand and has learnt to philosophically accept is suffering; his real difficulty lies in coming to terms with humbug, and even his wife is of no support to him in this. She, after all, makes excuses for the Deputy when Purni complains about his molesting her, and she tacitly sides with the pragmatist Bipin, even when Shibnath exposes his rank hypocrisy in wanting to use the freedom movement to his own selfish ends.

The question of Shibnath's madness is first posed by himself to Bipin, but later Shibnath comes to ask Bipin where the insanity really does lie:

> But who is mad? Me? Or you? Deputy...Party...
> Can't you see it has all started to stink?

Later, the old man who earlier had talked glowingly of him as a freedom fighter from Taherpur, asks him innocently and sincerely what it is like to step into 'free India'. Shibnath's reply is merely to raise his leg and fart. Indeed, he wonders whether whether he is better off being 'free':

> Perhaps jail was better. At least there I had dreams of a better world. But now I can see it is rotten. It stinks. I don't understand a thing!

Shibnath is able to perceive, in fact, that the significant question is not what is wrong with himself, but what is wrong with the world. Astutely, he covers stupidity, corruption and failed nationalism in a simple conversation with his son:

> You have seen this world for eleven years. How does it seem to you? Is it like an orange, a little flat on the head and on the arse? Actually, the world is like a banana, for lucky monkeys. Peel it and eat it! If you have to you can even divide it. If I knew the world would be like this I wouldn't have brought you into it.

The central reason that the world is fit for monkeys is that what was noble yesterday is derided today. We listen to Shibnath recite some patriotic lines:

> Oh wayfarer stop awhile.

> If you were born in Bengal, wait.
> If we are told to fight tomorrow we will fight,
> Even if the sun is going down.

Then we see Abdullah and his dwarf chasing after Jahanara in the background. The effect is established by an immediate cut to a shot, later, of Shibnath sitting alone under a tree as Abdullah and the dwarf pass by in the background. The juxtaposition clearly suggests the oxymoron, mad is sane and sane is mad. Sadly, it is often the case that majorities cannot be comfortable in the company of an Other; as long as their conviction of their own normality goes unchallenged, eccentrics may be tolerated. Hence, Abdullah and his dwarf are acceptable as entertainers who legitimately trade on their cultivated eccentricity, whereas those who are sincere in their ideological Otherness, for example, are frequently lambasted with vitriol in order to establish their disagreeableness and to strengthen the threatened values of the majority. The village boys who taunt and throw stones at Shibnath are ignorant louts who express their discomfort crudely; those who would chain him to his bed are more sophisticated in their response to Otherness, but just as crude in their expression of it.

Having established, gradually and with appropriate pathos, the discord and the callousness in the coming together of the man of dreams and the kingdom of caterpillars, Dasgupta uses very simple narrative with minimal dialogue to resolve the dissonance. Having been told about the fiasco at the Deputy's house, Hemangini resolves to take up Bipin's suggestion and chain Shibnath to his bed. This provides a dramatic peak in the film, having been carefully alluded to in conversation between Hemangini and a neighbour, and built up to with emotion, tension and duplicity. While the children make plain their abhorrence at the plan, Hemangini is determined.

> Don't I have any feelings? Do you think my heart has dried up? Every day people throw stones at him. I can't bear it any more.

While it remains unclear whether she is acting in her husband's best interests or her own, Shibnath can be heard in the background, singing of a caged bird. Later that night, when Hemangini and the blacksmith sneak into Shibnath's room to attach the chain, Jyoti awakens his father in time. He momentarily relives the horrible associations that a chain triggers in his mind, and in panic dashes from the house, never to return. Having watched her plummet to the depths of insensitivity, we have also seen the last of Hemangini.

The scene now cuts from night to the next day and the shot is of Shibnath's image in the mirror of the hawker, ominously confined, as it were. The hawker quickly sets off. Shibnath runs after him, but he is distracted by the drum beating the arrival nearby of Abdullah the Magician. All the disillusionment that Shibnath has experienced since coming home is encapsulated in this brief final episode. Abdullah selects him as a subject from the audience and, to demonstrate his powers, forces him to eat leaves. Mechanically, it seems, Shibnath submits, but Abdullah would humiliate him further, spitting on his hand and demanding that Shibnath lick it up. This is the point at which reason, poetry and dreams all desert Shibnath, and he attacks Abdullah and strangles him. There is a sinister irony in the echo of Shibnath's song about the bird:

> A caged bird flies away in search of fresh air.
> Bars cannot hold him.
> He spreads his wings and the cage breaks.
> A caged bird flies away.

There is also a poignant irony in the parallel between the dwarf's sobbing for his dead master and Jyoti's frantic running after the train that is taking the bird back to his cage. The first we saw of Shibnath was his hand at the window of the train, feeling the free air. That hand is now chained, and there is a wealth of spiritual truth in Shibnath's simple physical statement, 'It is cold.'

Tahader Katha is an intensely poetic film, remarkable for its elliptical dialogue, which is economic and tightly controlled, allowing for maximum concentration on the purely visual images.

These are enhanced, where appropriate, by an exceptionally fine soundtrack. Bishwadeb Dasgupta's intensely evocative music, introduced with the opening titles, is used sparingly throughout the film. Between sections of dialogue there is silence, interrupted only by the sounds of birds, rain or the singing of tribal women, giving the film a powerful intensity and providing it with a suitable context for its poetic expression.

Symbol and suggestion, then, are able to play a significant part without having to be over-used or laboured. The first shot, accompanying the opening titles, of a flock of birds against the sky, is a simple statement of freedom, which is complemented after the titles by an equally simple statement of confinement in the framing of the limited world in a hawker's mirror, so establishing two basic notions of the film without a word of dialogue. Mention has already been made of comments being suggested by simple juxtapositions, such as shots of Shibnath with Abdullah and his dwarf in the background or crossing the path of Shibnath and Bipin. Slow motion is used with excellent suggestive effect on two occasions: one is Shibnath's dropping of a book, which symbolises his eleven-year alienation from learning, and the other is the breaking of a mirror to express the depth of his hostility towards Bipin.

Effective as a counter to narrative realism is the film's impressionism, created by discontinuous editing to produce connected though non-sequential images, or by showing apparently inconsequential, isolated images, or sometimes by an unconventional treatment of time. With narrative realism, conventional perceptions of time are of paramount importance, but in *Tahader Katha* time definitions, at least in the present, have no real call to be made. The fact that the film's time-span is indeterminable and that it has no clear and obvious temporal perspective helps to highlight the particularly definite nature of eight years plus three as well as to allow for a kind of temporal amorphousness that is atmospherically important in establishing the confusions experienced by Shibnath as well as by his family. Especially effective is the transilience that Dasgupta employs on a number of occasions, such as when Shibnath, with Abdullah and the dwarf in the background, is seen during a storm, and in the next shot there is the same composition, but the day is fine. A similar effect is achieved when Shibnath runs from the house to escape the chain, and it is night; the shot is cut to Shibnath running to the hawker, but it is day.

Quite apart from the refinement of its techniques, much of the cinematography in *Tahader Katha* is exceptionally beautiful. The film's particular rural setting is indeed well chosen, and the camera has worked with splendid effect to impress on the viewer the natural beauty of the land. A shot of children leaving their swing in the woods and running up a hill to their home, shots by the river, occasional glimpses of the expanse of countryside that features so much in Bengali poems and songs, all help to establish that important element of nationalism, the physical beauty of one's homeland. This is, of course, something that affects Shibnath deeply, and this emotion is poignantly offset by the contrast it throws up—on the one hand the loveliness of Bengal, on the other the perverse self-interest of the people who now would hold the country's destiny in their hands. In this respect the cinematography is notably important in giving at least some inkling of the perception Shibnath has of the land of his birth, so that the audience fully appreciates his welling antipathy to Bipin and his ilk.

The visual impact of some sequences is especially memorable. One is inside the house at night; it is soon after Shibnath's homecoming and he and Hemangini are still getting to know one another. The camera follows a circular ambit from Shibnath on the right of the screen to Hemangini on the extreme left, showing them in two orbits, moving in proximity to one another but never merging. The lamplight and its shadows, the spatial arrangement of the characters, and the background sound of the steady rain, all highlight the absence of intimacy and serve to stress the distance between the two people, the woman groping to find a man who no longer exists, the man groping to find his bearings in a world in which he seems more and more to have no place.

And then there is a shot of Shibnath sitting alone against a tree beside the road, articulating his confusion, frustration and his sense of his own alienation. The camera encircles the tree, giving the effect of Shibnath being pinioned. As he utters his last lines the camera, quite incidentally, takes into its ambit Bipin in the distance, cycling down the road and then pulling up alongside Shibnath just as he finishes speaking. The simple circular trolley shot elucidates compellingly the perception that for men such as Shibnath the world is a jail and the Bipin Guptas are the turnkeys.

As is the case in Dasgupta's previous films, particularly *Bagh Bahadur*, sub-framing is very effectively used to enhance the meaning in *Tahader Katha*. In order to create the framing of a subject within the natural frame of the camera's lens, the obvious architectural devices—doorways and windows—are used to fine effect, as is the hawker's mirror and the children's swing. The wood is also effective, the lines of trees providing a natural framing along with the suggestion of confinement. This kind of framing offers the value of pinpointing a particular focus, often giving quite naturally an intensity to a visual image that might otherwise need to be achieved by a degree of artifice. It can also provide 'advance' continuity; for example, during a dialogue between Shibnath and Bipin, the camera moves easily to take in a window through which Hemangini can be seen coming up the path. The camera intimates clearly what is in store without interrupting the present shot. What makes this framing so interesting is its density—there is always a picture beyond the picture.

Technically, then, *Tahader Katha* bears most of the general characteristics of Dasgupta's previous films, but especially *Phera* and *Bagh Bahadur*. Yet, in some ways it also represents a departure and in some an advance. The film is as well put together as any of the others, but given the spare use of dialogue, the very careful restraint placed on background music and the notably thin narrative, intense potency is demanded of the visual images. This has engendered greater sophistication in composition, camera work and continuity than we have seen in any of his previous films. The film's continuity submits to the demands of metaphor, making the sequence of scenes notably impressionistic and apparently disjointed, but with an overall logic that reflects an exceptional breadth of artistic vision.

The theme, too, is an unusual and, indeed, a daring one—after all, people like to see their heroes as heroes, not as madmen. Moreover, Indians would like to think that their country deserved its nationhood and that the post-independence generations have been worthy legatees of what those heroes fought for. Yet *Tahader Katha* candidly attributes shame, not pride, to the beneficiaries of the freedom movement. The genuine idealists of nationalism, represented by Shibnath and Mohitosh, become fringe-dwellers or are put away. It is the pragmatic self-seekers, represented by Bipin and the Deputy, who set the agenda for the new nation, and it is their ideals of personal advancement and material profit which would seem to prevail. Dasgupta's view, that independence, as Gandhi understood the term, remains remote in modern India, might be true, but it is hardly popular. The utterly shameful treatment of Shibnath and, to a lesser extent, Mohitosh, must prompt discomfiting questions about the nature of contemporary Indian society and challenge some of the mythology of Indian nationalism as so much cant. Shibnath dreamed of a new India that would be free and just, yet his dreams are derided and his ideas scorned as inappropriate.

However, it would be a mistake to see the film too much in this historical light, for it is not so much a film about nationalism as it is a film about human suffering set against a nationalist background. What is prominent is the pain and the torment of people cut off, inexplicably, from one another—the woman who cannot know her husband, the children who want to love their father and continually find obstacles in the way of their affection, and the man who can find no rational perspective in his life nor a meaningful direction to the hearts of his wife and children. The physical and emotional suffering, particularly Shibnath's, can be readily understood; considerably more subtle and complex is the much deeper, unarticulated suffering that emanates from the cruelly enigmatic foreignness of all that ought to be familiar. *Tahader Katha* is the story of Shibnath's tragedy of alienation, an alienation made all the more stark by its apparent continuity with his brutal incarceration, and made all the more heart-rending by its consequent tearing at the natural bonds that tie a man to his family. The nationalist element of the film is really incidental to this human tragedy, drawing it beyond the bounds of its 1950s setting. Idealism is simply the particular vehicle for the portrayal of the universal experience of human suffering.

SIX

The Gilded Cage and the Lonely Sky

Now is the time. Come, let us go far off!
The promise has long been in the wind
Beckoning to fly away. Come!
Our tents are alive with readiness
The unwavering sun beckons with both hands,
Showing us the way.
Come! Let us go far off!
Off into the distance!
Come!

(*Now is the Time*)

Most of Buddhadeb Dasgupta's films contain characters whose lives are based on dreams: dreams of social justice, dreams of material success, dreams of artistic achievement, dreams of love, dreams of nation. Some dreams are realistic, some would seem to be beyond reach; some of the dreamers have their feet planted firmly on the ground, while others have their heads high in the clouds. The meaning and significance of dreams is often intensely personal, especially amongst the latter category of dreamers, and as Dasgupta has come to be interested more and more in less conventional, less ordinary characters, his films have taken on a focus correspondingly more personal. While his earlier films achieved their significance in a particular sociopolitical or socioeconomic context, *Phera*, *Bagh Bahadur*, *Tahader Katha* and *Charachar* concentrate on the personal, private world of a particular character. The major characters in the early films were often dreamers, but their dreams were tinged with a kind of realism, given the pertinence of the social context in which the characters lived and tried to make sense of their lives. But from *Phera* on, the social context becomes less and less important as the significance of the individual becomes gradually greater. While these later characters are entirely credible, they give the films colour and intensity of interest by their exceptional singularity and unconformity. The protagonist of *Charachar* is such a character; despite his simplicity, his marked unusualness gives the film its richness, and the power of his dreams provides it with its essential poetry.

Charachar ('The Shelter of the Wings') was made in 1993, and concerns Lakhindar, a bird-catcher (played by Rajit Kapoor), who pursues his profession not out of choice but in obedience to his hereditary caste and in accordance with what continues of Hindu social tradition. The overriding irony in his work lies in the fact that he has an exceptionally tender fondness for birds and an abiding fascination with their nature. As a professional bird-catcher he is a failure, rejoicing in setting free almost as many birds as he catches. Preventing this scenario from becoming comic are the social and domestic ramifications of Lakhindar's eccentricity. His older associate, Bhushan, constantly chides him for what he sees as his flippancy and irresponsibility, urging him to pursue with care the profession of his forefathers and so honour his debts to the middleman, Shashmal, and fulfil his domestic obligations to his wife, Shari. But right from the opening titles Dasgupta is at pains to establish that such conventional responsibility goes radically against the grain of Lakhindar's nature.

It is Lakhindar's nature that gives total significance to *Charachar*. He is central to every scene in the film, and even when he is not physically present, one remains conscious of him. It is important to note, then, that the earliest scenes in the film serve in establishing his character. The opening shots will reappear several times as the spatial context of Lakhindar's recurring dream of his dead son, Netai, while the opening titles appear against the picture of a hand opening the door of a cage and the strong, hairy arm of a man reaching towards the sky, gently coaxing the captured birds to their freedom. These two sequences also offer hints of the two kinds of dreams that will shape Lakhindar's behaviour throughout the film; one is a recurring dream founded in memory, the other is a more abstract dream of aspiration, symbolised by the hand reaching upward, offering life and freedom. In these opening sequences we discern a movement of focus from sky to cage to sky, a cycle which the complex arrangement of images throughout the rest of the film will substantiate. It is also interesting to note that the scene and music that Buddhadeb gives us to associate with Netai opens and ends the film, thus giving it a framework connected with the dreams of its central character.

Following the titles, the arm giving freedom to the birds is given narrative significance. The first shot is through a frame within the frame, looking from inside the cottage of Lakhindar and his wife, Shari, to the edge of the forest outside, and the sub-framing (the device is used relatively infrequently in *Charachar*) serves to make clear the distinction between the natural and the domestic. As the natural picture fades out of sight, the domestic one takes over as Shari begins expressing her serious concern for their material well-being, given that Lakhindar has the habit of setting free the only source of livelihood they have. Her quite reasonable complaint is greeted by flippancy from Lakhindar, who appears to be rejoicing in the new freedom of the birds he had only recently caught, and it is clear—even at this early stage—that he has little concern for material matters.

There are other early indications of Lakhindar's special concern for birds. He tenderly holds one of the birds caught in the snare set by himself and Bhushan, and remarks with obvious pleasure that this is the third time he has caught it. He admires its beauty and its lack of fear, then gently coaxes it to freedom. In what turns out to be a clear pointer to a major turning-point later, Lakhindar talks of how the thought of the birds he catches being killed and eaten makes him physically sick. And his special relationship with them is suggested in:

> I've heard the birds ask me, 'There are so many other jobs in the world. Why do you catch us? Why do you put us in cages? Why do you sell us?'

In one exceptionally moving scene he caresses a tree in which some of them perch, creating a picture not only of his affection for the birds, but also of his intimacy with their environment and his own remoteness from the world of work and domestic responsibility. To Bhushan, who is with him at the time, men who caress trees are simply mad.

But the most significant element in Lakhindar's feelings for birds is the memory of his little boy, Netai, who died some six or seven years earlier at the age of three. Lakhindar's dominant and recurring memory of Netai is of the child's distress at finding a dead bird and his subsequent burying of it in the belief that he was planting a bird tree from which many birds would bloom. The memory of his son pricks Lakhindar's conscience concerning the work he does, and he remembers how the boy would cry at the thought of his father catching and selling birds. Much of the film's poetry, the essence of which is given form by the dreams of the bird-catcher, is founded in the notion of Netai's being something of an *alter ego* for Lakhindar or, rather, a quaint inversion of the popular idea of the father living on in the son. Specifically, what lives on in Lakhindar are childlike innocence and an abundance of compassion for the natural world. Lakhindar believes that it is Netai's love for birds that lives on in him: 'By now maybe I love them more than I loved Netai.'

In his musing on the origins of birds and the infinity of their number there is further indication of Lakhindar's remoteness from the workaday philosophy of the straightforward, mundane and somewhat dour Bhushan. Lakhindar wonders at the vastness of the birds' horizon, as he looks into the distance through his own experience of a little river flowing on into a big river and then—as he has learnt from hearsay—down to the sea. This sets him thinking about the sounds of the sea and, especially, the flapping of thousands of wings over it. The poet in Lakhindar is marked by the contrasting retort of Bhushan: 'Why don't you talk sense?' To the audience, however, these musings are not as extraordinary as they might seem to Bhushan, given the great care taken by the director to establish the closeness of Lakhindar to the natural world at which he marvels. Moreover, it is clear on several occasions that birds are attracted to *him*. Particularly significant in this respect is a sequence that has Lakhindar waking from a dream about Netai to find a number of birds coming to settle on and near him, after which he proceeds to release those he had already caged.

The intimate communion between Lakhindar and the birds provides the basis for the yearning in Lakhindar's heart:

> I wish I could fly like them. From way up there I could look down and see you. You, Shari, Natobar, Shashmal. What a lovely life the birds have! No need to earn money, no house to look after. Just flying and flying.

On one level, this is an expression of a somewhat fantastic wish to be a bird, but examined more closely it reveals a cry for release from the cage in which Lakhindar is already imprisoned. His human condition is encumbered by responsibilities which are, to him, onerous—earning a living by work that is repugnant to his sensibilities, having to provide for a wife and pay a middleman, and facing the discomfiture of a marriage into which another man has intruded. While it would be absurd to see *Charachar* as a film about a man wanting to be a bird, it would be just as simplistic to see it merely as the story of a man wanting to escape from his disagreeable condition. What is significant is the constant tension between the desire to be and the desire to be rid of, and it is the gradually changing arrangement of the subtle complexities that make up these two desires that forms the film's plot dynamics.

The film's denouement consists in the ultimate easing of this tension, the logic of which is portrayed by a series of images rather than by any working out of narrative details. There are three particular images that might be singled out as principal stepping-stones. The first of these is the freeing of the birds Lakhindar had taken to Calcutta. Seen in its context—the intense reaction to having eaten birds' flesh and the singularly determined and stylistically drawn-out return home from Calcutta—this shows his decision to close categorically that part of his life that Shari and Bhushan would call his social responsibility.

This resolve is strengthened a little later when Gouri virtually offers herself to him as an alternative wife to Shari. She then asks him: 'If you love birds, you can still love a woman, can't you?' But he offers no reply; all his meaning is expressed by the simple physical separation of himself from her.

The third major image is Lakhindar's long slumber after Shari has gone away with her lover, Natobar. The length of the sleep, suggested by a variety and mix of camera shots, is significant in that it represents Lakhindar's break with married life prior to embarking on the solitary yet fulfilling life he longs for. Moreover, the length of the sleep to some extent implies its peacefulness, and it is quite obvious to the viewer that in this sleep Lakhindar is no longer troubled by domestic concerns and that his conscience, as far as the memories of Netai are concerned, is becoming clear.

Thus, in these three images, Lakhindar rejects conventional employment, the opportunity for love, and his marriage. Underlining this abandonment of society is his transition from householder to hermit, reflected in his serene unconcern for his livelihood. 'There's plenty to eat in the jungle.' Yet, while the audience may appreciate his removal from mundanity, Bhushan cannot, continuing to goad him: 'If you are a man, go there! Beat up that bastard and bring back your wife!' Despite the resolute rejection of his past, he does, nevertheless, make a sincere gesture to act on Bhushan's advice, but the endeavour proves futile. It is here that he poignantly underlines his contentment with the forest: 'There's the earth, the sky, the marshes, the birds. They'll take care of me. Just one life. It will pass.' The logical connection with the beginning of the film lies in the reiteration of the Netai memory, preceding Lakhindar's awakening into his new life that concludes the film.

Some will see Lakhindar as a rebel, one who bucks the established rules of social and familial responsibility. But this apparent rebelliousness is merely the effect, there being no consciously conceived anarchic cause. It is also possible to see him as a loser; in fact, he has to lose all that ordinary men would hold dear in order to gain the dream that is at the core of his life. Lakhindar's options—marriage with Shari and harmony with the birds—are mutually exclusive; there is no possibility of straddling both worlds. Ultimately, however, these notions of rebelliousness and loss are totally overshadowed by the ending, which is manifestly a triumph of the spirit.

Radical to this triumph is the breakdown of Lakhindar's marriage with Shari. Obviously, the experience is a painful one, but it is nevertheless essential that his new life contain no vestiges of the captive life that job and house and wife had meant for him. Indeed, the potential for rift in the marriage is set up in the early shots after the titles, where the visual distinction between the natural and the domestic is made along with the symbolic suggestion of the growing alienation of Lakhindar from Shari. As noted earlier, the camera is placed inside the small cottage of Lakhindar and Shari and looks through a window to the forest beyond; gradually the camera moves so that the sub-frame of the forest disappears and the frame is filled by the domestic interior. Now the visual image of distinction is reinforced by the characters, as Shari voices her concern over everyday bread-and-butter matters and Lakhindar responds casually. The wife's concerns are genuine, and she gains no reassurance at all from Lakhindar's making light of them. And this is the essence of the marital tension—not so much that the husband is irresponsible and does not provide properly for his wife, but rather that he does not seem in the least to share her worries. The two do feel and care for one another, but theirs is a dispassionate bond, for all romance has gone out of their marriage. Even when Lakhindar wants to talk about their relationship, Shari wants to sleep. Their life together has become a contract in which they create a mutual bind as each unwittingly and unavoidably smothers the aspirations of the other. The earliest shot in the film—a cage silhouetted against the sky—speaks much of this marriage: one partner finding meaning and the hope for security in the economic complexities of everyday life, the other seeking release from those same complexities.

Being without children has the effect of throwing their flimsy relationship into sharper relief and highlighting—perhaps exaggerating—the meagreness of the few positive threads that are holding them together. Lakhindar tells Shari, 'I feel scared sometimes that you won't stay with me any more,' and yet one can't help but wonder why this should trouble him. Perhaps he has simply grown used to her and as yet has not come to conceive of an unmarried life. Perhaps he sees her as the one remaining link with Netai. Shari, however, makes herself perfectly plain: 'Bring money home, and then I'll know you are a man.' In their unsophisticated, pre-modern rural society, gender roles and responsibilities are clearly defined; the essence of being a man is simply to work and to provide for his family. Lakhindar fails at that, and he is not noticeably moved by Shari's concern over her meagre diet and her shabby clothes. The one thing that brings a sparkle to her eye is the sound of Natobar's motorbike.

Lakhindar knows he is being cuckolded—Shari makes no attempt to deny it, and Bhushan constantly agitates him to do something about it. Natobar is good to Shari, bringing her gifts and sometimes money, wanting her to go away with him so that he can provide for her as Lakhindar cannot, promising her the security that she craves. When she asks Lakhindar to set her free like one of his birds, his reply is perfectly apt: 'If you fly away from here, you'll only enter another cage.' Yet a cage is attractive as long as Natobar, the provider, will be there.

As Natobar is the rival of Lakhindar, Shari sees the birds as her rivals. She tells Natobar:

> Sometimes I think he'll go mad with those birds. He catches them and lets them go. He talks with them. He dreams about them. There's no place for me in that world. But sometimes he is another man and he cares for me. I don't understand him.

Lakhindar's dilemma is that he must make a choice between Shari and the birds. She recognises that he probably loves her, after his own fashion, but it is patently clear to her that he loves the birds so much more:

> They've been coming between us for such a long time. They are always there. I can't reach you. [Natobar] wants just me. It's true it was a poor life with you, but don't think that's why I left.

He asks her if she is happy, and her reply encapsulates the pathos of this sad marriage:

> Happiness—what is it? I don't know. I eat twice a day now. I have some clothes. There is a good roof over my head. He gives me everything. If that's what happiness is, I am happy.

It would seem that the security of a cage is the nearest Shari will get to happiness. After the final, abortive attempt at reconciliation, Lakhindar sends her to the lurking Natobar, but as Lakhindar walks on alone towards the setting sun and Shari and Natobar get back onto the motorbike, there is a heaviness in the mood that obscures any thought of Lakhindar releasing a bird from a cage.

Lakhindar is by no means an oddball, not even especially eccentric. There are many people who do not fit into the world in which they find themselves, and he is but one. Gouri actually admires him:

> But I love to see you [releasing the birds]. It wouldn't seem you if you didn't. Your face shines when you do it.

Lakhindar can only rue the fact that Shari is not like Gouri. Yet there is nothing of the romantic in Gouri's father, Bhushan, who is appalled at Lakhindar's lack of response to his goading about Natobar. Yet Lakhindar must suffer humiliation at Natobar's mischief and Shari's unfaithfulness; he certainly feels ashamed about his indebtedness to Shashmal, his failure as a bird-catcher, and the public knowledge of him as a cuckold. So when we see him in the forest, welcoming the heavy rain that falls on his scantly clad body and embracing and snuggling against the trees, we see him in his element. Bhushan, however, sees him only as a fool. 'Better if you'd go and give Natobar a kick in the arse.' Lakhindar is intelligent enough not to do so and suggests dispassionately that it might, in fact, be Shari who is to blame.

Generally, the characters of *Charachar* are unremarkable, yet their simple ordinariness is sharply pertinent to the film's underlying aim of showing a humble man in pursuit of his own notion of a grand dream. Each of the characters is readily understandable, and none is really dislikeable. While Natobar might evoke a degree of disapproval in some, he is indeed sincere in his desire to make Shari happy, and she too is genuine in her appreciation of his looking after her. Bhushan is dry and unimaginative, yet earnest in his concern for Lakhindar's material and marital welfare, as well as that of his daughter, Gouri. The middlemen of the bird-trading business, while primarily concerned about their own profits, are hardly extortionists, showing Lakhindar a considerable degree of forbearing as well as a measure of charity. The two unsophisticated women, Shari and Gouri, both inspire pity by the softness of their hearts and the melancholy emptiness of their lives. Maybe the film's poignancy consists to some extent in the lack of a character who can be disliked, and by blaming who the audience gets a chance to redirect some of its feelings of sadness.

Charachar is an essentially gentle film, yet it is not without incidents of violence. While in another context these might be altogether overlooked, given this film's serene ambience their effects are profoundly emotional. As he showed so clearly in his previous film, *Tahader Katha*, Dasgupta can create moments of intense and lingering pity without any trace of sentimentalism, a pity that has been engendered by some element of violence felt intensely by an individual yet which might perhaps seem even trivial to an observer. One kind of violence suffered by Lakhindar emanates from the mental reminders he has of the actuality of Netai's death, reminders which, on the one hand, disturb his sleep and, on the other, destroy his ability to work at his inherited trade. Then there is the ongoing emotional violence he suffers from the awareness of Shari's affair with Natobar and his own corresponding inadequacy and growing unattractiveness to his wife. The most intense experience of violence—and the major turning-point in the film—comes from the appalling revelation, as far as Lakhindar is concerned, at a feast in Calcutta generously provided by Kalicharan, the bird-trader, that he has been eating a dish of the wild geese that fly in the skies over his own home. And finally there is the stock kind of physical violence when Natobar desperately attacks Lakhindar over Shari, comes off second best, yet wins the woman. Violence, a pervasive feature of our lives, is never treated by Dasgupta as particularly meaningful in itself, but rather for the sadness of its context and the pity that it generates. In *Charachar* the violence, for the most part, is carefully controlled and subtle, simmering rather than erupting.

The gentleness of the film is enhanced greatly by the elements of its atmosphere. Bishwadeb Dasgupta's music is beautiful in its wistful implication of dream and melancholy, and the director's typically sparing use of music intensifies its effect, especially the sadness of the solo flute. The most striking visual element is that of space, underlining the film's lack of business and action. It is all unhurried, the pace being set by the leisurely gait of the characters and the steady flow of the river. Lakhindar's return home from Calcutta, for example, might well have been effected by a single cut, but here it is beautifully drawn-out, to stress that Lakhindar belongs to the fields and the forests, and suggesting, by taking time and using quite a variety of shots, that his return is a major step in Lakhindar's growing self-realisation, similar to that suggested by his long slumber a little later. The importance of space and unhurried movement is enhanced by the contrast provided by the Calcutta segment of the film. The tranquillity of the forest is manifest in the skilled exploitation of colour as well as sound—especially the songs and calls of the birds, enhanced on several occasions by contrast to the sound of Natobar's motorbike. Many incidentals might be taken for granted, such as the marriage procession on the opposite bank of the river to where Lakhindar is sitting with Bhushan and Gouri early in the film. None of the characters remarks on it, and yet it is a simple image that suggests the notion of marriage —an idea basic to the film—and presages a similar procession much later when Gouri herself will be carried in a palanquin away from Lakhindar's dreams, away from her own. Pity is distilled just as subtly. Soon after Gouri's palanquin has passed by the spot where he is sitting alone in the forest, Lakhindar ventures, pathetically, to see the house to which Natobar has taken Shari. Hit by the harshness of the reality of their separation, Lakhindar, with no one in the world now to give him comfort, embraces a tree and sobs piteously against it. The contrast with his earlier joyous embrace of a tree becomes especially meaningful, and the pathos of Lakhindar's world is brought clearly into focus by the camera on a circular trolley moving around him, bringing his abject sadness out of the obscurity of the darkness of the forest into a silhouette sharp against the sunset sky. This simple camera manoeuvre creates a profoundly moving moment.

A metaphor that Dasgupta finds attractive concerns doors. Looking at life as though it is a meandering through a series of houses, we note that one is obliged to pass through doors. Many doors remain open after we have passed through them, allowing us to return; others shut behind us and remain barred. The notion of being trapped between locked doors might suggest a cessation of existence, so for every door that shuts and bars itself against re-entry, another one opens. Often we are able to shut doors ourselves and open others; more often, it would seem, this is done for us. Doors close on us and doors open up to us without our conscious instrumentality, giving to a life we would like to think is directed by our own deliberation a randomness that instills it with the constant promise of the unexpected. It is in such arbitrariness that life takes its shape and runs its course. Dreams may flourish there, for in a mansion where every door is known and predictability pervades, dreams can only be madness.

While Lakhindar is frequently shown opening actual doors for birds, the film sees a constant shutting of metaphorical doors against him. The death of Netai closed the door on the most beautiful part of his past; the affair of Shari with Natobar and the marriage of Gouri shut doors on other significant parts of his life; and Kalicharan's banquet closes the door on whatever efforts he might have made to restore his career. The conclusion to the film, however, represents a triumph of the spirit in that this chain of closing doors has ended with Lakhindar awakening to the opening of the door that leads, we may guess, to whatever is in store for the rest of his life.

In *Characbar*, Buddhadeb Dasgupta is characteristically positive in his interpretation of the elemental simplicity of the human condition as well as in his representation of human hopes, frailties and shortcomings. The gentleness through which the film's emotions evolves is enhanced not only by the simplicity and economy of the dialogue but also by the sustained beauty of the visual image. The camera work is superb, while the director's well developed and highly polished sense of perspective in framing and composition and balance in continuity have made this a splendidly crafted film. Poetic insight, intensity of emotion and an empathy with the sense of wonder of a simple rustic man are all sustained by the technical excellence of this truly beautiful film.

SEVEN

Insensibility and the Power of Red Beetles

Years pass, months pass, days pass—
two sets of teeth go to the market.
Days pass, months pass, years pass—
two sets of teeth cook, go to school.

Four sets of teeth sit at the table,
simply in order to eat.
Two sets of teeth suddenly shake in fury,
the other two tremble in fear.

Four pairs of gums are face to face
across the table. One day
a story of teeth is shown on the screen
and dentures watch in thousands before
they come home to spend the night
sitting in a bowl of water.

(*Teeth II*)

In seeking a source for *Lal Darja* ('The Red Doors', 1996), a film dealing with the spiritual ossification of life in the contemporary bourgeois desert, it is not necessary to go beyond

Buddhadeb's own poems, several volumes of which are replete with verse blandly exposing, humorously satirising or forensically criticising contemporary urban middle-class life. In all of this there is an unavoidable moral dimension, for quite plainly Dasgupta sees in the sterility, the philistinism and the complacent mechanical habit of the bourgeois way of life a turning away from the reality of innocence in a driven quest for a contrived reality that is based on notions of personal advantage, pride, insensitivity and ignorance. Much of Dasgupta's poetry is outrageous and often shocking in its frequent use of the absurd and grotesque, while its magnified focus on the trivial, its brazen essentialising and its inversion of perception—in which object becomes subject—enhance the surrealism of its impact.

It is *Lal Darja's* reflection of these features of Dasgupta's poetry, that indicates a turning-point in his cinema. The four previous films are aptly described as poetic, but their poetry is of a kind not readily discernible in the director's volumes of verse. Their poetic quality consists largely in the preference of the visual image over dialogue and a leanness of narrative detail in favour of suggestion. Needless to say, the metaphorical and the symbolic are characteristic of all Dasgupta's films, though especially from *Phera*. Of course, such distractions as the hijras in *Neem Annapurna* and the wrestlers in *Phera*, and elements of the bizarre such as Abdullah and his dwarf in *Tahader Katha*, do have their obvious counterparts in Dasgupta's poems (and, indeed, in *Lal Darja*), but it is difficult to push the connection between the poems and the films any further than this. The divergence of *Lal Darja* from its predecessors lies in Dasgupta's very successful endeavour to translate the artifices of his verse to the screen.

The overriding poetic intent of *Lal Darja* is established in the opening sequences, as are two of the film's three main narrative strands, the third being introduced soon after. The first sequence has a romantic setting in the hill country of northeast India, with low hanging clouds sweeping across the mountain tops. Here we meet a young boy capturing a small red beetle and reciting the 'magic' words that allude to the film's title, 'Tiny fat red beetle, open your red doors now!' causing the beetle to raise two of its legs. A radical contrast is effected by a cut to the streets of Calcutta as seen from a moving vehicle. A hint of contorted reality colours the distinction between the romantic and the mundane in the mirror-image view we are given of the city. There follows a shot of the man we will soon know as Dr. Nabin Datta getting down from his car just as a woman is gunned down on the pavement right in front of him by an assailant in a passing car. Nabin, only momentarily taken aback, then enters a large building and proceeds up its spacious staircase, establishing on the way a brief but possibly significant eye contact with a man on his way down, a character we will come to know as Kishori Singh. Nabin is then seen being examined by a doctor, a bizarre figure, to say the least, in connection with his complaint of the increasing hardness of his middle-aged body. It is no muscular complaint, but something seemingly fantastic, his hands and legs feeling as though they are turning to iron. Thus, the romantic world of the mountain tops and the expression of make-believe, the dissonant juxtaposition of two settings, and the dramatic incident with its unexpected reaction all point to something beyond the conventionally narrative, while the outlandish doctor's grotesque laughter at his own observation that Nabin might be turning into a robot underlines the promised connection between *Lal Darja* and Dasgupta's poetry.

The central narrative line aims to depict the dreary barrenness of urban middle-class life, focusing on Nabin Datta, a dentist with a very successful practice, who lives in material comfort with his wife, Bela; their son, Kushal, is at boarding school in Darjeeling. It is, of course, a truism that wealth and professional standing do not necessarily ensure happiness, and the picture we are given of Nabin is one of a man trapped on the treadmill of work for the sake of it and in a marriage that has become stale and loveless. Bela has resolved to leave him, to take a job as a teacher and to live alone close to her school. While she cites a recent domestic quarrel in which Nabin threatened her, this incident is clearly more a symptom than the cause of the breakdown of their marriage, although it does seem to be instrumental in Kushal's refusal to have anything to do with his father.

Bela, it would seem, has for some time been living in what is patently a loveless marriage. Sex has become an onerous duty for her and she has nothing to share or enjoy with her uncongenial and somewhat wooden husband. It is easy for Nabin to hasten to the suspicion that she has become unfaithful—after all, he has given her everything she could want, so what other reason could she possibly have for turning cold on him? Failing to see beyond his egoism, Nabin finds what he believes to be substance for his suspicions in one or two letters addressed to Bela that he secretly opens. She has, in fact, been receiving letters from an admirer, one Arnab Ray, a man she has not seen for nineteen years and whom Nabin sees as his rival and irrationally decides to have killed. Before doing so, he pays a visit to Arnab to see what he looks like. Ironically, Bela is in Arnab's house when Nabin comes to the front door, having come to inform him that his attentions are in vain as she wants to live alone and is fearful of embarking on another relationship. She pursues her plan to get a job as a teacher and move into a small flat close to her school, unmoved by her colleague's counsel that marriage is a social obligation and that it is her duty to endure and make the best of it. Indeed, the barrenness of this idea is underlined by the conversations between Bela and Nabin which, if they do not end in misunderstanding or frustration, are usually quite inconsequential.

The depression in Nabin's domestic life is complemented by the dreariness of his professional life. The few shots we see of him at work suggest that he goes about his job mechanically, without any interest in what he is doing and without any personal concern for his patients. Nor do we see any significant interaction between him and his colleagues; indeed, his life at work would seem to be as lonely as his life at home. As the love has gone out of his marriage, so too has the facility to dream gone out of his life. Later in the film he complains to the bizarre doctor that his dreams have been replaced by tormenting morning visions of deep gaping mouths baring rows of decaying teeth—an adequate indication of his professional life as well as an eloquent metaphor for his morbid outlook on life.

The representations of Nabin's domestic crisis and professional ennui are enhanced by several elements of the absurd, involving in particular the doctor and Kishori Singh. Nabin's first encounter with Kishori, on the stairs to the doctor's chamber, is significant. Although they do not know one another, the two men still make eye contact and Kishori, once Nabin has passed him, gestures in displeasure at Nabin's not having greeted him. The rapport is not actual but more of a suggestion of Nabin's being drawn to the wrong means of solving problems. (Later Kishori, with appallingly decayed teeth, will come to Nabin for treatment and Nabin will seek Kishori's help to eliminate Arnab.) The crazy doctor, too, is a useless source of help, given that Nabin's 'disease' is incurable, being more a case of corrupted values and diminished love of life than something physiological. Kishori, a mysterious thug with rotten teeth and apparent connections with the underworld, is ridiculously beyond Nabin's orbit, as is the bizarre doctor with his unwittingly meaningful jokes about robots, a practitioner who finds nothing physically wrong with Nabin and is perceptive enough to point out the seriousness of his loss of self-esteem, but who is totally unable to make any significant improvement to his life. His utter irrelevance is highlighted, ultimately, by his simple replacement by a cloud of smoke.

In mundane terms Nabin's complaint is bourgeois boredom, poetically seen by Dasgupta as the eclipse of innocence by sophistication. In Nabin's case, at least, sophistication—in the form of material prosperity, professional accomplishment, social advancement—is characteristically self-centred. He has become something of an island, complaining to the doctor that he feels remote not only from his family and his work but from the country as well, a perception that is well illustrated by the apparent indifference he shows to such things as the murder of the girl on the street and various items of news on television. Yet whereas Nabin feels incapable of loving anyone, he does indeed suffer from that inability. The cure, it would seem, is not in doctors and prescriptions, but in the recovery of innocence.

However, the real import of the film is not to be found in the core narrative, and its remove might suggest that the answers we seek are not necessarily to be found in the obvious places, just as what seem to Nabin to be obvious ways out of difficulty prove to be quite inappropriate. Dasgupta has contrived quite an intricate structure through which to discern the essential significance of his film: in addition to the central narrative the structure comprises a medial narrative, a counter narrative, and a series of seemingly incidental or even irrelevant distractions.

The medial narrative is complementary to the core narrative in that it offers a sense of the completeness that Nabin's life lacks, and it also brings the dullness and seeming unreality depicted in the Nabin theme to mingle with the vibrant reality of the life of Dinu, his driver. Given that Dinu is something of a petty rogue, not averse to the occasional shady deal, it might not be appropriate to describe him as innocent, but he is certainly unsophisticated. Unlike Nabin, he is not well-off, works at a lowly job and is socially less than commonplace; again unlike Nabin, he is carefree, plainly happy and successful in marriage. Nabin is amazed at Dinu's habit of falling asleep in the car every time he has to wait for his boss (and is irritated by his habit of lying across the front seat with his feet poking out of the window), but Dinu's ready propensity to sleep is indicative not of laziness but rather of a man simply at peace with himself.

Dinu's extraordinary matrimonial situation—two wives, two households—intrigues Nabin, given his own obvious marital melancholy. Legally, of course, Dinu is acutely culpable, bigamy being a criminal offence except under certain religious circumstances that clearly do not apply to him. Moreover, the law might also take offence at his pilfering of petrol from his employer's car, and he might certainly lose his job if Nabin were alert to his lies about being ill when in fact he has taken on a temporary job for someone else. Notwithstanding his malleable honesty, he is evidently quite right in describing himself at the end of the film as someone who has never sought to hurt anybody. His two wives and his daughter suffer under no illusions about his faithfulness, none of them demanding exclusivity as a necessary precondition of Dinu's love. When he is asked by Pratima, a refugee from Bangladesh, to help her out of her difficulties, it is more a case of his generous heart softening than any macho leap to the chance of conquest. His eventual love for her—his third woman—emanates out of a tender urge to be kind and supportive.

Yet there is also a touch of rationality in this apparent liberality of passion. On an unscheduled visit to his second wife, Malti, Dinu finds her not at home and he goes to the nearby ruins of an ancient fort, sentimentally significant in their relationship. It is there that he chances on her in the embrace of another man. Malti is distraught that she has been found out and, fearful of being beaten by Dinu, tries to run away, but Dinu convinces her, kindly yet firmly, that what is acceptable for him must be acceptable for her too. Malti's indiscretion has to be judged, if at all, on her loneliness without Dinu and by the fact that the other man's fingers 'are so much like yours.' Later, when Nabin meets Sukhi, Dinu's first wife, she describes both her love for him and her appreciation of the devoted care he gives to their daughter as having nothing to do with what he does anywhere else. While many men pursue affairs in secret, Dinu's candour and his steadfastness—though shared—are offered as saving graces. Loving, in the sense of self-giving, comes easily to Dinu; Nabin's facility for love has been corroded by egoism and middle-class form and custom. After meeting his driver's wives, Dinu is revealed to Nabin as a man of surprising moral dimensions.

To the majority of viewers the Dinu narrative, though not difficult to accept, might seem somewhat extreme. Indeed, the notion of credible unreality that is fundamental to the counter narrative also tempers the medial narrative in its polygamy theme as well as the core narrative in its overwhelming ordinariness. The credible unreality of the counter narrative is simply more blatant, focused as it is on a child and not dissembled by the wiles and stratagems of adulthood.

The counter narrative offers something altogether different from the life depicted in the central narrative. It is the shortest of the three narrative strands, has the least amount of dialogue and is hardly a narrative at all as much as a series of impressions of a boy's life in the high hill country of northeast India. The boy is also called Nabin, and there are obvious connections to be drawn between his life and that once enjoyed by Dr. Datta. However, it is important not to interpret the hill sequences as flashbacks in the conventional sense but rather as depicting a state of innocence which the older Nabin might once have known and to which he might yet return. Obscuring the 'flashback' nature of these sequences is a confusion of time, allowing for the suggestion that much of the apparent past abides in what is perceived to be the present. Most notable to this effect are the mother's letter and ultimately, the young Nabin's intruding into the central narrative.

It is worth remembering that the opening and closing shots of the film are set in the counter narrative, and clearly it is the director's intention that the optimism it articulates should prevail, for *Lal Darja* is a film of hope, not of submission or despair. Underlining its element of optimism is the striking visual beauty of the setting which, given the special purpose of the counter narrative, is as articulate as any dialogue might be. In this romantic atmosphere of sweeping hilltops, soaring snow-capped mountain peaks and low, floating clouds, the interest is in make-believe, focusing on a children's rhyme uttered while holding in the palm of the hand a small red beetle:

> Little fat red beetle
> Open your red doors, open them now!

and the beetle obligingly 'opening its doors' by raising two of its legs. Young Nabin takes the 'magic' a little further, using the beetle in his hand and the utterance of the rhyme to cause actual doors to be opened for him. Whether we accept this phenomenon or not is quite beside the point, for what Dasgupta is trying to establish here is not the power of magic but the reality of make-believe, the strength of belief, the innocence of trust. This optimism is reinforced in the boy by his parents, who refrain from polluting his mind with facts and reality but rather, encourage his make-believe by endowing it with notions of faith and love. The doors open for him because he has faith in his heart and they in turn love him, and now we start to see clearly that 'doors' are really to be thought of in a metaphorical sense, as was noted in the discussion on *Charachar*. When, at the end of the film, Nabin returns to his empty flat without his keys—significantly after his revealing day with Dinu and his women—he tries the old childhood trick. Again, whether it gets him into his flat or not is unimportant; what is significant is that faith and love, thanks to Dinu, might seem to be returning to Nabin and that he is ready to re-enter that state of innocence from which egoism and materialism had alienated him.

The counter narrative offers some significant contrasts. There is the obvious visual one distinguishing the beauty and peacefulness of the hills from the bustle of Calcutta, which, while not represented as ugly, is obviously manufactured. The peace of the one and the unrest of the other is well indicated by quiet and noise but might well be discerned also in a distinction between people: in the hill sequences there is a warm kindliness radiated by Nabin's father and mother and the old tribal man on the road, while in Calcutta there is the bizarre doctor, Kishori Singh, and his shady friends, and the murder of the girl on the street. Nabin is the contented child of a happy marriage; Kushal, the dentist's son, is the disturbed child of a very unhappy marriage.

The medial narrative dilutes these contrasts to some extent. The Dinu strand begins, away from the central narrative, at sunset, by the ancient ruins on the bank of the river, evoking an atmosphere closer to the young Nabin's home in the hills than to the older Nabin's home in Calcutta. Dinu's marital happiness has no counterpart in the young Nabin's life but does evoke a semblance in that of his parents, while the genuine love between the latter and their words to him about unconfined and unselfish love are echoed, albeit rather unconventionally, by Dinu. His daughter, Basanti, despite her relative poverty, has more in common with the young Nabin than with the son of the wealthy older Nabin. Like the young Nabin, Dinu is at one with his world while his boss is very much at dissonance with his.

And yet the central narrative does offer indications that the gap between it and the counter narrative might indeed be traversed. Nabin's mother, important to the counter narrative, appears in the central narrative by letter, offering affection and tender concern for her son and his family, as well as affirming her resolve to remain where she is, in the realm of that which gives the counter narrative its peculiar nature. There is also her singing of the well-known song, 'Boatman, take me across', evoking the transition between life and the world to come but also suggesting the crossing that Nabin will eventually make—in a sense—back into life. Nabin's wistful asking of Dinu whether he had ever sought to know anything of his boss's family background or where he had lived as a boy is also an indication of his emotional survival in the realm of the counter narrative. And ultimately, of course, the young Nabin intrudes quite blatantly into the central narrative to draw the older man away from his world of discontent to one where beetles can be believed to open doors.

The film is structured, then, on a clever weaving of these three narrative strands: the central one suggesting submission to banality, the medial one hope, and the counter strand promise. As well there are the several apparent distractions that lend poetic significance, sometimes in a most unlikely way, to the central narrative and its relation to the other two. There is, first, the street murder, which becomes an ongoing item on the television news along with an on-the-spot interview with a beggar; also appearing as part of a television programme is an interview with a man hoping to be included in the *Guinness Book of Records* for having the world's longest beard, then three more news items: a note on the increasing number of Indian students studying in the United States, mention of the Prime Minister's visit to Sweden and a report on the outbreak of a new disease afflicting many in the U.S.A. and Europe but yet to reach serious proportions in the developing world.

These sequences, incidental to the three-part narrative, would also appear to be utterly irrelevant. The story of the street murder is pursued only as far as the arrest of a suspect, and it is suggested that the motive for the crime might have been 'love-related'. The interview with an eye-witness, an old beggar, is something of a distraction from the distraction in that the main interest here is in the brief projection of a personality rather than any advancement of the murder story. While the man with the extraordinarily long beard might also be interesting as a personality, the interview with him is evidently pertinent to nothing. One might also wonder about the relevance of the reports about Indian students abroad, food supply and the Prime Minister visiting Sweden, but when mention is made of a strange disease that hardens the body, we are taken straight back to the beginning of the film and Nabin's visit to the weird doctor.

It could be asserted that the reference to the allegedly love-related murder is what prompts Nabin to pursue the idea of taking out a contract on Arnab Ray's life, but this would seem to be an elaborate means to a somewhat unimportant end. However, we might find it remarkable that after a second or two of shock Nabin was able to walk away from the murder that occurred right in front of him and that he continued to be inattentive to reports about the crime on the television news services. Quite clearly, then, the murder is of no interest in itself but is presented as an indication of Nabin's self-absorption, his withdrawal from the world around him. In a sense, the Indian students going to study abroad are also withdrawing from their own world to seek the kind of panacea that Nabin finds in his bizarre doctor or through the services of Kishori Singh. The absurdity of Nabin's world is illustrated by the curious desire to achieve notoriety on account of the length of one's beard, the exceptionally confident precision in the prediction about the food supply, and the Prime Minister's turning away from his work on the multitudinous problems of India to visit northern Europe. The exotic disease emanating out of the West is obviously a metaphor for the kind of automatism that is threatening the humanity of Nabin and which Dasgupta—poet and filmmaker—sees as the product of an acquisitive, technological and ultimately banal society.

These apparent distractions are of considerable value in highlighting some of the more important abstract notions that the film seeks to convey. They also have the secondary effect of enabling the dialogue to remain unencumbered and the action to be, for the most part, bold and compelling. While the distractions seemingly emanate out of nothing and conclude abruptly, the three narrative strands are at one time or another entwined: first the central narrative mixes with the medial narrative, and after the tidy bringing to a close of the latter with the prospect of Dinu's third marriage, it melds with the counter narrative, now that the doctor, Kishori Singh and Bela have simply drifted away. As the opening lines of the film focused on make-believe, so too does the ending, where the Nabin of the core narrative is sublimated to the Nabin of the counter narrative.

The highly original development of the narrative structure is enhanced by the film's carefully conceived and tightly executed continuity. The editing is sharp and determined by a quest for logic and balance of the major narrative elements, along with a vivid diversity in the presentation of the visual images. Indeed, some of the contrasting cuts are quite splendid, such as the cut from Dinu's bibulous revels on the river bank to Malti's approach to the little rural church the next morning. An especially revealing example of dialogue substitute is a cut from the doctor's eerie chamber that provides an answer to his question to Nabin, 'What do you do?'; the subsequent shot is a close-up of a gaping mouth from which a tooth is being extracted. There is also an overall excellence of composition that provides the basis for the superb camera work, while the composition of shots is effective in underlining many of the abstract notions of the film, such as alienation, banality, melancholy, affection and absurdity, as well as in giving rise to the various contrasts offered by different juxtapositions of those notions. One of the real strengths of the camera work lies in the lighting that so clearly establishes the characteristic mood and temper of the narrative elements and the connection between the apparent distractions and the central narrative. There is a very close visual affinity with the contrasts between the hill country, Malti's village by the Ganges and the various parts of Calcutta. Indeed, the visual variety is rich and never flags.

One might be critical of certain features of the work. The presentation of Nabin's visits to Dinu's women is unable to avoid a touch of the didactic, exacerbated by the rather patronising demeanour of Nabin, where a humble quest for what he cannot comprehend might have been more appropriate. Throughout the film Nabin is appropriately boring and Bela is appropriately apprehensive, but neither is much more than that. Of course, Nabin, in keeping with his imminent robotic transmogrification, is logically incapable of development, and this creates something of a performance problem. Moreover, many might have been happier with a more assertive Bela, providing not only a contrast to Nabin but also enhancing the narrative with a vibrancy appropriate to the idea of the modern, independent woman, even if such a character is not really consistent with Bengali realities. However, the seemingly somnolent flatness of these two characters is made up for by the vivaciousness of all the characters in the medial narrative, especially Dinu, as well as by the eccentricity of the doctor, the sleaziness of Kishori Singh and the contrasting charm of Nabin's parents. Indeed, the smaller parts are all very well rounded.

If one looks at *Lal Darja* as the tenth of Dasgupta's feature films, one may well be struck by its originality. Indeed, Dasgupta is an exceptionally original filmmaker who has always seems to find an alluring corner to turn just when he might be tempted to come up with a polished offering of more of the same. What was to follow this highly original tenth film would pursue the filmmaker's quest for something different, while cherishing his well established skills as a craftsman with narrative, his poetic conceptualisation of narrative ideas, and his exquisite talent in exploiting the visual aspects of his art.

EIGHT

And Even the Stones Did Groan

One chair sits
beside another empty chair.
Day after day a book stands
beside another book.
Slowly one sorrow falls in
beside another.
You simply scurry away, unable at all to care about
anything, dashing into one hole and
out again through another.

(From *Mouse II*)

The short story *Uratiya* by Samaresh Basu helped to inspire Mrinal Sen's film *Genesis* (1986) as well as Buddhadeb Dasgupta's *Uttara* ('The Wrestlers', 2000). The two films could hardly be more different from one another, and each has its variations on its literary source. *Uratiya* tells the tale of two men employed at a flag station some distance from a remote village, which in turn is some considerable distance from a not very important provincial town. The two railwaymen are unmarried and have only each other for company. In their otherwise oppressive isolation they manage quite easily to obviate loneliness and boredom through their mutual passion for wrestling, an activity which is more an obsession than a pastime with them. Into their life of simple though somewhat eccentric self-sufficiency comes a woman, Uratiya, who had many years before been betrothed to one of the men when they were both children. The girl is good and innocent and utterly devoid of malice, and yet her mere presence—in itself a threat to the well established way of things—becomes a catalyst for the destruction into which the trio descend.

Mrinal Sen's film has as its philosophical basis the Marxist paradigmatic process of thesis-antithesis-synthesis, and his debt to Samaresh Basu lies in little more than the story's odd social structure. Although Buddhadeb Dasgupta alters much of the detail, his film does, however, take up much more of the original story—the setting, the two railwaymen and their wrestling, the coming of the girl, even much of the psychological complexity of the personal relationships—but the genius of the film lies largely in what he adds of his own to the substance derived from Basu. The story of the wrestlers and the girl becomes a strand in a much more complex creation, the ultimate interest of which is cultural rather than personal and is infinitely removed from the doctrinaire contrivance which gives from to Mrinal Sen's film.

At the time when Dasgupta was conceiving the substance for this work, many people in India and other parts of the world were shocked by a ghastly crime committed in a rural outpost in the state of Orissa. An Australian medical missionary, Dr. Graham Staines, and his two young sons were deliberately incinerated in their locked car on the night of January 22, 1999. Given the political climate of the time and the incidence of certain other crimes of violence against Christians and Christian establishments in various parts of India, it was easy to jump to conclusions about who—at least, in a very general sense—might have been responsible. The Bharatiya Janata Party, which was in charge at the time, had never denied its widespread description as a Hindu nationalist party, nor had it ever shied away from being associated with the other elements of the broader international community of Hinduism, the Vishwa Hindu Parishad— particularly the Rashtriya Swayamsevak Sangh and the Bajrang Dal, two organisations noted for their open hostility towards non-Hindu communities in India. In the early months of 1999, while the destruction of the Babri Mosque and the horrible communal violence let loose by that act were still fresh in memory, there was a genuine fear of a rise of fascist extremism threatening Indian life.

It was this perceived threat that prompted the other narrative strand in *Uttara*, which focuses on an Indian Christian pastor working in a rural community. We see him ministering to his small flock and working as a paramedic amongst leprosy sufferers, always in the company of his foster-child, Matthew. There is nothing overtly evangelical about the pastor, and the quest for conversions would not seem to be on his agenda; anyway, he is far too busy tending the sick and feeding the poor, both Christian and non-Christian alike. Indeed, there is nothing at all remarkable about his life; what lends it significance—at least, in cinematic terms—is the sinister interest taken in it by a small group of extremists who lurk, as it were, in the shadows of the film.

The two narrative components, then, are provided by the wrestlers and the pastor, but there are also several minor elements that serve to highlight, to cohere, or to sunder associations in the two narrative strands. There are the three extremists who loom over the pastor and his work; there is a dwarf train guard and a party of little people; there is a group of itinerant natuas, or singers and dancers; and there is a small group of impoverished rustics whose purpose to some extent resembles that of a classical chorus. These are the accompanying ingredients of an exceptionally beautiful and unusual film.

These elements are all introduced in the first ten minutes, and it is worth taking a careful look at how this is done. The film opens in a forest with a motif shot of leaves falling from a tree, an image offering a simple suggestion of regeneration which will carry considerable significance as the film makes its final statement. Then the picture becomes an open expanse; in the distance a girl is bringing a herd of cows home in the dying light at the end of the day. Into this picture of rural commonplace Dasgupta intrudes a jeep, its headlights serving to point to its ugly extraneousness in this environment; an interior close shot reveals three men, and a crude wolf whistle to the girl herding the cows confirms their apparent unpleasantness. It is the throwing of an empty liquor bottle from the moving car onto the rocks beside the road that points—in retrospect, of course—to the destruction that these men will have brought about at the end of the film.

There is a simple cut to a hill. It is early the next morning, still a little dark, so that the time distinction from the previous shot is vague: we are not concerned here with particular narrative dynamics but with the general abstractions behind the images. We see, at first in silhouette at the top of the hill, a large party of little people heading off together to their various jobs in the working world. (We learn later that they all come from one village on the other side of the hill beyond the river.) Their small stature is well stressed by the silhouette shot and then more clearly as they approach the camera on the downward slope. As they pass through the forest, they go by the place where the three outsiders are camped with their jeep, and one of them, a train guard, is ridiculed as he stops to observe the strangers, one of whom is practising his knife-throwing. There is a clearly significant intention in this juxtaposition of guard and knife-thrower, horribly realised at the end of the film.

We then see the bus carrying the guard to his station hurtling off along the lonely country road; passing it in the opposite direction is the pastor, riding his bicycle laden with goods from the market, with Matthew sitting behind him on top of a large pumpkin. There is then a shot of clothes being thrown in the air on the other side of a rise, and then two near naked, burly men come running over the top to their pit, where they are seen to commit themselves with great enthusiasm to a bout of wrestling.

So far not a word of dialogue has been spoken, yet most of

the narrative agents of the film have been established and already two interconnections have been made. At the sound of a train's whistle, the two wrestlers are torn from their indulgence into the workaday world where, dressed in railways shirt and dhoti, they perform their duties at the crossing while the pastor and Matthew wait for the train to go by. Here, in a brief passage of small talk, we learn of the pastor's work amongst the sick and his feeding of the hungry. His observation, 'We have many people who are short of food,' is the first pointed indication we have of the poverty that afflicts this region, an allusion that will recur from time to time to underline the condition of various characters.

As the pastor continues on his bicycle with Matthew and their goods up the road to the church and their home, the church is held in an extended long shot. Its isolation is apparent, and into this can be read several things, including its foreignness and its alienation from the majority of Indian society as well as its vulnerability, given its physical prominence. The former of these possibilities is underlined when the pastor is conducting his service and Matthew has rung the bell; the boy's attention is distracted by the first appearance of the natuas, moving rhythmically across the screen to their song and the sound of their simple instruments, dressed in oddments and most of them wearing gross animal masks. Matthew's attraction to them is obvious.

At the natuas pass by, the film cuts back to the interior of the church. Several men seated at the back, more concerned with their stomachs than their souls, slip out during the prayer to be first at the table where Matthew and the pastor will serve a hearty lunch to them and other destitute men. As the men talk of regional poverty and unemployment, it becomes clear that the church has more appeal as a social service than as a spiritual institution. We also learn that there is some degree of hostility suffered by those who take to Christianity. Finally, they articulate their dream: they will go to America, where everyone is of the same caste as they, the women are like fairies, babies are born with white skins, and everyone eats every day as well as they have eaten just now. They are not sure where America is—or even what it is—but it can't be too far from Calcutta.

Of the main characters it is only Uttara who remains to be introduced, and all the narrative agents and accompanying elements have now been established. It is interesting that in this film Dasgupta lays out the ingredients before any significant narrative progression is made. It is important to his purpose to start to evolve the basis of his film's atmosphere and to present his elements, almost as though they were interesting in themselves. This is done with an exquisite sense of the visual and an exceptionally spare economy. We might note that the first word is not uttered until sixteen minutes into the film, and to the point where the group of destitute men come to the screen and all the elements—except Uttara—have been introduced takes but a further fours minutes. We might also note the terseness of what dialogue there is, the director using no more than sufficient words to present whatever it is he wants us to know, and of that there is little at this stage.

As well as introducing his ingredients, Dasgupta starts, in this opening section, to suggest interconnections between them. There is a pre-existing association between the pastor and the wrestlers, as there is between the pastor and the destitutes; in an ugly moment, the little train guard comes into brief contact with the outsiders who, in a short time, will also have crossed paths with the wrestlers.

As has been noted many times already, narrative detail and complexity are not characteristic of Dasgupta's films, and the story told in this one is as simple and uncluttered as any of the others. The effect of such simple directness is as riveting here as in *Tahader Katha* and *Charachar*, and in those masterly works it is also necessary—and by no means difficult—to look beyond the minimal plot for the full import of the film. The story element of *Uttara* is of considerable interest, but frugally presented, nevertheless.

The prominent narrative strand deals with the two railwaymen, Balaram and Nimai, or the wrestlers as they are better known, even by the postman, who does not even know their names. There is an element of pathos in their story: two lonely men, destined perhaps to a life of loneliness, whose good fortune it was to be brought together in this remote outpost of the railway system and to discover a mutual passion for wrestling. As their work is undemanding, they have ample time to indulge in their sport. An indication of the power that it has over them is given when Nimai suggests a bout at night, something they had not done before. The continuity is interesting here, for the shot of the night bout cuts directly to a shot of the two limbering up before their morning bout, almost as if they have not stopped between the two.

Wrestling also allows them an escape—from the baggage of their earlier lives, perhaps, and from the perplexities that they might confront in the present, such as the surprise they get when the three outsiders approach them one night seeking directions for the procurement of carnal comforts. A brief dialogue of wondering aloud about the men and what they might be doing dissolves into:

> The world is full of odd people, but we don't need them. We've got each other and our wrestling.

There is a clear indication here of introspection, even of obsessiveness. Neither man is experienced in the ways of the world, both are functionally illiterate, and they would seem to be sexually inexperienced. It is easy, then, to appreciate their contentment in their present situation. (There might be some academic satisfaction in sniffing about for indications of latent homosexuality, but this would be to miss a much larger and more significant point.) The sequences involving Balaram and Nimai, at the railway crossing or in their wrestling pit, bring out their simple fondness for one another, their ingenuousness, and their pathetic vulnerability.

It is an innocent and kindly girl, not the outsiders with their mission of fanaticism, who inadvertently lays bare this vulnerability. Balaram's aunt—on the pretext of her 'imminent' death—manages to turn a long-standing betrothal into a marriage. The girl is Uttara, whom Balaram brings back to the flag station, much to the consternation of Nimai. Nimai is no misogynist; it is just that his limited philosophy does not allow him to see how a third party can live with them without upsetting their profoundly cherished and firmly established way of things. The warmth of Uttara's smile and her innocent laughter are enough to melt Nimai's frostiness, and for a time the trio live in harmony and happiness.

However, cracks start to open up. Balarama and Uttara go alone to see the 'bioscope'—a rural outdoor screening of a popular Hindi movie—and Nimai's nose is put out of joint. Uttara is concerned that Balaram and Nimai's obsession with the physical has left them mentally and emotionally sterile. Indeed, Balaram's approach to sex has become almost as boisterous as his approach to wrestling. Nimai is jealous of Balaram for being replete with what he himself intensely needs, and he tries to cover this envy by chiding Balaram for his growing slackness in the pit, which 'comes of spending all night with a woman.' The two men are dashed into conflict when Nimai spills his frustration to Uttara, telling her that she should leave the two men the way they were, then declaring that he wants to have her as Balaram does. It is just then that Balaram appears and sees Uttara struggling to escape from Nimai's grasp. The wrestling bouts continue, but they are now hostile: the former mutual appreciation has been transformed into an urge to hurt, to bring down and to defeat. An obsession with wrestling has become an obsession with hatred.

In India the fine line between ignorance and hatred is crossed every time there is communal violence. Representing the forces of blind reaction and intolerance are the three outsiders, ignorant and with tunnel vision themselves, who prey on the ignorance of simple folk to provoke social disintegration. The inability of the two wrestlers to adapt to change instead of turning their frustration into hostility is a very simple and persuasive way of representing a perennial problem in a multicultural society.

Somewhat less prominent is that aspect of the narrative involving the pastor, although once the wrestlers' strand becomes fraught with unremitting tension, interest is focussed on him and the three outsiders. It has been noted that the initial perception of the pastor's role is one of charity in the feeding of his flock and tending the sick, as is suggested by his concern for Balaram's minor ailment and then in a visit he makes with Matthew to a dairy village to tend a woman suffering from leprosy. It is here we see the pastor as an object of hostility, a notion that will colour his role through the rest of the film.

The dairy village sequence opens with Matthew having a milk can filled. Then there is an interesting cut, showing in the foreground, but in part silhouette, the pastor and the woman sitting inside her hut; in the background, internally framed, is her husband, sitting outside the door and tinkering with a radio set. Matthew asks him about his work, and he makes a clumsy joke at the expense of the boy's innocence; it is this and his cruelly insensitive remarks about his wife's leprosy that set the tone for the sinister role he is to play. Matthew runs off to watch birds with another boy, and as the pastor is leaving, the man plies him with questions, through which we learn that five years back Matthew's parents were found dead and that he, once known as Rakhal, has been with the pastor and his church ever since. The man vents his distaste for the boy's now being known by a Christian name. 'He's one of us,' says the man, so raising the notion of the enemy Other. The pastor leaves without reply as the man goes on to express his hostility against people becoming Christian. A little later the man is seen riding his bicycle through the forest towards the outsiders' camp, and then in close conversation with them. These few brief shots make quite clear that dividing lines are now established for a burgeoning conflict.

There are two confrontations between these three extremists and the pastor before the film's horrible conclusion is played out. There is one sinister moment when, as evening is falling, the pastor calls Matthew, who is outside. There is a shot of the boy running through the forest in response, and then we see one of the thugs lurking behind Matthew and watching him. The first actual confrontation is played out on the road when the jeep is being driven towards the pastor and Matthew, who are coming along on their bicycle. As the jeep approaches them, it swerves dangerously close and runs them off the road. Uttara and the little guard witness the incident, and lend assistance to the pastor and Matthew. It is these four who, in one way or another, will be the victims in the final act of destruction, to which this incident would seem to have been a prelude.

The second confrontation is less dramatic and seeks simply to reinforce an already suggested attitude and purpose. This time the pastor and Matthew are riding on a narrow track through the forest when they again encounter the jeep. Two of the men have gone among the trees to relieve themselves, and Matthew enthusiastically asks the driver about the jeep's horn, to be answered only by a callous face and stony silence. Undeterred, he runs off to join the other two in relief of his own bladder and is spurned by them as well. Not a word is spoken between the pastor and the men, and the one who remains in the jeep avoids any eye-contact with the pastor. The warning signs are obvious.

Just as the opening section brings the various elements of the film together, the closing section sees their disintegration. The cataclysm is directed at the pastor; since tension between him and the three extremists has been simmering for some time, it is not entirely unexpected, although its ferocity does come as a shock. The attack on him and his church is very well prepared, but Matthew is able to run from the clutches of the men who would consign him to the flames they are about to ignite around his foster-father. Pursued by the knife-thrower, the boy hides behind a large tree into which a knife is thrown just as the natuas appear. They encircle the tree, giving refuge to Matthew and warding off the thug. What is perhaps the film's most cogent statement is made in the offering of an animal mask to Matthew, who joins their procession under the protection, as it were, of the earthy culture of the common people. This is the film's note of triumph, and it will be reaffirmed a little later.

In the meantime, Uttara sees the thugs running in and out of the church and, as she gets closer, she is shocked by the sight of the pastor bound and gagged and being doused with kerosene.

In desperation she runs to Balaram and Nimai, the two heroes admired so much by the innocent Matthew for their physical indomitability, heroes whom no one can hurt. They are wrestling, of course, and so intense has their hostility become that Uttara cannot even get their attention. By chance she meets up with the little guard who, in telling contrast to the big and strong men, does not hesitate to run to the good man's aid. It is too late, of course, and as Nimai and Balaram wrestle unaware of anything but antagonism towards each other, the pastor is incinerated with his church. Uttara's judgement is simple: 'They could have saved him. They're not human.'

A final exchange between Uttara and the little man is ended by a frightening shot as the jeep appears; its headlights, as in its first appearance, are made to look like a pair of ugly, monstrous eyes. During the brief attack on the guard, whose murder is senseless beyond all comprehension, and the first stage of the flight of Uttara, these 'eyes' remain central to the shot, the appalling action taking place outside of the frame. Now there is no more dialogue, for as the film grew at the opening out of an extensive segment without words, it will now, in tidy balance, reach the closing titles in the same way.

This coda, as it were, is in itself a very powerful piece of cinema. In terms of story, the film is ended: the brutish zealots drive away, presumably to bully and threaten someone else; the pastor, the little guard and Uttara are all dead; Matthew joins the natuas; and Balaram and Nimai go on doing the only thing they know. The narrative can go no further. The purpose of the coda, however, is to show the tragic consequences of the narrative in perspective, the director's perspective.

The coda offers a series of exits. The first is the flight of the three murderers. We see the back of their jeep disappear into the distance, and we need not let them take up any more of our attention. Then, coming at a snail's pace along the road behind them is the party of destitute men setting off for America to realise their dream of perpetually replete stomachs. It is a gently comic shot, not out of place, for the ingenuousness of the men is in harmony with exactly the same kind of rusticity, so remote from the modern world, seen in other parts of the film, and serves as a final reminder of the innocence and simplicity of the common people, who are also the life of the songs and dances of the natuas.

The strength and dignity of the little people as they carry away the body of their slaughtered friend is prominent in the next exit, which takes the form of a funeral procession. Their formal mourning betrays no sign of hysteria or even righteous anger. (One remembers Mrs. Staines' exceptional dignity after the murder of her husband and two sons and her public forgiveness of their killers.) As their funeral procession passes by the dead body of Uttara, it pauses in respect while one of the women goes and gently shuts the eyes of the tragically destroyed girl.

But as sure as there is death, there is also life, and here is sounded the triumphal note of the film: the natuas cross the screen as they have done several times before—and will go on doing long after the film has ended—singing the songs and rejoicing in the values of a humble people. Their number has been augmented by Matthew, whom they saved, without any kind of conflict, from the agents of wild hatred. The fact that the knife-throwing thug retreated from them is a simple yet cogent assertion of a set of values more powerful and enduring than any held by fanatics. The natuas' art is rustic, earthy, an expression of the higher yearnings of rural people in the context of the natural world, whose laws govern so much of their lives. It is a joyful expression of a way of life and a litany of praise that sings of itself; it passes by whatever may seek to resist it, just as a river flows around obstacles, and it gives refuge and succour to the innocent. It is the antithesis to the anti-culture represented by reactionary bigots such as the three who have just wrought such pointless destruction and then callously disappeared from its consequences. The procession of the natuas, as they cross the screen in the opposite direction to the funeral procession of the little people, is a triumphal march, notwithstanding the realistic surrender to emotion by the little boy. Indeed, his tears are the tears of all of us and are absorbed in the supremacy of the natuas, who have been both a stumbling block for the zealots and a refuge for the innocent child. It is a simple triumph, liable to be missed or, at best, taken for granted. It is a joyful celebration that asserts that the rains will fall and the crops will grow, that birth will follow death, and that the leaves that wither on the tree will give way to shoots of new life. There are some easy extensions to this: that leprosy can be cured and the hungry can be fed, because good men will always arise, even when the evil-doers have had their day. The natuas' triumph is the continuing triumph of life itself.

The final statement, in harmony with the enduring of the people's soul, belongs to nature. As the funeral procession, the dance of the natuas and the migratory trek of the destitutes wend their several ways across the screen, the two wrestlers, oblivious even to life itself, continue in their frenzied obsession on a hill in the background. As though tired of them because they will not be part of it, nature is seen to reject them in a wonderfully surreal shot of a large boulder near their pit rolling of its own accord down the hill, accompanied by a thunderous groaning, away from these blind, stubborn, wilfully lost men. The camera makes a cyclic return to the forest, to the shot that opened the film, where we see the leaves falling from the trees. It then tilts up to a shot of the vast, open sky before the closing titles roll down.

It is obvious that three elements in the film have no narrative significance: the natuas, the little people (except the train guard who has a minimal involvement, with tragic consequence), and the group of destitute men. Although they do not in any way advance the narrative, they may not be thought of, however, in the same way as the 'distraction elements' in earlier films, such as the hijras in *Neem Annapurna* or the wrestlers in *Phera*. Rather, they are closely pertinent to the narrative—as the distraction elements are not—in a representational sense.

The natuas are an image of the people's culture: their values, their aspirations, their faith and wonder. This grand personification has the effect of magnifying the counterpoints of the drama, of universalising its agents. Three thugs conflict with a Christian pastor and his adopted son; they celebrate the gratification of their blood lust with their carnal lust, raping and killing a woman after slaying the little man whom they had mocked at the start of the film. It is the representative portrayal of the natuas that broadens this perspective to a clash between the forces of fundamentalist fanaticism and the strength of basic human interests. As the narrative plays itself out, all the characters are affected in one way or another and all relationships change. The natuas, however, remain unwavering and unaffected. At the end, the force of intolerance is seen running away in its jeep, while the force of rustic humanism, borne in the masks and costumes of the earth and its creatures, dances across the screen just as it had when it first appeared: as it always has been, so it always will be. Fanaticism and its viciousness will appeal only to bitter souls like the leper woman's husband, but the entrenched values of the people will abide, beckoning to all.

The power of the common people is highlighted further by the portrayal of the community of little people. There is a very potent irony here, for lack of stature might normally be an easy representation of weakness and submissiveness. Dasgupta's clear intention is different, of course. The community of little people is portrayed, indeed, for its strength and self-sufficiency, not for any helplessness that might be ascribed to it. Additionally, a sense of mystery is suggested by the procession of little people coming over a hill in the early morning, at first seen in silhouette. We might note their apparent sense of purpose, as we might be impressed later by their obvious dignity when they march funereally at the film's end. What one of the big, strong wrestlers dreams of becoming—a guard on a train—one of the little people actually is. The wrestlers' naive perception of the world as one vast wrestling pit reflects the inferior notion of power through conflict that the guard, in the final dialogue with Uttara, puts down as one of the false values of tall people. And when, in their self-absorption, the brawny wrestlers ignore Uttara's plea on behalf of the pastor, it is the alacrity of the little man in running to her aid that carries so much meaning. As the natuas articulate the dreams of ordinary folk, the little people, represented by the guard, dream of a world of harmony and goodness. He says to Uttara, 'If we married, our children would be good like you.' Her candid reply, 'But they'd also be dwarfs like you,' allows him to assert the morally positive aspect of his community, an assertion that is underlined by contrast to the brutish extravagances of the thugs. There is simple idealism represented in the little people as there is in the pastor, and both are targets of the hostility of bigots. One of the little people is lost, but the community endures by its moral strength, as does the troupe of natuas and all that they represent.

The small group of destitute men resembles in an odd sort of way the chorus in classical drama. Although they are seen attending the pastor's church service—as well as surreptitiously extricating themselves from it—and being served food by him and Matthew, they are never part of the narrative. As the classical chorus, uninvolved in the action, indifferently comments on it, so too do these men, albeit in a limited way. In their detachment they make observations on the small world of their own experience and dream of getting away from it to a new 'village' where only happiness prevails. (Unwittingly, they dream of what the community of little people already have, just as Nimai dreams of becoming what the little guard already is.) It is from their simple, uninformed conversation that we learn of the serious problems of unemployment in rural areas, and that many people, driven by hunger, turn to the church in order to benefit from its charity. Well fed as they are by the pastor, they decide, nevertheless, to follow their dream, on foot, to some place called America which surely flows with milk and honey. Our amusement at their innocence has a cloud of sadness hanging over it, for we know that their dream will turn sour as their feet become blistered and that they will have no pastor to feed them when they return. A dream may have compelling power, but when it arises out of ignorance, it will usually give rise to disappointment.

The parlous state of the rural economy that is driving these men in their fantasy is alluded to a number of times. Simmering beneath the apparent quietude of the rural world and belying its serenity, there is genuine hardship. Very early in the film, when

Balaram remarks that the pastor has bought many things at the market, the reply points to the great number of hungry people in their vicinity. The existence of leprosy, very much a disease of the poor, is another indication of hardship. A young woman at the rustic post office, dictating a letter to her husband who has gone away in search of work, offers some detail of the difficulties she and her children have to endure, while the old woman sweeping up leaves in the forest, referring to her daughter-in-law (whom we have seen prostituting herself to one of the thugs), gives Uttara a brief yet poignant picture of the pain wrought on ordinary people and their families by unemployment.

However, it is also important to remember that Dasgupta offers a realisation of the ideal of contentment, despite the reality of poverty and deprivation, in the train guard's description of the village of the little people—across the river that flows on the other side of the hill—where everyone lives for the good of everyone else. This allusion comes as part of the final dialogue and may well be seen as a summary statement of faith and hope in the meek.

While we may note with some admiration the dedicated endeavours of the selfless pastor to alleviate some of this hardship, we may also note the utter indifference of the three zealots—whose energies are spent on self-indulgence and bigotry—to the suffering of others. Fundamentalism is not interested in reform or in charity; its self-righteous destructiveness is a mere distraction from reality. Smoke-screens are as much a part of Indian political life as they are anywhere else in the world—if not more.

But the sin of indifference must also be ascribed to the two wrestlers, who have no interest in anything outside their own bodies. Here is a very clear and simple indication of the effectiveness of smoke-screens, in this case a wrestling-pit and a world view defined by its perimeters, in cultivating social blindness. As we watch them, helpless in their descent into mutual destruction, we may remember the admiration for them expressed by the innocent Matthew, who marvelled at their strength and invulnerability, unaware that the strong can have weaknesses. Ultimately, they can be judged no less harshly than the thugs, for at the crucial movement it was their unforgivable indifference that facilitated the fulfilment of hatred.

Essential to the audience's awareness of such subjective elements as personal attitudes and emotions is the film's atmosphere, which is not simply a natural outcome of the narrative and the *mise-en-scène*; rather, it has been carefully conceived and its development is tightly controlled. At the opening the partnership of music and visual image creates a feeling of peaceful optimism in the forest, and this is reinforced by the subsequent shots of the girl leading the cows home at evening. The jeep creates an obviously discordant note, although the cut to the morning shot of the clothes of the wrestlers flying in the air with evident abandon serves to restore the optimism. However, the discordant note will resonate in the background, gradually and insidiously becoming louder as the film progresses. In this early stage the tranquillity is threatened; in the final stage it will be shattered. The progression from one stage to the other is subtle, without any obvious crisis or turning-point, but it is felt as an almost palpable simmering that is as unobtrusive as it is inexorable. (The jeep is an obvious visual indication of the presence of wickedness, as certain visual images make clear: an empty liquor bottle is thrown from the jeep to smash against the rocks beside the road; behind it a poor woman is sexually exploited; in an act of crude hostility it runs the pastor and Matthew off the road; it is the focus of confrontation and tension in the forest; it conveys many jerrycans of kerosene to the church; and, with 'eyes' blazing, it is a grotesque spectator of the final horror committed by its masters.)

The setting of *Uttara* is remote. It is characterised by a simple rusticity and outward serenity, typified by the shots of the pastor and Matthew getting about on their bicycle, passing the postman on his bicycle on an otherwise deserted country road, or riding through the forest. The only motorised traffic is the occasional bus, crowded with simple folk going about their daily business—and the jeep, the ineradicable discordant note.

The dairy village is marked by an apparent peacefulness, though the potential serenity is minimised by the affliction of the woman with leprosy and the cynicism of her husband. The home of Balaram's aunt is a rustic gem—a once-splendid mansion now in utter disarray, haphazardly adorned with tatty pictures, and through which cows wander with total freedom. The bus carrying a crowd of people and animals, both inside and on its roof, with Balaram and Uttara in their wedding clothes, is another delight, as is the forbearance of them all when a flat tyre renders the bus out of action. The rural weekly market and its photographer's 'studio', with its ancient camera and its backdrop of London's Tower Bridge, offers another picturesque image of rural happiness. There is a lovely episode depicting Balaram and Uttara's outing to the bioscope. It is an outdoor showing of *Coolie* with the popular star, Amitabh Bachchan, presented on a makeshift screen—a sheet tied between two trees. A storm comes up and Amitabh and his dancing chorus are blown away by the elements.

All of these aspects of rural life provide a calculated diversion from the resonance of the discordant note. They also provide a very important contrast between the simple though difficult life of the rural people and the forces of bigotry brought in from outside. Whatever hardship the people have to endure, it is at least natural to them. The values of the outsiders are alien, offer them no good, and are intruded into their world. These men do not belong to the forests and fields; they have come from outside, not to contribute or to share, but to disrupt and to destroy. Whereas the natuas are a substantiation of the natural rural life and are integral to it, the fanatics are from elsewhere and, after their evil has been wrought, they leave in anonymity.

The isolation of the setting—which is both spatial and qualitative—is underlined by evidence of illiteracy and poor communications. The jeep may be seen as a recurring image of alien intrusion, while the trains that pass by suggest a reminder of an outside world. The notion of distance, intrinsic to the remoteness of the setting, is further suggested by the unfamiliarity with the telephone and the adventurousness that would seem to characterise even the postal system. Balaram makes a seemingly long journey to his aunt's house although it is situated in relative proximity, while Nimai dreams of being a guard and relishes the notion of travel over distances that might, in less remote regions, be almost commutable.

The setting and atmosphere of this film have been represented with exceptional skill. To a large extent Dasgupta has depicted an archetype of rural India, with all the outward signs of pastoral loveliness. He has also very carefully drawn the underlying economic stresses and the regressive isolation that undermine such loveliness. Isolation might have the effect of being uninfluenced by undesirable forces, but as the jeep-borne zealots show, isolation cannot be total. The aspect of isolation that Dasgupta focuses on, the isolation of mind, is that which, in fact, increases indifference and underlines weakness. The total picture that emerges is of a very fragile, vulnerable world.

So much of the subliminal meaning of the film is exuded in exquisite poetic suggestion and intrinsic interconnections of ideas. For example, the first encounter of the guard with the outsiders is while one of the latter is practising his knife-throwing, and it is knife-throwing that is central to his final encounter with them. When Uttara puts her ear to the post box hanging from the tree and explains to Balaram that she is listening to all the letters talking to one another, he looks at her dumbly, obviously unable to share her romanticism; in the last dialogue, it is easy to appreciate the declaration of the guard that those who cannot dream are bullies. Again, Uttara sets out on her journey with Balaram with great optimism, wearing the anklets that had been handed down to her through her mother and which she looks forward to passing on to her own daughter. Balaram blandly describes their jingling as sounding like chains. In her final meeting with the guard she takes them off and throws them away, now seeing them as symbols of a marriage which has become nothing more than thraldom. The grim irony in her setting herself free glares out of the headlights of the jeep emerging from the background. Earlier there was a brief sequence in which Uttara shelters under a tree from a sudden downpour. The rain is shown as a harbinger of regeneration, a notion already established by the falling leaves in the opening shots in the forest. In this natural regeneration even a snake, which glides close to Uttara's feet without any demur from her, has its place; this shot suggests a telling contrast to the three outsiders. The idea of an indifference which in time becomes callous is adequately kept in prominence by the frequency of the wrestling sequences, effectively placed on a rise so that they may be seen in long shot as well as in close and medium shots. While *Uttara* offers a persuasive warning against extremism and the indifference by which it might thrive, it is also a film of hope and celebration, recognising the strength of the spirit that will endure and overcome, the strength of the underlying good that buoys ordinary people. While one might draw particular inferences from the film that are directly pertinent to the rise of Hindu extremism at the end of the twentieth century, the quality of *Uttara* lies in the universality of its subject matter, which transcends any particular historical phenomenon. The film is also remarkable for its form and structure, its carefully conceived syntax and its superb control over the evolution of the narrative and the emanation of the atmosphere. The ultimate effect of the work is all the more riveting for its simple, direct statement and the absence of any narrative or philosophical complexity. Put simply and directly, it is an exceptionally beautiful film.

NINE

Life at the Throw of a Dice

We think only of setting out, of
journeying off into the distance.

Moving from one window through another
we go out into
the great beyond

and one day reach the bathroom.

Cold water keeps on coming
out of the tap, really
making us cringe,
and in the flow of the water
we set out into the distance
from that small, cold hole

and we'll not come back again.

(*Cockroaches*)

One of the remarkable things in Raja Rao's pastiche of stories, *On the Ganga Ghat*, is the way in which seemingly mutually exclusive opposites—the living and the dead, the sacred and the profane—are melded into an accommodation. The less sceptical reader can never be really sure whether this reflects a miracle of

Benares, the literary skill of Raja Rao or even, indeed, an aspect of the essence of creation. 'The unreal and the real are so co-adjacent in Benares,' writes Rao, 'you lose trace of the one, while you are wholly with the other.' Presumably, it is not always easy—or even possible—to discern which is 'the one' and which 'the other'.

In all of the films of Buddhadeb Dasgupta the distinction between reality and unreality is often similarly unclear. Indeed, there are instances where unreality is often difficult even to recognise, as it is often confused with dream or disorientation or madness or even simple difference from some kind of norm. As early as in *Duratwa*, Dasgupta was experimenting with those moments in experience, those perceptions of life, where reality and unreality would seem to overlap, where there is a difficulty in discerning one from the other, or where the actual is not necessarily to be equated with the real. These experiments continued to one way or another until the permeation of the 'real' with the 'unreal' was given focus in *Tahader Katha*, and thereafter such confusion of perception would be prominent.

In all of Dasgupta's films so far, the real is often punctuated by the unreal; sometimes the two are juxtaposed, sometimes they embrace one another or are intertwined. It is in *Manda Meyer Upakhyan* ('The Tale of a Naughty Girl', 2002), however, that any acknowledgement of the real and the unreal as separate entities is altogether rescinded and one is left more than a little uncertain of whether the film is about unreal aspects of reality or about reality impinging on unreality—or even about something else altogether.

There is nothing so abstract about the source of the film, which is Prafulla Roy's charming story, *Akasher Chand ebang ekti Janala* (literally 'The Moon in the Sky and a Window'). It tells of the fourteen-year-old Lati's quest for emancipation from a life that has been determined for her by her mother, Rajani, the madam of a provincial brothel. It is not as though Rajani is heartless in resolving that her daughter will become just any ordinary whore, for she has something better in mind for her—and for herself. Rajani finds a wealthy, middle-aged man who will take Lati as his mistress—along with her mother—in a house he has had built especially for her. Not surprisingly, the girl is appalled at the prospect of a life as the plaything of a man more than four times her age; moreover, such an arrangement would obviate her own ambition of pursuing her education. However, Rajani has taken Lati out of school in preparation for her new career, and the little girl's only contact with learning and the teacher she so greatly admires is through her young friend, Shibu. So desperate is she to learn, as well as to repudiate a life of prostitution, that she eventually runs away to Calcutta with her teacher, who has been promoted to a school there.

What gives Lati's flight something of an epic quality is that it occurs on the same day as the first moon landing. The proposed lunar voyage had been discussed by Lati and Shibu with immense wonder and an element of incredulity. But just as Neil Armstrong took his legendary small step for a man, Lati took what was for her a giant step in breaking free of the shackles of prescription and defying established attitudes that would bind women to the interests of men.

Dasgupta takes up this story quite faithfully and gives it centrality in his film, but he also sets it in a broader, diverse narrative context. Natabar Paladhi, the would-be patron of Lati, is drawn more fully; Shibu is presented not as the son of a teashop proprietor but of a washerman; there is an additional story of three young prostitutes who seek to break free from a profession that binds them in thraldom; and a quaint adaptation of an idea from another Prafulla Roy story, *Barshay ek Din*, dealing with an infirm elderly couple, complements the element of the absurd in the film.

Manda Meyer Upakhyan opens in a provincial cinema hall. It is interesting to note that, apart from one brief and amusing scene in *Uttara*, cinema has not previously featured in a Buddhadeb Dasgupta film. Here it is used as a ready metaphor for unreality. Before the matinee show begins, Natabar Paladhi, also the proprietor of the cinema hall, is seen somewhat somnolently watching a screening of a piece of pornography. The piece has been culled from something more extensive—

perhaps it is the one juicy part—and is being shown as a film loop, held by a projectionist who too sits sleepily at an ancient projector as the extract is repeated time and time again. The illusoriness of it all is highlighted by the sleepiness of the projectionist and his audience of one; it has all been seen before, and represents mere fantasy.

The pornographic extract is of some interest in itself, however. It is something of a caricature of Indian soft-core pornography, with loud and frantic music, gaudy colours and an amazing unconcern for subtlety. It represents the attempted gang-rape of a woman by three burly, ugly thugs. However, strong and brutish as they may be, they have their work cut out for them, as the lady's unwillingness to accommodate their desires is expressed by some quite impressive footwork, which sends the thugs flying one after the other just as each would seem to be about to get a mouthful of some part of her flesh. Apparently, the piece once titillated Paladhi, as it is shown repeatedly, creating for the genuine film audience an element of burlesque. In its farcical way, however, this brief loop foreshadows two things: the notion of male exploitation of women as represented by prostitution, and, in the refusal of the woman to submit, the three girls who later seek to leave the profession as well as Lati's flight to Calcutta and an education. Most significantly, it establishes a basis for the blurring of the line of demarcation between actuality and illusion.

As the private pornography screening comes to a hurried end, the first customers for the matinee show are seen arriving outside the hall in a large jeep driven by one Ganesh. From the crude fantasy of the cinema screen we are taken into another illusory realm, the world outside. Conventionally, of course, movies are seen to be a world of make-believe, while the real world goes on outside of the cinema; in this case, however, there is nothing of a 'real world' to be seen. The cinema hall is situated way out in the open country, with no sight of even a semblance of a town or human habitation anywhere, nor are any people seen coming to the matinee show other than those of the one family pouring out of the jeep which, it appears, serves as a taxi.

The jeep is a central image throughout, drawing otherwise disparate planes of the film into relationship with one another. Except for the brief appearance of a small car, it is the only motor vehicle to appear in the film. In the early scenes we note that the jeep is a recent model, and hardly the rundown bomb we might realistically expect in a film set in such a remote region, although, despite its newness, it has a noticeable propensity for refusing to start except with a kick. However, we may wonder about the significance of this when, later in the film, we learn that preparations for the lunar voyage of 1969 are underway; evidently, the trappings of period are not seen to be important. Perhaps this says more about the illusoriness of the moon landing than the apparent anachronism of a late model jeep in a film set in 1969. Conspiracy theories aside, how real is the historical fact of the moon landing to most people living in the world today, particularly the hundreds of millions living in pre-modern circumstances beyond the modern metropolises? The sheer wonder of the lunar landing must not be underestimated, for it will be seen to equate even with the wonder of the flight of a little girl from the bonds of a tradition-bound, predetermined life. That flight might give greater inspiration to millions than the momentous walk of Neil Armstrong.

The other significant aspect of the jeep is the landscape through which it travels. The countryside is bare and dry, its only visual interest lying in its undulating topography and the occasional tree and less frequent copse. In the evident absence of human habitation and cultivation, the land seems unwelcoming and inhospitable, and the millennia-old relationship between man and the soil is not to be noted here. One major effect of this is to deny definition to the landscape, so that the notion of location, for example, becomes immaterial. Thus, the long shots of the moving jeep easily give the impression that the vehicle is travelling from nowhere to nowhere.

The viewer might also wonder about the nature of Ganesh's business. In fact, as we come to learn, he is the driver of Natabar Paladhi. But given Paladhi's minimal needs for travel—perhaps his special fantasies make too strong a claim on his time—

Ganesh would seem to have ample opportunity for making a little money outside of his regular duties. Thus, we see him taking the large family group to the cinema at the beginning of the film; soon after, he takes a girl from somewhere to an open expanse; he drops off a male passenger short of his destination when the jeep breaks down; and he drives Lati to the station at the end of the film. He is underpaid for the first of these jobs and only partially paid for the second; we may assume he does not collect a fare for the third, for he helps Lati as a genuine favour. Hence, his business is hardly a thriving one; indeed, it is hardly a business. And yet he is kept busy throughout the film, most of the time driving an elderly couple, again from nowhere to nowhere, and with no prospect at all of remuneration.

The focal point of the film is the brothel, its life and its characters, especially Lati and Rajani, and this world is introduced by an interesting cut from the cinema hall with Paladhi calling to his pet cat, Gufo, to a room in Rajani's quarters where the cat is seen in the act of stealing food intended for Lati and her mother. While the direct link in this cut is the cat, the indirect link is Lati, the subject of discussion in the next scene. As Lati and Shibu run off with the cat stowed in a gunny sack to 'lose' it in the woods, preparation is made for the upcoming scene as some of the women talk about how Rajani is looking for a patron for her fourteen-year-old daughter, but would seem to be satisfied only with 'Prince Charming on a white charger.' We then see Paladhi with his lackey, Nakul, ambling among some trees while the latter extols the virtues of a fourteen-year-old virgin he has found for the pleasure of his master.

The life of the brothel is indicated further through Ganesh and his meandering taxi. The girl he drives from somewhere to an open expanse is a prostitute called Bakul, and she is actually travelling from the station to the house of Aunty Jamuna at Gosaipara, where she intends to embark on her carnal career. It is when she states her destination that we note the moral conscience of Ganesh who, in righteous indignation, refuses to take her there, telling her instead to get out and walk the rest of the way. His morality is put to the test, which he almost fails, when the girl cannot pay the entire fare, and offers him use of her body as payment of the balance. On instinct, Ganesh cannot resist the temptation, getting out of the car and moving towards her, but the distance between them gives him enough time to reflect on what he is about to do, and he quickly changes his mind, hurries back to the car and drives off. This helps to make sense of Ganesh's later abhorrence, expressed contemptuously to Nakul, of their boss's intentions regarding Lati, and his own alacrity in hurrying her away to the station at the end of the film. His strength of principle and decency, along with his solicitous care for the elderly couple, helps to portray him as a pillar of moral hope in a realm of moral anarchy.

The subplot involving the three young prostitutes continues after the survival of Ganesh's threatened integrity. As Bakul sets off on foot on the last stage of her journey, a car is seen to pull up nearby, roughly where Ganesh had let Bakul out of his jeep, and a young woman and a hump-backed servant carrying a suitcase and a bundle get out. The woman is peremptorily dismissed by the front seat passenger after offering her a wad of money, which she accepts with studied disdain. Then she too sets off on foot to where, presumably, the car and its respectable owner will not be seen. Immediately, she meets up with Bakul, and both girls are amused to learn of the coincidence of their meeting, as she, Basanti, is returning to the same brothel after an assignment 'in town'. A little later they are joined by another young woman, clad in a burka; this is Ayesha, who had left the brothel some time before but has been obliged to return to do the only work available to her. The two experienced girls, overjoyed at their reunion, strike up an immediate friendship with the newcomer.

In the introduction of this subplot, we have revealed for us some of the emotional baggage the three girls are carrying with them. Brief reference is made to poverty as a cause for a girl's turning to prostitution—after losing so much in a flood, even Ayesha's own father presses her to return to work in the brothel —as well as to the perfidy of men, whose only concern is for 'the few inches dangling between their legs.' In the girls' expression of contempt for their work and for the men who exploit them for a pittance, there is also established an important aspect of the ambience from which Lati is determined to escape.

The elements of the film so far established bear at least some loose relationship to one another, but in the cut from the three girls in the bare expanse we move to something quite extraneous. There is a close shot of an elderly couple being carried on a bier by a group of men in a state of some agitation. As Ganesh approaches in his jeep, he is flagged down and, without any discussion, the two old people are transferred from their stretcher into the back of the car, while Ganesh is told simply that they are in urgent need of treatment and he must taken them to hospital. One Lakshman, apparently responsible for the couple, is called but is shown running away, and it would appear that we have a common case of two old people, having passed the limit of their usefulness, being dispensed with.

For the rest of the film the two old people will be driven about by Ganesh, not exactly looking for a hospital, but rather hoping for one to appear. Suggestions of a 'hospital' for cars and one for cows are raised, but the general notion is never taken really seriously, especially as it comes to be realised that there does not seem to be anything noticeably wrong with either of the old people. And so Ganesh spends his days driving them around, seeming to look for what is not to be found. Ultimately, they find their fulfilment in sitting under a tree playing Ludo, a board game that requires no skill other than the ability to throw dice and count in low single figures.

On the immediate plane this element of the film has nothing at all to do with the story of Lati, the life of the brothel, or the fortunes of Natabar Paladhi, the owner of the vehicle in which the old couple are aimlessly transported. On reflection, however, their significance lies right at the core of the film.

It is often observed that the geriatric condition and that of the infant bear many similarities. The comparison is significant here in that in a number of films, especially in *Phera* and *Lal Darja*, Dasgupta has portrayed children or childhood as symbolic of innocence, a kind of morally neutral state of nature. While children may be the potential victims of injustice or immorality, they are not—at least in the films of Dasgupta—deliberate agents of virtue; they simply are what they are, in a state that may be challenged but not compromised.

The elderly couple in *Manda Meyer Upakhyan* are both as helpless and dependent as small children; they are trusting; they take delight in simple pleasures. They are also at the mercy of those in positions of power over them: first, the people who get rid of them, and then Ganesh. Similarly, Lati and Shibu, while not really helpless, are certainly dependent on their parents, whom they trust, and their pleasures are simple and pure—chatting with one another, marvelling together at the imminent moon voyage, and pursuing an education. And like the two old people, Lati also is vulnerable—to her mother and the social condition in which she has been brought up, and to a future determined by her mother's values, values which welcome a place in Lati's life for one such as Natabar Paladhi.

Thus the elderly couple serve two purposes in the film. One is to reinforce the notion of innocence as represented by Lati and Shibu. The other—in their utterly disoriented state and their ultimate fulfilment in a children's board game—is to offer yet another perception of reality. Because the only people to have genuine experience of age are the aged themselves, their world remains very much a mystery to everyone else. Those who carry the arrogance of youth and all its self-importance may see them as remote, dwelling somewhere beyond life and short of death Their twilight world is an alternative state of reality, unexplored, alien and uninviting.

However, the world of the brothel is also shown as an alternative state of reality—not fully explored by those who visit it, alien to 'respectable' society, and uninviting even to those who people it, and especially to Lati.

The brothel accommodates both the plot and the subplot, yet these two remain separate from one another, the one significant thing common to both being the dream of escape. Whereas Lati's dream is clear and attainable, however, the dream of the three young prostitutes is vague. They simply want to leave the brothel and find a life free from deceit, exploitation and humiliation. There may well be many prostitutes who actually enjoy their work, but Basanti, Bakul and Ayesha certainly are not among them. In one scene, as they get ready for their evening's work, each expresses in her own way how her sexual experiences with men disgust her, how no amount of soap can wash away the filth that would seem to accrue from being physically used by men. In their first scene together they made it clear that it is only economic necessity that forces them to do this work; if there were another way, it would be embraced.

Each of the three girls can feel a ready sympathy with the experiences of the other two, and while they may not find true love (whatever that may be), they do find a mutually sustaining alternative in their compassion for the plight and aspirations of one another. As they daydream about a life together beyond the brothel and its business, they broach the possibility of doing without men. The counter-suggestion—that they themselves can attend to one another's needs—may be flippant and it evokes giggles, yet it is complemented at least to some extent by another dressing scene whose visual intention is unmistakably erotic. The three young woman had once dreamt of love with men, and that dream has turned sour; for them, orthodox love has become a realm of unreality. Who is to say that the love they may give to one another—as a group rather than as couples—would be less genuine?

The depiction of the brothel is deliberately intended to negate realism. Like the cinema at the start of the film the brothel has no urban context but is situated seemingly in the middle of nowhere. The intention here is that it should not be related to anything; if it has no connection with anything that suggests a 'normal' or 'everyday' world, it might be seen much as a world unto itself. Nor does the building suggest the sordid realm that it accommodates but rather something grand, particularly at night, when the well-lit pillared cloisters are peopled by glamorous looking women and reasonably well-dressed men, giving an effect even of classiness which, in terms of simple realism, is patently absurd. On the other hand, the depiction of the interior and the conversations that take place there is quite naturalistic, while the aspect of the absurd lends to this naturalism a telling distortion.

The use of cliché reinforces the aspect of the absurd, at the same time intensifying the sinister element of the distortion. The women smoking (smoking is very uncommon in India amongst women), the hackneyed ribald humour, and the studied gestures, postures and facial expressions all evoke a very theatrical bordello atmosphere. The imposition of Basanti's extortionate husband is realistic, though clichéd nevertheless, while there is even an element of melodrama in his being dispatched by the knife-wielding hunchback, so intensifying the fantastic realm of the brothel.

Just as the cinema and the brothel are seen as islands in an ocean of the unknown, all of the characters in this film are also seen as cut adrift from any recognisable social moorings, such as home, family, friends and work. The contempt in which the three young prostitutes hold their work and the sheer economic necessity that keeps them shackled to it have already been noted; what is suggested here is the irony of survival coming at the cost of doing something that is repugnant. While sexual commerce is shown to be bizarre—at times even grotesque—given its foundation in fantasy and make-believe, so too are the other references to work that occur in the film seen as somewhat exceptional. Ganesh's job might seem everyday, although his devotion to aimlessly driving the old couple around the countryside would certainly seem to compromise its ordinariness. There is the projectionist at Paladhi's cinema hall, yet all we ever see him doing is showing a pornographic loop to an audience of one, a process that is soporific for both worker and client. There are also Nagen, the schoolmaster, and Shibu's father, the washerman. The schoolmaster is much admired by Lati and Shibu, but for most of his time on screen he is seen meandering about on a bicycle—we see no school, no students. The only aspect of the washerman's work which we see is his laundering for whores; moreover, of far greater interest than he is Pyarelal, the donkey who helps in his deliveries.

While the most basic economic convention is work, the fundamental social reality is the family, from which support, too, the characters are presented as detached. Lati is presented with mother but not father, and Shibu is presented with father but there is no indication of a mother. Indeed, radical to the crisis in Lati's life is her perceived need to run away from her mother, so nullifying whatever little family life she has. Natabar Paladhi makes mention of his wife and family, but we see nothing of them. There is no reference to a wife of Ganesh or of Nakul, and Nagen, the schoolmaster, tells us he is unmarried and without children. The old couple have each other, yet have been rejected by any larger family they might have.

Given these various kinds of detachment, it might be suggested that Dasgupta sees the world, at least in this film, as lacking in cohesion. Underpinning the conflict and tension in most of his films (*Neem Annapurna* is the exception) is a serious failure to communicate and to understand, leaving characters cut off from one another, unable to fulfil one another; indeed, there are characters such as Shashanka in *Phera*, Nabin in *Lal Darja* and the two wrestlers in *Uttara* who are cut off from themselves in some way or another. In *Manda Meyer Upakhyan*, however, we are taken into a world of arbitrariness, a quasi-society of transient connections, misunderstood relationships, and thwarted aspirations. There is no malice to speak of here, only an indifference to the interests and feelings of others. Dasgupta's world is not yet a realm of chaos or anarchy, but, in its non-cohesion, it is very much a world of meaninglessness.

It is in this detachment from simple human values and social integration that we might note—in passing—Natabar Paladhi's fascination with the ants that labour together and in harmony in the bark of the trunk of a tree, and his concern for whether or not they talk to one another. Of something more than passing interest is Pyarelal, the washerman's donkey, whom Dasgupta endows not only with intelligence that serves to entertain, but also with a prescience that clearly suggests that the film's human characters are unable to read the webs of life they are in the process of weaving. Perhaps lacking in intelligence and prescience, but not in wilfulness and assertiveness, is the cat, Gufo. When Paladhi calls for it at the end of the first scene in the cinema hall, it is in the process of being 'lost' by Shibu and Lati for its constant thieving of food. But a cat is not as easily fooled as perhaps a person is, and despite having been taken to the forest in a gunny sack, it eventually finds its way back to where it is content. And so, at the end of the film, when Lati has embarked on her epic journey, the three young women have set out on their road to a dream, and the elderly couple find fulfilment in Ludo, one shot makes an eloquent comment on the world of confused realities that has been the setting of this film: sleepy Paladhi is seated in his cinema hall in front of the same pornographic loop, Gufo sleeping contentedly in his lap.

Given the historical disjointedness of the film as suggested by the juxtaposition of the recent model jeep and the imminence of the 1969 lunar voyage, one might wonder at the actual significance of the moon landing to this film. In fact, it is learned of in this remote rural area not from a television or radio news bulletin but from a scrap of newspaper used to make a paper bag for fast snacks and carelessly cast from the window of Ganesh's jeep. The scrap of paper might well be very old, but in this rustic outpost the news it conveys is not. And so what is important to the film is not the actuality of the lunar landing, but the simple idea that it might happen.

The significance of Lati's flight is the same. When Ganesh drops her off at the station, we get a visual surprise. At any station in rural India, when the one train a day is about to leave for the state capital, there would be a bustling crowd of passengers, well-wishers, hawkers, porters and so on. When Lati arrives at the station there is no one there at all, and instead of people looking out of the windows and leaning from the doorways, there are only empty windows and doorways, indicative of an empty train. At Lati's calling, Nagen the schoolmaster appears at the entry to one carriage, and takes Lati on broad as the train pulls out with, presumably, two passengers only. Again, what is important is not Lati's actual going to Kolkata, but the mere idea of it.

It is of more than poetic significance to say that, to Lati, Calcutta, with its promise of education, is like the moon to Neil Armstrong. In some ways, it is even further away and harder to get to. But there are other moons to be reached, too, such as the promotion in Calcutta to which Nagen, the country schoolmaster, is headed. The moon to which the three young prostitutes aspire is freedom from exploitation, where there is mutual love and fulfilment. Absurdly—perhaps not—the elderly couple find their moon on a Ludo board. The sphere of acquisitiveness and venality that is Rajani's moon depends entirely on others for its attainment. Perhaps Natabar Paladhi, entrenched in his world of fantasy, is altogether unaware of the moon, and so is content to remain in his cinema hall dozing in front of a pornographic loop, while the utterly undiscerning cat, Gufo, aspires to nothing but someone else's lunch and Paladhi's lap.

Although the three young prostitutes know what their moon is, they would seem to have very little idea of how to reach it, and their journey to it is likely to be as arbitrary as has been the journey to fulfilment in Ludo of the elderly couple. Whether they are ultimately successful or not is of no interest; what matters is that they are human enough to dream and courageous enough to chase their dream. Rajani's moon can be reached only if circumstances out of her control should change—rather like winning a lottery—but Lati's journey to her moon is clearly determined. Nevertheless, the arbitrariness of the world in which Dasgupta has placed this young girl is hardly minimised by the execution of her intention, for the most prominent determinant in this film is chance.

Manda Meyer Upakhyan advances the idea that maybe life does progress by chance, as though it is determined by the throw of a dice. The importance of chance as a determinant in life is indicated in a number of ways. It is quite by chance that Bakul meets Basanti just after she is put out of Ganesh's taxi, and it is chance that brings Ayesha along the remote and lonely road soon after that. It is chance that brings Ganesh together on the road with the party seeking to rid themselves of the elderly couple. It is chance that the hunchback with a knife happens to be outside

Basanti's door when her husband becomes menacing, and it is chance that turns the ensuing confusion into an unforeseen opportunity for Lati's escape which, in turn, puts paid to the carefully worked out plans of Natabar Paladhi and the dream of Rajani.

The prominence of chance is best highlighted by a series of shots featuring a piece of newspaper carrying the story of a man's intention to go to the moon. The piece of newsprint starts off as a paper cone containing the snack of puffed rice that Ganesh has bought for the elderly couple. After they hungrily devour the rice, the old man drops the cone from the window of the moving car. The camera cuts from the car to a medium long shot of the paper being gently tossed about on the road. It is then elevated—physically and connotatively—by the wind, and we get a long shot of the piece of paper floating about on the breeze against an expanse of sky. Held for quite some time, this shot is enhanced by an exaggerated—even clichéd—sound effect of wind and an occasional four-bar snatch of atmospheric music. There is another cut to a medium long shot of the schoolmaster, Nagen, approaching the camera on his bicycle, slightly obscured, perhaps romanticised, by a haze of dust. There is a cut to a long shot and we see the paper bag being blown towards him from the foreground of the frame. A medium close shot sees Nagen dismount, attracted by the piece of paper. The paper is then blown to his feet, and he picks it up and reads the headline proclaiming the imminence of a modern miracle. The sequence ends with a reflective long shot which has Nagen and his bicycle on the far right edge of the frame, which is divided equally between the expanse of sky and the barren landscape, broken only by a scraggy tree in the centre of the shot.

All this visual attention given to a mere scrap of newspaper has to have some justification. Quite clearly, the effect of Dasgupta's making this shot so pointed is to highlight the notion that pervades this film—that life is illogical and arbitrarily determined. A haphazard act of littering sets in train a series of events that form the substance of the rest of the film. But there is another aspect to giving prominence to chance. There is a suggestion, at least, that it has some kind of inexorable, unavoidable power, an idea that is prompted by the schoolmaster's being drawn to the piece of newspaper (it is, after all, the sort of thing that most people cycling along a country road would instinctively ignore); the look on his face as he deliberately gets down from his bicycle suggests a degree of enthralment. However, of particular significance is that the shot shows the piece of paper actually coming to him, rather than being chased and fetched by him. The last shot of the sequence lays emphasis on the notions of detachment and isolation, cogently lending intensity to the sequence as a whole.

Manda Meyer Upakhyan is quite different from all of Buddhadeb Dasgupta's previous films in that it is essentially a film of ideas and abstracts rather than a film about people. In all the previous works it is the essential humanity of individuals that gives interest and development to the narrative; but *Manda Meyer Upakhyan* is much more an expressionist work, where the characters, quite credible as people, are human representations of abstracts. The whole idea of cutting characters away from the usual moorings of human life—familial and social interactions and so on—is to strip away the significantly personal, to essentialise the characters to the abstractions that the poet-filmmaker wants to explore.

Manda Meyer Upakhyan is an extraordinarily original and imaginative work in which so much that is trite and hackneyed is candidly taken up and sculpted into an intensely complex view of the randomness of life. The intellectual domain of the film is significantly removed from the simple elements of its narrative; those viewers who can readily bridge that gap will welcome the work for its exceptionally skilful melding of philosophical insight and quirkiness. While the technical hallmark of Dasgupta's cinema —tightly constructed narrative, intensity of sparse dialogue, and brilliantly conceived visual work—are well in evidence, the one problem that some may have will be in the assessment of the worth of what the film ultimately has to say. Many will hail it with enthusiasm, some will find it somewhat inconsequential. But none will deny with conviction its superb artistry.

TEN

The Dream Machine

...And as no word
could adequately name the moonlight
I held out both my arms, calling the sun
out of the mist.
There was love immeasurable in my heart
and heavenly music in the air, and any
words might stir me deeply and spontaneously
such as art is art or a rose is a rose.

(*Descent*)

Contemporary India is a myriad of contradictions and anomalies. Perhaps the most striking is the prevalence and acceptance of violence in the land that gave the world the Buddha, Mahatma Gandhi and the ideals of *ahimsa* or non-violence. The newspapers carry daily reports of domestic violence, of suicide and enforced suicide, of the lynching of suspected criminals, of protesting mobs burning buses, of fights between rival political gangs. From the countryside come all too frequent reports on brutal class conflict between organised landlord militia and self-defence groups of 'untouchables', of human sacrifice in the name of religion, and of female infanticide. Horrible communal riots, often with oblique political patronage, still take place, destroying any remaining credence in the notion of Indian tolerance. Particularly sinister is the use of organised terror in pursuit of various territorial separatist agendas. And then there is commercial cinema, dominating television screens, flaunting all manner of brutality as a form of entertainment. Emanating from this widespread violence is an air of callousness that colours so much in social relations.

Swapner Din (literally 'Day of Dreams' but going under the English title 'Chased by a Dream'), released in 2004, makes incidental though significant use of two manifestations of contemporary violence. The more general, immediate one is the separatist movement in the northeast of the country and the illegal gun-running industry that nurtures it. The particular violence, taking place in the background, are the appalling communal riots that occurred in the state of Gujarat in early 2002. Given the apparent bleakness out of which much of the film emanates, one might expect a work similar to *Uttara* in its gravitas. On the contrary, *Swapner Din* is one of Dasgupta's most positive and optimistic films and, perhaps, his most light-hearted.

Prominent in the film's thematics is the notion of commitment, or its absence. The two central male characters are committed to nothing tangible. Paresh has a job to which he is mechanically committed: he is responsible and reliable, though goaded perhaps more by the fear of the consequences of losing his government job than by any element of dedication he might have to it. His work is to travel throughout rural Bengal showing educational films about such things as family planning, the dangers of smoking, and the social injustice of dowry. He has no expressed idealism in any of these areas. He is a projectionist, and the nearest he is expected to get to voicing values is in his spoken introductions to the films. His purely formalist approach to his work is further underlined by his occasional unwillingness to do the introduction, in which case his assistant must present it. There is also his frequent need to lend buoyancy to what is, apparently, his somewhat dull life by recourse to the bottle.

He has two assistants in the film. At the beginning we meet

Shamu, and from what little we learn of him through his brief appearance we may conclude that he is a committed womaniser. He is evidently inattentive to the films about condoms that he has been assisting Paresh in showing, for in his one scene he is preparing to abscond from work for a week in order to help settle the inconvenience of yet another unwanted pregnancy for which he has been responsible. In other words, whereas he has some commitment to his own sexual gratification, he has none to any higher personal or emotional ethic.

So that Paresh won't be left to do the work on his own, Shamu has arranged for the assistance of one Chapal, a fundamentally decent young man but one who will bow when necessary to the superiority of pragmatism over moral principle. His only—and quite reasonable—commitment is to finding a secure future, and his vision is directed westward to the Eldorado offered by the wealthy Gulf states. Getting there is his problem, and he has had to engage the services of a money-lender and a middleman. For some reason which he does not explain, he will have to travel on a stolen passport under the name of that document's rightful owner, Makhan Das. Early in the film Paresh will identify Chapal to the officer at a police roadblock as Shamu Biswas. And so his identity comes into question: who, in fact, is Chapal?

Both Chapal and Paresh have virtually no ties. Paresh's only family is his elderly father, a sad old man whose wife had left him for another man when Paresh was just two. Paresh meets his father only when he comes to him for money, and on the one occasion when we see such a meeting he treats the old man courteously but with obvious coldness. Chapal's mother had died some twelve months back and he, like Paresh, is alone, for neither of them is married. For Chapal, personal survival comes first, and so he pursues the somewhat nebulous hope of a ticket to Dubai and well-paid work. Paresh must find his perfect woman, and he pursues the even more nebulous ideal of an anonymous actress from one of the films he shows to his rustic audiences. Nevertheless, underpinning each man's life is the pursuit of a dream.

Amina, the young woman the two men meet up with on the road, certainly has dreams, but she is decidedly in pursuit of reality, her pronounced commitment being to the welfare and security of the baby she is expecting. Amina's realistic perspective on life has been conditioned largely by her experience of suffering; still young, she has endured more than her share of poverty, physical terror, grief and despair. She and her husband had been illegal immigrants from Bangladesh, presumably in quest of a more secure material existence. The husband got work as a stone-mason, but then they got caught up in the ghastly anti-Muslim riots that shamed the state of Gujarat and its government. Amina survived the riots but her husband did not. His murder by fanatical thugs not only deprived her of the man she loved and who adored her, but also cut her adrift in a foreign land—impoverished, pregnant and illegal. Having survived the terror and her grief, she has somehow crossed the country and is now in the last stage of going home in order to provide her baby with roots. She is a strong character, determined and resolute, yet just as vulnerable as any of us to forces greater than herself, such as governments and the legal restrictions they place on people's movements, as well as the prejudices and incompetence of some of their functionaries.

The notion of dream pervades Dasgupta's cinema, but very rarely does he portray an actual dream sequence. The artifice of the dream sequence in cinema might be considered to be hackneyed and often a cheap and easy way of dealing with complex problems, but here the three brief snatches of dream while the characters sleep in a jeep serve to underline concisely what may well lie in the foreground of each one's mind at this stage. Before retiring to the vehicle to sleep, the three companions play out a somewhat sentimental scene, one that is touching rather than syrupy. Paresh is easily aided by his booze to make brief mention of the lack of a mother in his life and then to take up a sentimental song, which prompts Chapal to suggest a sad irony in the nostalgic observation that his mother used to sing that song beautifully. A discussion on the meaning of love ensues, by no means intellectual but leavened by Chapal's gentle and amusing cynicism and strengthened by the inferences of Amina's courage in coping with the absence of a greatly loved husband. In this context, which underlines their vulnerability and the reality of emptiness in their lives, they then retire to sleep.

The three slumber dreams commence with Paresh's somnolent vision of his dream girl, who is also the substance of his waking dreams, and then fades into a picture of his elderly father imploring him to forgive the man for whom his mother deserted them both when Paresh was still an infant. Chapal in his dream is seen to get out of the jeep and run across a bridge after another man, all the while shouting out that 'this' is not his passport, that he is Chapal Khar and not Makhan Das or anyone else. That dream merges into Amina's, which shows a crowd of agitated Muslim men and women running the other way across the bridge, fleeing from some apparent catastrophe. Central to this is Amina's obvious distraction as she looks in panic for her husband.

While their waking dreams are all positive—Paresh dreams of a girl, Chapal dreams of the golden gate to his future, and Amina dreams of the new life she is carrying—their slumber dreams are totally lacking in confidence and expose the fear and insecurity that pervades the mind and emotions of each of them. The presentation of the dream sequence without the conventional signs of contrived fantasy underlines the depth and immediacy of this fear and insecurity. All three are seeing in their sleep what is or has been an actual part of their lives; hence, the three dreams, so briefly stated, offer a summary statement of the psychological condition of each character, underlining pointedly and cogently the tension between the actual and the sought after.

It is Paresh's waking dream, however, that Dasgupta chooses to make central to his film, in the context, of course, of his slumber dream and the sleeping and waking dreams of the other two characters. We first learn of Paresh's dream when he and Chapal are drinking together in a rustic country liquor dive on their first night together. Paresh would seem to be trying to drink away the gloom that has descended on him after he had to abandon his attempt to show a film on birth control to a group of local people, who had staged a mass walkout; the rural audience had been quite resentful that anyone should presume to interfere with what is an amalgam of their sexual, social and religious values. Paresh startles Chapal by telling him that he has actually brought the girl of his dreams with him. Chapal thinks he is talking through his drink, but takes him up on a bet, obliging Paresh to produce her. The other drinkers in the liquor den are called on to witness the resolution of the wager, and they are all led out into the fields by Paresh to the screen where the film show had been aborted. As Paresh starts to set up his projector, the rustic tipplers believe they have been hoodwinked and return to their den, leaving only Chapal to learn that the girl is not here in flesh and bone but in celluloid: she is the rejected bride in a film condemning the practice of dowry. Nevertheless, whatever the nature of her manifestation, she is the dream of Paresh's life, his obsession.

In fact, we have already seen Paresh's dream girl twice before, although probably without knowing it. When he leaves his house in the morning to set out with Shamu—who will then be replaced by Chapal—he is seen carrying his projector, on the case of which is pasted a paper cut-out picture of a girl's face. Later in the day, when the rural audience is getting itself settled to listen to Paresh's introductory words about contraception, we see that same girl among them. We see her again when their jeep comes across a car, in which she is a passenger, stopped beside the road having a tyre changed. She next appears at the jeep at the beginning of Paresh's part of the dream sequence. She will be the girl who actually leads him to whatever his destination might be when at last he finds himself alone across the border.

(After the girl's first appearance in the film at the open-air picture show, Dasgupta offers an interesting image to underline the merging from time to time of dream with reality. As the crowd departs, the projector's lamp is still on and lighting up the screen, so allowing the shadows of the crowd to play on it. The people of a few moments before are now but shadows, and Chapal takes up the concept, after the people have gone, by playing hand-and-finger shadow shapes onto the screen, accompanied by Paresh's 'playing' the tabla on the bonnet of the jeep. Any personal actuality that might have been manifest before, including the girl whose giggle ever so slightly seemed to distract Paresh, has now been consumed by fantasy. People have become shadows, and those shadows have become imaginary figures and shapes, figments of a creative mind dancing to the rhythm played out by another creative mind in a context that is neither certainly real nor a dream.)

The term 'dream girl' is to be taken literally. While she is certainly the girl of his dreams, she exists for him only in dream—at least, until the film's end. Paresh is obviously a trifle disconcerted by her giggling at the open-air picture show, but plainly he does not recognise her, even though he is aware of her. When he and Chapal come across her leaning against the car with the flat tyre, he seems momentarily taken aback before telling Chapal to drive on, again not having recognised her. When she appears in his slumber dream, she simply walks around the jeep, quite detached and alone. It is only when Paresh, at the end of the film, finds himself alone on a country road in another land, a place strikingly green alongside a vast expanse of river, that he asks a local girl for directions. Just a few moments earlier we saw the missing projector with the girl's picture pasted to its case going by on a cart; that image is now completed as the girl—again, the dream girl—turns to Paresh, engages with him for the first time and beckons him to go with her. The dream girl would seem to have assumed a dimension of reality. The earlier theft of the projector, which had seemed to herald disaster for Paresh, is now seen to be the beacon drawing him to the fulfilment of his dream. It is, of course, futile to ask who the girl is or who stole the projector. The point of this ending is merely to show that actuality and dream—like the actuality and nightmare elucidated earlier in the film—are often confused, intending quite without restraint on each other's territory. Significantly, the final shot is of a squirrel, as much beyond the reality of human dreams as an earlier one was beyond the reality of human nightmares.

The major narrative crisis point in the film occurs soon after Amina has been picked up on the road by Chapal and Paresh, and would also seem to be founded beyond reality, its nature being much closer to dream than to mundanity. The three stop at a dhaba, or roadside eating-house, to have a meal, after which they return to the jeep to find that the projector is not there. The seriousness of the loss is obvious: the machine is not only the basis of Paresh's livelihood but it is also government property for which he is responsible. But for Paresh there is an even greater reason to rue its loss: it is indeed the embodiment, as it were, of her whose picture is pasted on its case. When Paresh laments 'I'll never see her again,' he is not referring with intimate affection to the projector but to the girl of his dreams. The projector makes her manifest, and without it she is but a memory. So Paresh must fear not only for his reputation and his job, but also for his heart.

Paresh quickly launches into an investigation of the machine's loss, although his inquiries go no further than the questioning of remotely possible witnesses to an apparent theft. A rather comic sequence of scenes ensues as Paresh questions people about what they may have seen, and for a time reality is transcended as the locals he talks to drift with alacrity from actuality to fantasy. Telling someone what one knows is very often not as pleasing as telling him what he would like to hear, and from this predilection to please rather than report, a suspect by the name of Sudhangshu emerges. After two men contrive for themselves a lengthy ride in the jeep in quest of this Sudhangshu, Chapal is directed to drive to a nearby pond where the suspect 'is virtually certain' to be fishing. Of course, Sudhangshu is not found, but emerging from the water's edge comes a man who claims to know a Sudhangshu in a village not far from there, the sort of man quite likely to steal their projector as he has, apparently, spent a bit of time in a police lockup. It is Amina who suddenly realises that they are being given the run-around by people simply looking for a comfortable ride to where they live some distance away. The three drive off acknowledging their wild goose chase and the hopelessness of recovering the projector.

However, the audience has been given a clue—and an utterly meaningless one at that—as to the fate of the projector. During the chase after the mythical Sudhangshu, there is a cut to the first of three brief shots of a dwarf hurrying across the fields with the projector—recognisable by the picture pasted on the case—on his shoulder. We see the projector for a fourth and final time on the back of a cart going along a country road, drawing—as it were—Paresh towards his dream in a new land. Who the dwarf is is immaterial. What is significant is that he is the agent of Paresh's liberation from one 'life' into another, and that his stature puts him in obvious contrast to the men of power who perpetrate the violence in our lives: the gun-runners and arms dealers, the initiators of communal violence, the police, the border security forces. Paresh is translated from being a dreamer to being the object of a dream, and the essential poetry of this overrides any pointless concern for a detective-story solution to the theft of the projector.

As is the case in so much of Dasgupta's cinema, the narrative dynamics of the film are largely determined by chance. The liaison of the three central characters comes about by chance and is taken wherever chance may see it go. It is by chance, as far as Paresh is concerned, that his regular assistant and driver has business elsewhere and has arranged for Chapal to help him out. It is by chance that Paresh and Chapal form a ready friendship, and it is by chance that they come across Amina trying to hail a ride. For Amina, it is only chance (although she might think it to be the will of Allah) that it is Paresh and Chapal who come to her aid. It is easy to see the two men as having been swept about on a sea of fortuitousness, with more dream than direction pointing to their futures. Amina and her husband had tried to take charge of their own lives, but found themselves swept up by the unforeseeable and especially cruel vicissitudes of a world conditioned by prejudice and unreason. Like the two men, Amina may have her dreams, but like them too she will have to bow to whatever chance has in store for her and over which she holds no sway at all.

With consummate skill, the director weaves these chance occurrences together to form the structure of his film. While events might seem to happen purely at random, and with chaos ruling over order, Dasgupta's arrangement of the manifestations of chance is in no way *ad hoc*. It is some time into the film that Amina meets up with Paresh and Chapal, but she is introduced to us much earlier than that. Soon after Paresh has set out with Chapal as his driver, we see a pregnant woman on a train, unable to produce a ticker for the inspector. From her face we discern that she is troubled, not so much by not having a ticket but preoccupied by some greater concern. She is sitting beside the window, through which we see on the road that runs alongside the railway line the jeep carrying Paresh and Chapal. Thus the imminent link between them and Amina is established.

The jeep is then seen to approach a bridge, the scene of that morning's massacre of policemen. There is a hold-up of traffic as the police facilitate the loading of bodies into ambulances and make their routine checks. Chapal is directed to stop and wait, Paresh is questioned briefly, and so another link is suggested, this time with the perpetrators of the morning's atrocity. This suggestion is substantiated further when, a little later, we see a convoy of police vehicles going over the bridge; once they have passed, the camera moves down to reveal two arms thieves in a temporary hideout underneath the bridge. As night approaches, we note the two men's concerns for provisions, for a bath, and for a car to get themselves and their illicit cargo away from their present insecure situation. As one of them goes off to get some provisions, he sets afloat at the water's edge a paper boat he has just made. The implication is that just as the boat will float to wherever unseen forces take it, so too will the characters in our film. The image of the vulnerable paper boat is a particularly fine punctuation point between the scene under the bridge and the subsequent scene at the country liquor den where, among the hands thrusting out money and reaching for bottles of cheap liquor are those of both Paltu the arms thief and Chapal, quite unaware of one another. Now the link between the three companions and the two arms thieves is clearly indicated. A more ominous signpost is among the shots later that night of the three companions asleep in their jeep. Chapal sleeps slumped over the steering wheel, disquietingly reminiscent of the gruesome shot at the beginning of the film of one of the dead policemen. Thus, a coming event casts its shadow on the present.

Finally, there is the fortuitous link between Chapal's problem of identity and his fate. This is prepared for by the three being picked up on the road along which they are trying to hail a ride to the border. The driver who stops for them does not do so out of kindness; rather, because his car is in poor running condition and keeps spluttering and stopping without warning, he needs a couple of able-bodied men to push the vehicle for him when it misbehaves and stalls. When he is forced to stop at a police road block, it transpires that his name is Makhan Das, that his passport—his usual form of identification—has been stolen, and that he has reported the theft to one of his close connections in the upper echelons of the police force, who is now working on the case. Chapal is mortified and alarmed. The immediate thought might well be that safety is best found across the river with Paresh and Amina.

The ending of the film, of course, underlines the fatuousness of many of our confident predictions, suggesting that the only certainty is uncertainty. On the surface, their simple scheme would seem to be perfectly feasible. They will take a boat and be rowed across the river that divides two sovereign states. If they should be stopped on the other side, the two men will offer a well-rehearsed story that would get them by with Amina and then to her family's home. However, in the course of conversation, the boatman forebodingly suggests that there has been some difficulty in the past few days, so leading us to suspect that things will not go as easily as planned. The three boatloads of immigrants without documents are stopped by armed border security personnel, amenable to bribery but not to humanitarian concerns. They turn back Amina, who accepts her rejection stoically, vowing to do her best for her unborn child, albeit under such daunting, unforeseen circumstances. The men decide to make a run for it; the border guards open fire and Chapal is felled by a bullet, proving all too late that his decision to seek refuge across the river could not have been more wrong. Paresh's luck, however, enables him to survive the attack. It is then that the film suspends naked realism for realism clothed in the garb of dream.

Crucial in the narrative development is the removal—assumed to be theft—of the projector. Its disappearance is presented entirely as a matter of chance, since no perceptible clue to explain it is offered. This chance disappearance gives rise to other, quite comic, chances, in that a series of rustics seize the opportunity to contrive rides for themselves in the jeep until the hapless projectionists see themselves as being taken for a ride. Just as it was chance that had Paresh and Chapal come across Amina on the road, it is purely by chance that they are confronted on the road by the two terrorists, a meeting that leads to the blatant theft of their jeep. Left entirely to their own devices, they are picked up on the road, as the two men had earlier picked up Amina, by a man who just happens to be the rightful owner of Chapal's stolen passport. The absurdity of the coincidence serves brilliantly to underline the ludicrousness of a world in which chance holds such mastery. The final part of the film moves from this notion of ludicrousness to a depth of absurdity that is almost black, and where the element of dream temporarily evolves into nightmare. Assured as Amina is of the appropriate procedure for infiltrating the other way across the border, she does not reckon on the role that chance, in all its perversity, might play in thwarting her simple and reasonable scheme.

Despite the prominent light-heartedness of the film, much of it is concerned with violence. While the central theme might be the three protagonists' quest for identity and self-fulfilment, their endeavours are set in the context of a sustained violence, which is not only around them but to a large extent directed against them. It is important to bear in mind the ordinariness of Paresh, Chapal and Amina, for it is that which serves to make them typical; the fact that they are so utterly unremarkable makes them as vulnerable to violence as anyone of us. Normally, ordinary people do not get caught up in violence because of what they do but rather because of where they might unwittingly happen to be at a certain time or, in somewhat more special cases, who they happen to be. Amina's being Muslim, for example, makes her more vulnerable to the violence of communal hostility; it is, therefore, greatly ironic that ultimately she suffers from the hostility of her own compatriots and co-religionists.

It is interesting to note the spectrum of the agents of violence in the film. On the lowest level we have Ghana and Paltu, the two petty thugs engaged in the theft and, presumably, smuggling of arms. There are the self-appointed fanatics claiming to represent the majority and perpetrating communal hostility. We may be amused by Paresh's boss, but his threats and intimidation are, nevertheless, violent in tone and intent. The bullet that kills Chapal is fired by a member of a government agency. At the top of the range are the invisible men who orchestrate beyond and against the law the sinister machinations served by the fruits of the labours of the petty Ghana and Paltu.

The opening somewhat insidiously intrudes violence into the film. The opening titles are presented over the serenity of an early morning sky. The camera then lowers to a view of a rural scene, lovely except for the bodies of dead policemen strewn about, while another policeman, shot and still slightly convulsing in the last moments of his life, is draped hideously over the steering wheel of his jeep. Stepping efficiently from corpse to corpse, Ghana and Paltu gather up the rifles of the dead policemen. Soon after, there is a shot of a squirrel scampering about inquisitively on the bonnet of the jeep, suggesting the indifference of a life of busy simplicity to an 'advanced' life of mutual exploitation, conflict and hostility.

There is an ironic and highly significant cut to what appears to be the start of a mass bicycle rally, with some of the cyclists bearing banners denouncing separatism and proclaiming the virtue of national unity. The point of this, of course, is to make sense of Ghana and Paltu, who apparently are functionaries of some secessionist movement. In multilingual, multiracial, multicultural India, individual militant movements to withdraw from the national republic and set up one separate state or another have been numerous in the years since Independence, causing considerable local destruction and loss of life. In northeastern India, in particular, there has been sustained separatist unrest and, in the times recent to the production of *Swapner Din*, such turbulence has been prominent in the state of Assam, much of its activity flowing over into northern Bengal. In *Swapner Din*, however, the only indication of any such cause are the banners carried by a couple of the cyclists. Dasgupta sees no need to develop the issue any further, for there is no point in trying to justify in any way at all violence as it impinges on the lives of ordinary people; a man shot and a man shot for a cause are both as dead as each other.

Paresh, Chapal and Amina are brought by chance into contact with the two arms thieves, Ghana and Paltu, and so into this vague realm of hostility. The two thugs are without a vehicle, have a heavy load of guns to deliver to somewhere or other, and are well aware that there is an intense police search for them. After hiding out for a time under a bridge, they decide to flag down a car and commandeer it to their own needs and purposes; that car just happens to be the jeep driven by Chapal. Chapal continues to drive, but now at gunpoint and with two unwelcome strangers as passengers whose intention is to go to a deserted house that serves as a hideout. On the way, Chapal is forced to stop near a group of hens beside the road. The men are ordered out of the jeep and told to catch one of the birds for lunch. There is an element of black comedy in the bumbling endeavours of the inept Paresh and Chapal, black because of the utter humourlessness of their captors and the stark reality of the guns they keep pointed at them. It is, indeed, a bullet that purchases their midday meal, a bullet that might just as readily have gone to either or both of the two harried men. At the hideout, Amina is set to cook the lunch while Paresh and Chapal are made to load the jeep with more bundles of rifles and then to change the number plates. Chapal manages to do something mischievous with a screwdriver that brings the thieves to some degree of grief a little later, but for the moment all the suffering is endured by Paresh and his companions as they watch aghast as their government jeep is driven away by the two thieves.

The theft of the vehicle and the previous day's apparent theft of the projector have to be seen in context as blows not so much violent in themselves but in the potential of their consequences. Now, without the projector and the jeep, Paresh is virtually without a job, and the possibility of the police becoming involved and bringing a case against him and Chapal is also quite real. The potential violence exists in the injustice of the situation. It is this realisation, made abundantly clear to Paresh by a bombastically threatening boss, that leads him to the extreme decision to flee across the border with Amina, enticing Chapal to go with them. As we have seen, their illegal entry into Bangladesh will have serious consequences for Amina and claim the life of Chapal.

As well as the various kinds of hostility the three companions inadvertently meet up with, there is also the hurt that they carry with them in their emotional baggage. Chapal's inability to find a personal identity and so exercise mastery over his own life might seem trivial in the light of Amina's experience of devastation, yet it still represents a kind of psychological hostility which he must overcome if he is to attain anything approaching happiness. Paresh's desertion as a child by his mother is obviously more serious, and would seem in some way or another to militate against his ability to love or be loved. Indeed, on the morning when we see him setting out with Chapal on this present journey, he has had to come to terms with the hostility of his landlady, who first denies him water during a municipal emergency, and then orders him to vacate the premises as she does not trust him near her nubile daughter; Paresh, in fact, would be perfectly happy if it were the nubile daughter who was going away, as he is irritated by the interest she has in him, one that he cannot reciprocate. As though Amina has not suffered enough from the violence that emanates from intolerance and unreason, her eventual endeavour to return to her homeland brings down a blow to herself as well as to her unborn child. The border patrol officials refuse to believe that she is returning to her homeland and treat her with callous disdain when it is clear that she cannot bribe them.

And so, after a time of trying to cope with the hostilities of life, the three companions are resolved from their predicaments in different ways. Chapal's succumbing to a bullet, like that of so many thousands of others before him, is a realistic resolution. Amina has no choice but to return to a country where she does not belong and has no right of citizenship, and her determination in the light of such an immense setback to provide an identity for her child against all odds is an idealistic resolution. It is Paresh's resolution—and the film's—that is fantastic, though indeed credible. He finds himself in a new country, to which he has been drawn, even pursued, by his own dream. It is a typically Dasgupta touch to have the dreamer seemingly being pursued by his dream, and one that gives the film a conclusion of such optimism. While Chapal represents the many who are destroyed by the violence of a few and Amina sets her face against all manner of hostility for the sake of her unborn child, Paresh represents the hope of all that violence will eventually prove to be futile.

There was a time when a Buddhadeb Dasgupta film would concentrate intensely on a particular character or group of characters in a particular set of circumstances describing a particular story. *Charachar* is a fine example. The subsequent *Tahader Katha* is another, although here the concentrated vision is notably expanded by the hawker of trinkets and the bizarre Abdullah and his dwarf assistant. It was with *Lal Darja* that Dasgupta truly embraced the cinema of expanded vision and pointed his films in a new direction.

Swapner Din is a consummate expression of this conceptual elasticity. There is a remarkable pluralism in the substance of the film: the various misfortunes of an itinerant projectionist and his two companions, the diversity of their backgrounds and their aspirations, their being subsumed in a realm of violence quite beyond their own experience and expectations, and a totally new perception of reality imbued by a wholesale intrusion of dream. The characters also are diverse: the two city men, the pregnant Muslim refugee, assorted rustics, thugs, the real Makhan Das, and the persistent inhabitants of dreams. Moreover, the film evokes a variety of moods: general light-heartedness, occasional black humour and the comedy of perversity, an element of seriousness in the consideration of the reality of all manner of violence, and the challenge to the imagination made by the depiction of the reality of dream. It is a truly remarkable film in that this vast disparity is presented so cohesively, and that its significance emerges with such compelling cogency. No less than any of Dasgupta's previous films and more than most, *Swapner Din* is a visual gem, brilliantly composed, trimmed of any suggestion of excess, and smoothly fluent in its dynamics.

ELEVEN

The Poet as Filmmaker

> Then slowly something started to happen to me. It was poetry that made me.
>
> Slowly I started to see a film coming through the words of a poem.

Buddhadeb Dasgupta had been a published poet for quite some years before he took to making films. Thirteen feature films and numerous prestigious Indian and international awards later, he continues to write and publish poetry in which he pursues ideas similar to the abstractions which find expression in his films. There is a general concern with notions of individualism, particularly its vulnerability in an increasingly commercialised society, the unsuitability of an individual to a particular sociopolitical context, and the problems of individuals whose hopes and aspirations have become dislocated from their times. A number of poems deal specifically with the perceived security of domestic serenity and the underlying reality of its vulnerability. Poems with a more psychological focus reflect the sterility and predictability of modern life, while others, conversely, are concerned with the often dangerous unpredictability of life's vicissitudes and the very real problems threatened by the thin and fragile line between various extremes of human behaviour.

As well there are some very beautiful poems dealing with the complexities of love and the ramifications of self-interest.

While there is a consonance of subject matter among much of Dasgupta's verse and his films, certain technical and artistic similarities are also evident. Indeed, there is a strong sense of cinema in much of his verse: for example, the images are strikingly visual, sharp and clear, and set in a perspective that is, indeed, well-framed. This is illustrated nicely in *Umbrellas*:

An umbrella comes out into the street.
One umbrella leans on the back of another.
On a passing umbrella's shoulder one
rests a hand. Hurt and angry after
waiting a long time at a bus stop,
a little umbrella disappears in a crowd,
when an expected umbrella fails to come.
Overhead, in the distance, is a strange
big white umbrella. Out of nowhere
a thickening cloud suddenly appears,
bearing down on the white umbrella,
spreading itself. Here and there
the umbrellas huddle in groups.
One runs to catch hold of another,
clashing against its teeth. All day long
the umbrellas pass and re-pass.
Now the last umbrella has gone home.
It stands quietly in a dark corner, and
water drips from it, and drips, and drips.

There is a filmic, visual realism here if we think of the poet or camera looking down on a busy street from a rooftop in the rainy season, but there is also the personification of the umbrellas—a fantastic notion, perhaps even an absurd one, but a notion nevertheless capable of being realised cinematically without any trick or device. The essential unreality is made real simply by the absence from the picture of what is obscured by the umbrellas; they are seen to be in a world where they are dominant and unchallenged, even exclusive. The poetic fantasy in the verse or what might have been the film emanates merely out of looking at things from a particular, unconventional angle. After all, put in the very simplest of terms, that is what poetry does.

While we might say that there is a strong sense of cinema in Dasgupta's poems, perhaps it would be more correct to say that there is a strong element of *his own* cinema in his verse. Consider, for example, these lines from *Fingers*:

> Slowly across the dining table
> fingers move toward cigarettes.
> Fingers take hold of a pencil,
> fingers turn page after page.
> Five pairs of fingers pursue
> one pair of shoes, come out into
> the road, return, light a candle;
> illuminate a head with thirty years
> behind it, thirty years before it,
> and an unchallenging period in between.
> Fingers leap to take hold of a razor
> as it flashes in the sunlight
> and a finger runs along its edge to
> test the keenness of the blade.

The images are simple, concrete, pictorial, and there is some aural suggestion in the hint of the sound of pages being turned or a match being struck, as well as the tactility of the flesh against the edge of the blade. However, the second half of the poem becomes less concrete as it reaches its abstract consummation, and the simple images of the opening lines now take on quite a surrealistic nature, very much a characteristic of the later films. Nevertheless, the strikingly visual quality of the verse remains dominant:

> Fingers make many things known to
> other fingers, and as they come down
> through the lather as the
> razor nears the throat, fingers begin
> to force the razor into the neck,
> through the skin, the blood,

moving with the razor through the flesh
towards a myriad of windpipes.

While the intention in this chapter is more to offer a concluding view of Dasgupta's films and their salient characteristics than to offer a critique of his poetry, the intimate connection between the creative artist who expresses himself in verse and the one whose medium is film should become clear, as should the potential intimate connection between poetry and cinema; hence, to seek to know whether the verse is cinematic or the cinema is poetic is to miss a more fundamental point.

It has been said elsewhere in this book that Dasgupta's most poetic films are those from *Phera* on; that is to say, it is in these films that the meld of poetry with cinema is closest. On the chronological order of the thirteen feature films discussed in the previous chapters, a qualitative, philosophical development might be imposed, one that involves a move away from narrative structures to the more extensive use of images in the communication of the filmmaker's ideas.

In *Duratwa, Grihayuddha* and *Andhi Gali*, the particular sociopolitical context is of basic significance, while it is of considerably less importance in the later films; indeed, in *Bagh Bahadur* (despite the reference to the Cuban blockade) and *Charachar*, there is no significant sociopolitical context at all. In the three 'Calcutta' films, however, the characters behave as they do because of, or in response to, their immediate history; hence, in these films, the emphasis is on the perspective, logic and ramifications of human behaviour, or, more simply, conventional narrative. In *Andhi Gali*, the action is cluttered and drawn out, labouring the narrative and minimising whatever poetic content the film otherwise might have had. The narrative in *Grihayuddha* is much more carefully constructed, and in those aspects of the film that deal with ideological agitation, human grief that comes from human loss, and the disappointment that arises out of thwarted expectations, the director's imagist approach is considerably more effective than it ever could have been in *Andhi Gali*. Nevertheless, such an approach is by necessity restricted, given the peculiar demands of logic and dialogue that pertain to the detective-story element that runs throughout the film. It is *Duratwa* that offers the most promise of a poetic cinema. It rests on the same Naxalbari narrative substructure as the other two do, but here it is more incidental and is never allowed to intrude into the intensely personal arena which is Dasgupta's focus. Plot is minimal, serving only to present the people of the film and their responses to a private dilemma, and therefore, many images of loneliness, isolation, anxiety and confusion are portrayed by the camera alone, without the encumbrance of dialogue. The title itself, 'Distance', is abstract and descriptively applicable to the film in hardly any tangible sense at all, and yet the *notion* of distance, rather than 'distance' as some specific aspect of plot, is portrayed in a variety of ways by image and mood, an approach which is effectively poetic. (The all too common translation of the title as '*The* Distance' is inappropriate and reflects a careless reading of the film.) Moreover, in stressing the importance to poetic cinema of the *unstated*, Dasgupta's first film gives a significant indication of what is to come in the films of his greater artistic maturity.

Although Dasgupta certainly cannot be described as an ideological filmmaker, it was his altruistic concern for the poor and dispossessed, based on a loosely Marxist political outlook, that inspired his sympathy for the Naxalbari movement and which is at the foundation of the three 'Calcutta' films. A similarly altruistic concern inspired the making of *Neem Annapurna*, and that concern would evolve into a sensitivity to a different kind of poverty and dispossession in the later, more metaphorical films. In some ways, *Neem Annapurna* is unusual compared with the rest of Dasgupta's work. While the visual image and the soundtrack, against the characteristically minimal plot, do much more than the dialogue to evoke the pervasive despair and helplessness that create the film's mood, the film might well be described as a social documentary, particularly in a purely visual sense. The camera is used to meticulously document not only the physical nature of slum life in Calcutta, but also the social and moral ramifications of deprivation, exploring and recording the frighteningly self-perpetuating nature of poverty. Indeed, in none of his other films does Dasgupta show anything like the concern for social issues that he shows here. Nevertheless, the extent to which *Neem Annapurna* might be described as social documentary is limited by the essentially poetic purposes of the exploring and recording. In all, the film goes far beyond the description of documentary realism.

Seet Grismer Smriti is the first of three films to deal with the integrity of the artist in a modern, industrialised society, where the urge for material profit brazenly obscures reverence for artistic value. However, the issue is dealt with immeasurably more successfully in the other two, *Phera* and *Bagh Bahadur*. In these two films, plot is compressed even more, and dialogue, while subordinate to visual image, is charged with a tightly economical intensity of meaning. Whereas *Seet Grismer Smriti* might seem to threaten a polemical, somewhat cerebral phase in Dasgupta's work, the two films dealing with the traditional artist in Indian culture proved, happily, that threat to be a hollow one. In both these films, as well as in the two that followed, Dasgupta's use of the camera to create rather than reflect is the major factor in the advancement of the poetic over the narrative. One might consider, for example, the shots of the Tiger Man in costume and makeup dancing across the countryside: on the surface the idea is fantastic, bordering on the absurd, yet in its artistic context the picture is exceptionally natural, credible and, indeed, exciting. Some of the more recent films are generally characterised by a sensuous and aesthetic logic in the length, angle and lighting of shots, while shots are rarely if ever taken for any intrinsic attractiveness of their own. Used relatively sparingly, as in *Tahader Katha* and *Charachar*, the circular trolley can be made to give a peculiar intensity and extension of meaning to what might have been an ordinary closeup. Dasgupta's intelligent, creative and sometimes provocative use of subframing with doors, windows and mirrors has generally been immensely effective in portraying notions of confinement, alienation, separation and distinctiveness, as well as creatively asserting emphasis or laying the ground for something that is to come.

Whatever may be the requirements of narrative, they never dominate the essentially imagist aims of the editing.

Thus, as in poetry, the best images are effected with an economy of language; the presentation of image and idea bears meticulous attention to an appropriate relationship with form; and the piece has a clear integrity which accommodates the emotions as much as the intellect. These are some of the salient poetical features of Dasgupta's films. However, in this context the substance of his cinema, its values and predominant ideas, which, needless to say, are more akin to the interest of a poet than, for example, a social realist or a story-teller, should also be considered.

In dealing with violence, the emphasis is more on the idea than the action. Violence in Dasgupta's films is acknowledged as a fact of life rather than an element of entertainment, as it is in so many commercial films throughout the world. Violence feeds on itself and pervades our lives. It is not only physical, but takes a multiplicity of forms and is perpetrated to varying extents. As violence is subject to degree, it might be measured as much by its effect as by the action. It need not be simply physical but can be verbal, sexual, intellectual or cultural. Even a deliberate unwillingness to understand others, for example, is a kind of violence in that it militates against harmony.

The portrayal of physical violence in Dasgupta's films is generally subtle and restrained. The murder of Prabir, the beating of Braja, and the rape and killing of Kalyani and Uttara are depicted adequately without the point being laboured in any way at all, although the frightening frenzy of the thugs in *Uttara* as they prepare to conclude their work is exceptional. The mental and sexual cruelty of Hemanta to his wife, Jaya, is protracted enough to make sense of her suicide, while the sexual violence exerted by Shashanka over Saraju is not allowed to become lascivious or even 'sexy'. The violence suffered by Shibnath in *Tahader Katha* is largely intellectual, as he sees his dreams and ideas beaten down by men of straw, though he also suffers physical violence from the stone-throwing joys, just as he had already experienced physical and perverted sexual violence at the hands of his prison guards. Here as well as anywhere, the cruelty is exposed by its effects. Further, there is the reality of socioeconomic callousness, or the violence of selfish unconcern, as it is depicted in what is, in effect, one of the cruellest of modern Bengali films, *Neem Annapurna*. An extension of this social callousness is developed very broadly in *Lal Darja* and specifically, in the context of the brothel, in *Manda Meyer Upakhyan*. The pervasiveness of callousness is basic to *Swapner Din*, where violence is depicted in its consequences rather than its actuality.

In assessing the violence, its major victims spring to mind—Anjali, Nirupama, Ghunuram, Shibnath, Lakhindar, Nabin and Bela, Uttara, the guard, Matthew and the pastor, Lati, Amina and Chapal. However, it would be missing the point to forget the others—Mandar, Bijan, Radha and Sibal, Hemangini and her children, Shari and Gouri, the pastor's small flock and the community of little people, and the prostitutes—who are inevitably caught up in one way or another in the suffering. Yet fundamental to the reality of pervasive violence is the gentleness of approach that is characteristic of a Dasgupta film, along with easiness of pace, subtlety of exposition and development, and a focus on human simplicity rather than cerebral complexity, all of which serves, ironically, to actually intensify the impact of the cruelty on the audience.

In all of Dasgupta's work notions of time are particularly important; common to the thirteen films discussed in this book is a concern with the alienation of the individual in the context —or, maybe, under the threat—of changing times. In the 'Calcutta' films the major characters are victims of time; they sought to change the times, but failed, and the times in turn changed them. Once an activist, Mandar becomes withdrawn and unsure of himself and his milieu; once a self-sacrificing Marxist, Bijan becomes a profit-seeking, acquisitive businessman; once a fighter for the uplift of the downtrodden, Hemanta becomes self-seeking, cravenly willing to exploit even his own wife for the attainment of his goals. Caught up in the maelstrom of history and unaware of the direction it is taking, all three have been dislocated by time—Mandar personally, Bijan and Hemanta morally.

In *Neem Annapurna* the starkness of having fallen on hard times is intensified by the memory of better times. The use of a train at the beginning and end of the film is obviously to represent spatial movement, but with the voice-over it also suggests a movement through time that is cyclic and which presupposes a deterioration, while the camera more than adequately strengthens this notion. The film also suggests the tension of time caused by the utter uncertainty of one's condition. Braja and his family might well wonder how long their plight must last, whether they might be restored to their former Bhadralok status, whether things could get even worse, whether they might indeed descend to the condition of the old beggar—or lower. The frequent picture of Pritilata helplessly sitting inside the doorway of their squalid room shows her as having surrendered to time; the most she is capable of is mere survival, a goal which negates the value of memory of time past and makes time future inconceivable.

As well as causing dislocation and ill fortune, changing times also bring about a change in values that comes from the inevitable conflict of modernity with tradition. As technology and commerce march forward hand in hand, that which was once cherished becomes questioned and, very often, is seen as irrelevant, of no further interest, and fit to be discarded. The transformation of society is reflected quite clearly in the entertaining arts, where advertising and sponsorship, transistor radios, live leopards and the popular taste for the vulgar are all symptomatic of the passing of something precious and the embracing of plastic values that treasure titillation and glitter. As changing times give rise to changed values, the consequent distortion of established perspectives threatens the self-esteem of the individual. In the case of *Phera*'s Shashanka, for example, modern times cause the eclipse of pride in himself by self-pity and bitterness, as he sinks further into drunkenness and becomes nasty and deceitful. There is more than passing significance in one of the scenes being set amongst the tombstones of his estate, allowing him to invoke the rich tradition of which he has so long felt himself and his art to be a part. And into the hitherto simple life of Ghunuram, the onslaught of the new throws up the monster of betrayal, distorting so radically the Tiger Man's judgement and sense of perspective that he consciously and deliberately enters the leopard's cage to fight the beast bare-handed.

The most tragic example of the individual being buffeted by time is Shibnath in *Tahader Katha*. Like the young activists that Mandar, Bijan and Hemanta had been, Shibnath had once been dedicated to making history, but unlike his later counterparts he has not become a victim of time or history, for his imprisonment meant that time and history effectively ceased to exist for him. He had fallen out of time, as it were, living for eleven years in a virtual temporal vacuum. On his return to the real world, where nothing stays the same, he is not only eleven years behind but, having been drained of any genuine sense of temporal context, he is quite ill-equipped to understand the world in which he finds himself. After his long incarceration (without family and home, eleven years might be an eternity), he has to suffer the profound shock of a world which appears to have simply hurdled a decade and is in no way consonant with the dreams which gave meaning to an earlier time, helping him survive being locked away, but which now indicate his perceived madness.

The tyranny of time is perhaps more subtle in *Charachar* than in the other films. Nevertheless, past and future are significantly entwined in Lakhindar's present, producing the intricacies and giving rise to the worries that beset him, and bringing into relief his dreams and the values and the elements of nature he treasures so much. So much of the man Lakhindar is has been fashioned by the dominance of memory. His lasting love for Netai is appropriate to the time in the past when Netai was alive, yet it will not leave him, finding expression in his peculiar love for birds. In this sense Netai lives on in Lakhindar; in a sense he lives on in the birds, too. Lakhindar is forced to think about where all this is leading him, but his future remains obscure, if indeed it exists at all, and it is only in the final shots that he is able with jubilation to transcend his imprisoning present.

Time is not so obviously represented in *Lal Darja*, although in the sense that the self-centred and self-absorbed Nabin has let life pass him by—as Dinu and the young Nabin would suggest—he bears some slight comparison with Shibnath in that he is out of step with time. In *Uttara* temporal change is expressed by the counterpoint of the dissonance of the outsiders and the harmony of the natuas. The dissonance is used to try and force the good out of time, an attempt that is more than partially successful, and to give the wrestlers the opportunity to opt out of time altogether, which they accept. The natuas represent the natural rhythm or the course of nature in which the film finds consummation—the times have been put right. In *Manda Meyer Upakhyan* there is almost a disrespect for time in its deliberate confusion by such concrete images as the late model jeep and the apparent historicity of the film's setting. Here time is seen more in terms of states of being and value, such as childhood and hope, or old age and contentment. In *Swapner Din* time is not employed as an ordering system of narrative, but serves rather to give context to memory, which in turn conditions dreams, which in turn point to some notion or other of future.

As well as a diffused concern for perceptions of time, in all of Dasgupta's films there is an attention to dreams. The dreams themselves are not always of particular interest to Dasgupta, but an intimate concern with their dreamers is. His cinema is by no means didactic or ideological; rather, it is predominantly personal. Hence, while values and ideas are important, of greater importance are the people who hold them. In *Charachar*, for example, Dasgupta shows a genuine affection for Lakhindar, although the exact nature of his dream is never spelled out. Similarly, in *Tahader Katha*, we are not regaled with the substance of Shibnath's nationalist idealism; for Dasgupta that is incidental to the generally unloved and misunderstood man and the pity he inspires. In the three 'performing arts' films the director is, of course, vitally sympathetic to the ideals of Shaibal, Ghunuram and Shashanka, yet the emphasis of interest is always on the man: Shaibal in conflict with his troupe, his sponsors and himself; Ghunuram struggling to maintain a rich pride in the face of abject desertion; and Shashanka treading the path of personal decay and being brought back to creative aspiration by the power of the innocence of youth. The naive quest for a new life in the big city of unlimited opportunity and the simple desire for a full stomach highlights, in *Neem Annapurna*, the pathos of Braja and Pritilata and the poignancy of their dreams. The interest in the central characters of *Duratwa, Grihayuddha* and *Andhi Gali* lies in the fact that they all—Mandar, Bijan and Hemanta—have placed their newly realised personal interests in counterpoint to the more lofty idealism they had once espoused; once grand dreamers have become self-interested dreamers. Again, the dream is incidental to the dreamer. The notion of dream is contorted somewhat in *Lal Darja*, in that we may discern the root of Nabin's unhappiness to be the fact that he does *not* dream, so that his life is sterile and devoid of promise. There is, of course, in *Uttara*, the promise of a better life, expressed on a very mundane level by the chorus of destitute men, and more loftily articulated in the dreams of the little guard and the idealism of the pastor. The dreams of the destitute men are frustrated by simple ignorance, whereas those of the little guard and the pastor are cut down by violent fanatics. In all these films, the dreamer is trapped—at least for a time—between the dream and its realisation. Indeed, in all the films except *Phera* and, we may imagine, *Charachar*, the dream remains unrealised. The notion of dreams coming true is played out candidly in *Manda Meyer Upakhyan*—at least as far as the narrative takes us: the young girls leave the brothel (but they have done so before) and Lati boards the train to Calcutta; and Natabar Paladhi is left with his dreams which, in their baseness, would seem to be sufficient in themselves for his desires. It is in *Swapner Din* that a distinction is drawn between waking dreams and slumber dreams, the former being fantastic in that they may be directed by the dreamer, the latter being realistic in that they are largely conditioned by memory. More significant in this film is the deliberate conflation of dream and reality.

As the dreamer is of greater interest to Dasgupta than the dream, so too is the individual of greater interest than society. In his first four films there was the opportunity—had he wanted to take it—to launch an attack on, let us say, the selfishness and lack of moral fibre of the middle class, blaming it for the failure of the Naxalite dream or the poverty of Braja and Pritilata. However, despite his academic background in economics, Dasgupta does not seem to think in such general societal terms. Real people, however, have faces, names and addresses, families and friends, joys and sorrows and, of course, dreams. Seen in their essentially personal contexts, real people are rarely *typical* of society, even though they are credibly part of it. A social realist might make an excellent, yet very different, film out of one of Dasgupta's scenarios, but a poet is much more likely to find in those scenarios golden opportunities for the exploration of the essential humanity of particular individuals.

One of the most eminent of Dasgupta's individuals is Shashanka, simply by virtue of his claim to a noble lineage, albeit a moribund one. In reality, Shashanka is merely a bitter, drunken, unemployed amateur actor. Indeed, none of the major characters is at all heroic or even especially important. Generally, they are ordinary, unremarkable people, who may enjoy middle-class or professional respectability or have some particular talent, but who remain ordinary, nevertheless. Yet this very ordinariness is quite significant, for it is the foundation on which the films base the playing out of their dramas and the pursuit of their dreams, so bringing into proportion the real magnitude, as they experience it, of their worries and their aspirations. Given the actuality of context, the death of the old beggar in *Neem Annapurna* can be as shattering as the killing of a prime minister.

The central characters in Dasgupta's films all find themselves in a world in which sadness has to be confronted, a world in which melancholy and sorrow inevitably evolve out of alienation, the loss of faith, the evanescence of love, the thwarting of hope and the shattering of dreams. Generally, they are people who are affected, in one way or another, by the tension between their ideals and their personal sphere, and the endeavour to resolve that tension draws them into a process of self-discovery. In some cases the process is a happy one, and mostly it is a creative one. *Duratwa* ends with an indication of optimism for both Mandar and Anjali, as does, a little less obviously, *Grihayuddha* for both Nirupama and Bijan. Nirupama, of course, suffers intense disappointment, but it is a small price for saving herself from a life of bourgeois acquisitiveness and venality, a life that Bijan might now happily pursue without the inconvenience of a conscience. Pritilata's experience of self-discovery is indeed a wretched one, her ideals of gentility serving merely to underline the despair into which she and Braja are relentlessly drawn, while Hemanta loses everything except the negative desire to escape. Lakhindar, however, is liberated from the bonds of the mundane, just as Nabin is presented with the hope of a similar blessing, and Shashanka is inspired with renewed optimism. In *Manda Meyer Upakhyan*, Lati has a moon of her own to strive for, as do the three young prostitutes, while the elderly couple find release from callousness in utter simplicity. *Swapner Din* shows how the cruelty of chance makes the quest for fulfilment result in death for Chapal, a desperate reassessment of the future for Amina, and a dream come true—whatever that may mean—for Paresh.

It is easy, perhaps, to see Ghunuram and Shibnath as losers: one is killed and the other is returned to prison. Yet, while Ghunuram loses his life, his sacrifice represents a moral victory in the Tiger Man's resolution not to bend to the winds of change, and the film ends on that positive note, reinforced by the triumphal beating of Sibal's drum. Similarly, Shibnath has not been won over to the values of the 'caterpillar raj', and his return to incarceration and the physical suffering it might entail is also a removal from the stench of corruption and self-seeking, a retreat from a dreamless world. (Of course, it cannot be denied that philistine values and the caterpillar raj come out on top.) In *Uttara*, while evil does indeed have its day in the senseless slaughter of three good and innocent people, its designs are not fully realised, as the natuas save Matthew from its agents and proclaim at least a symbolic victory over them; the real losers in this film are the two simple wrestlers who sacrifice themselves on the altar of indifference. While Chapal's death is downright bad luck and Amina's rejection demands, for such a strong character as she, that it be overcome, *Swapner Din* proclaims the triumph of innocent dreams over senseless hostility.

Despite the pervasive sadness of Dasgupta's films, pessimism is prevalent in only two: *Neem Annapurna* and *Andhi Gali*. Dasgupta's view of life is in fact a positive one, recognising the value of happiness where it is appropriate, but also recognising that happiness always comes at a cost if values such as truth and honour are to be more highly esteemed. If one is willing to sacrifice one's ideals, as Nirupama would have done had she agreed to marry Bijan, happiness of a kind is cheap. Dasgupta's world view sees personal integrity as paramount, and if this ideal is to be maintained in a world of individual ambition and materialist self-seeking, then suffering is inevitable. The extent to which one is willing to pay the price determines the degree of worthiness to which one may aspire.

It is here that mention might be made of the importance of the notion of innocence in Dasgupta's films. In eight of Dasgupta's feature films children play a meaningful role, although admittedly the significance of Anjali's baby boy in *Duratwa* is essentially an indirect one. More obvious is the importance of Juthi and Lati in *Neem Annapurna*, where the cruelty of poverty is assessed by its effects on those who are most vulnerable to it. The two girls, like most children born into poverty, have no control over their situation and are destined simply to suffer it, unheeded by a callously indifferent world. The untimely death of Lati merely underlines the utter helplessness that marks the thraldom of the poor. The two children of Shibnath in *Tahader Katha* are also innocent victims of circumstances over which they have no control, and have to suffer the awful emotional confusion resulting from their father's homecoming turning out tragically rather than being an occasion for joy. The little Matthew, in *Uttara*, may well have become a victim of the march of fanaticism, yet it is his innocence that so readily draws him to the natuas, the embodiment of the film's triumph. In *Phera, Charachar* and *Lal Darja*, children are represented not so much to enhance the atmosphere or as narrative agents but as beacons signalling the light to confused adults who would seem to be lost in the dark. It is through Kanu that Shashanka is able to see a more positive and creative hope for himself, while in *Charachar* the remembered Netai serves as something of a clarion call within the soul of Lakhinder. The young Nabin in *Lal Darja* bears similarity to the immediacy of Kanu and to the Netai of memory; of course, he is immediate in a sense beyond reality, and he is more a gentle stirring in the heart of Dr. Datta than a clarion call. Nevertheless, he is there as the simple and accessible answer to the problems of the older Nabin, if only the man will trust in the child-like simplicity signalled by the boy. There is a somewhat different approach in *Manda Meyer Upakhyan*, where Lati is presented as an innocent child, though to a significant degree she is independent in so far as her intelligence and propensity for critical thought lend her an element of self-possession at variance with her domestic environment. She is presented as one not so much seeking experience as seeking to escape the experience being imposed upon her. In this film it is the elderly couple, depicted in their dotage—or second childhood—with their game of Ludo, who appear as symbolic of innocence, simplicity and vulnerability. In *Swapner Din* the only obvious symbols of innocence are Amina's unborn child and the squirrels.

While the examination of character is usually focal in cinema, an interesting feature of Dasgupta's films is what might be called the poetry of distraction, in which passing focus is given to the seemingly irrelevant. In a number of his works prominence is given to some feature or other that has apparently nothing to do with the film. For instance, we might wonder about the actual importance of the transsexuals in *Neem Annapurna*, the pilgrims in *Andhi Gali*, the wrestlers in *Phera*, the celebration of Diwali in *Bagh Bahadur*, the festivities of the tribal women in *Tahader Katha*, or the religious procession while Paresh is phoning his boss in *Swapner Din*. It is easy to be tempted to try to find some metaphorical connection between such elements and the main theme. In *Tahader Katha*, then, Mohitosh is married to a tribal woman and in *Phera* the wrestlers have their place along with whisky and the theatre in Shashanka's dissolute life. Nevertheless, one cannot help feeling that the element of distraction is more than a little strong. What value or relevance can there be in underlining Mohitosh's marriage to a tribal woman, or any woman, for that matter? And is there not already enough indication of Shashanka's decadence? If we assert that the transsexuals are living in a world of unreality, as are the gentle family in their world of poverty, that the pilgrims in Bombay reflect the pilgrimage that Hemanta has set for himself, and that Diwali is another aspect of the same traditional culture from which the tiger dance derives, have we done anything more than proffer a kind of cleverness, interpreting imagery as though it were some sort of code?

And yet, perhaps, these elements of distraction need not be taken quite as seriously as all that. Unusual as transsexuals or private wrestlers, for example, may be, none of these elements of distraction is in any way out of place in its particular context, nor do they in any way minimise the credibility of that context. The beguilement is due to the contrast that the distracter highlights. Shashanka's wrestlers are content in their utterly simple life of predictability and mutual dependence, while Shashanka himself must endure something quite different. Bizarre and unreal as the transsexuals are, they are apparently resigned to their condition and content with it. One might, in fact, assert that Hemanta has set out on a pilgrimage, but how different it is from that of the more orthodox pilgrims who cross his path. The trilling of the tribal women underlines their harmony with their culture, while Shibnath must suffer extreme dissonance with his. But in all these distractions we are also reminded, albeit in a peculiarly striking way, that life goes on indifferently, in all its diverse forms, outside of the world of our immediate focus, and while a more general reality is being indicated, a certain callousness is also being suggested, given the essential detachment or alienation of the subject of the diversion.

It is in *Lal Darja* that we see the use of distractions taken to a new level, while in the two films that follow, this element is no longer to be found; the device has a brief appearance in *Swapner Din* in the form of the religious procession. However, in *Lal Darja* the bizarre elements are only *apparent* distractions, for whereas all the previous films and *Swapner Din* might well have been done without such elements, at least as far as mere thematics are concerned, here they are integrally entwined with the narrative and, although they are minor ingredients in it, they are nevertheless indispensable to it. The murder in the public street, the beggar man, the man with the extraordinarily long whiskers, and the odd snippets of television news all serve directly to magnify our understanding of the central character. Indeed, the bizarre elements have become, in fact, images of the absurd, and are not to be thought of in the same way as the elements of distraction in the previous films. Similarly, in *Uttara* and in *Manda Meyer Upakhyan,* what might have been distractions in earlier works are intricately woven into the main current of the film. In *Uttara* the destitute men provide a highly original way of establishing context for the pastor and his role in the film; the little guard offers a highly significant moral contrast to the thugs and to the wrestlers; and the natuas are basic to the work's prevailing symbolism. In the strange *mélange* that is *Manda Meyer Upakhyan*, the odds and evens are so thoroughly integrated that the idea of distraction elements has now become irrelevant. One might consider the dwarf with the apparently stolen projector in *Swapner Din* as integral to the film as the bizarre elements are to *Lal Darja,* yet in the regime of dream that conditions that film it seems pointless to try to define him.

In the films from *Bagh Bahadur* on, Dasgupta expresses most candidly his interest in what might seem to be a condition beyond what we normally take to be reality. Dream as perceived reality is important in all of Dasgupta's films, but in the later films often what is taken to be real is expressed more as an extension of reality, a condition beyond reality. In this kind of 'metareality' any distinction between what is conventionally real and what is perceived to be real is blurred, and in this sense it can be said that Dasgupta's cinema is starting to take on one of the essential characteristics of his poems. However, as the films portray character and personal circumstances to an extent that the poetry does not, it is the subjectivity of particular characters that becomes prominent as the distinction between the actual and the imagined becomes obscured. As with the representation of dreams, the interest lies not so much in the particular nature of this metareality, but rather in what it means to the characters who perceive it.

Mundane reality is portrayed very simply in *Bagh Bahadur*: the real is seen as a moving, breathing beast and the cash takings from the people who come to marvel at it. Thus, when Ghunuram dances through the streets of Nonpura in his tiger costume and make-up, he is scorned for being unreal. It is easy to appreciate the popular mind's perception of the beast as real and the dressed-up man as pretence. It is a little less easy to appreciate Ghunuram's perception of himself, not so much as a real tiger, but as being real in the guise of a tiger. However, he lays claim only to the worth and authenticity of his performance; he does not claim to be an animal. Here we should note the difference between the artist and the philistine, or the difference between sublimity, a state to which the artist aspires, and mundanity, a condition in which the philistine finds contentment. It is the reality of the artist's aspiration—eccentric, perhaps, to the popular mind—that gives life itself to Ghunuram. The fusion of movement with the rhythm of Shibal's drum brings Ghunuram, appearing as the tiger, onto a higher plane than he has known all the preceding year. This for him is the real, the sublime, the fulfilment of his most earnest aspiration. Extreme as it may be, there is a clear and simple logic in his climactic entry into the cage of the impostor and his resolution to overwhelm it.

In *Tahader Katha* reality is blurred by a confusion of subjectivities. For example, those whom Shibnath sees as the lackeys of a caterpillar raj are seen by others as pillars of the community; the lofty dreams of Shibnath are seen as the visions of a madman, while credibility is extended to the inane conjurer,

Abdullah, and his assistant, a transvestite dwarf. These deviations in perception make reality—or sanity—difficult to discern except by the negative reference to the 'unreal'—or insane—Other. But whereas the fact of difference might, perhaps, determine one to be mad and the other to be sane, it does not necessarily determine which is to be which. Moreover, Shibnath's realm of the real has become intensely internalised over the years, as is also the case somewhat with Mohitosh, who may experience his realm of the real only by removing himself from the society of the majority.

In *Charachar*, Lakhinder is far from certain about reality. His communion with trees and his almost worshipful care for birds are clear indications that reality for him is not to be found in the world of men, in established forms of society and economy. His dramatic return to the village after attending Shashmal's feast is forcefully portrayed as a categorical rejection not only of common human values but also of human commerce, domestic economy and even marital relations. The coming of the ocean to Lakhinder at the end of the film is a peremptory manifestation of Lakhinder's perceived reality, from which all his former human relations are excluded, except, perhaps, for the one with his dead son, which has become so internalised that it has merged harmoniously with the new reality.

In *Lal Darja* images of metareality become intermingled and even fused with the seemingly commonplace to a much greater extent than in previous films. The apparently unremarkable slaying of a woman on the streets of Calcutta, the eccentric people and items of news on television, Nabin's bizarre doctor and the unconventional domestic life of Dinu are all presented in the guise of the normal and everyday. It is Nabin, sane and rational, who is seen as odd in this world and in his apparent insensibility to it. There is, as in *Tahader Katha*, a significant confusion of the 'mad' with the 'sane', and there is a similar though more clearly articulated representation of value inversions —death in life, failure in success, hostility in love—that characterise urban middle-class life in much of Dasgupta's poetry. While the red doors might be for Nabin what the ocean is for Lakhinder, it is the impossible reality of the young Nabin that offers the most potent agent of persuasion for the desensitised and unhappy older man.

In *Uttara* there are some simple perceptions of a realm beyond the immediate, such as the pie in the sky of the destitute men and the idealism of the pastor, to suggest two extremes. The excessive introversion of the wrestlers might be seen more as a denial of reality, for the story of Nimai and Balaram as it is told in this film is the story of a gradual and inexorable withdrawal from the world to the wrestling pit. Genuine extensions of reality, however, are seen in the natuas and the community of little people. Although the natuas are representative of that which is rooted firmly in the mundane, like all cultural expressions of any worth their art is at least outwardly removed from it. Their singing, their rhythmic movement and their masks and costumes are the trappings of their anonymity and their aspiration to a plane beyond the ordinary. There is a pronounced element of mystery about the community of little people as they first appear in silhouette and later as they encircle the body of the dead train guard, but there is no denying their actuality; we see them in close-up as they come over the hill in the morning to go off to work in the everyday world, and we see them just as clearly again when they come to take up the body of their dead companion. The guard, however, is the only one of them to engage with other characters in the film, and it is, indeed, this interaction and dialogue that suggest most clearly a reality beyond ordinary perceptions. He describes their village, beyond the river on the other side of the hill, as peopled only by little folk, a place where everyone lives for the good of everyone else. Such a utopia is fantastical in the context of the many negative—yet manifestly 'real'—notions raised in this film, and to have it populated exclusively by dwarfs—who are depicted here as strong and self-sufficient—underlines the evident metareality of the idea, while in no way minimising its credibility. What is of particular significance here is that the community of the little people is considerably enhanced by its remoteness from the ordinary world rather than obscured or diminished by it in any way.

There is a zany fusion of various realms of reality in *Manda Meyer Upakhyan*. The brothel context of the film is almost by definition removed from reality if the commoditisation of love, with the clear implication of people groping for that which might give meaning to their lives, is to be seen as at all abnormal, at least by comparison with more conventional forms of sexual relations. Outside of this commerce in unreality there is a donkey that exercises judgement on human character, and there are also visions of a more fulfilling world beyond the immediate, found by the abandoned elderly couple in the simple and utterly undemanding joys of Ludo, and yearned for by three of the prostitutes who find themselves trapped in an ugly thraldom. The focal notion of aspiration is seen in the young girl, Lati, who aspires to personal emancipation through learning. On the day that a man first travels to the moon—hitherto a notion of fantastic science fiction—Lati too breaks through the caul of confinement within what her mother perceives to be the real. While the discerning donkey and the finding of fulfilment in Ludo may be seen as bizarre, there is nothing odd about the aspirations of the three young women and of Lati, except for the ways in which their release is presented. The escape of the girls is seen on the silver screen, an easy metaphor for a state beyond the real, while Lati's flight is clouded in uncertainty, first hinted at by the peculiar focus on the fluttering scrap of newsprint at the feet of the schoolmaster, and then painted in plainer colours at the railway station, where no other people but Lati and Nagen are to be seen.

The concept of cinema is basic to the narrative dynamics of *Swapner Din*, in that Paresh is, by profession, a projectionist of educational films. While it would be difficult to discern any elements of metareality in films about birth control, the unacceptability of dowry or the dangers of smoking, it is the perception of these issues by rustic audiences that would seem to distort the common sense notions of reality held by educated urban folk such as Paresh. The film on birth control never gets shown, so bizarre is its premise to an audience of people with their own set of values and customs that are rigidly subscribed to. The overriding role of chance in determining the causes and consequences that are the episodes of characters' lives is also seen to be considerably removed from the rational, lending an undesired element of chaos to lives we would like to be in control of. Indeed, the run-around sequence where Paresh and his companions are sent on a wild goose chase by characters who have no interest whatsoever in engaging with them on any given set of terms, so making communication totally random and without any anchorage in reason or purpose, would seem to grab reality by the neck and point it wherever chance would have it go. The distinction between slumber dream and waking dream, with the former set in mundanity and the latter in fantasy, points to the film's frequent intrusion of dream into reality and the modifying of one by the other. Given that the agency of dream is more fully realised in *Swapner Din* than in any other of Dasgupta's films, the apparent theft of the projector and the lodestar role of Paresh's dream girl can be interpreted only within the realm of metareality.

In the cinema of Buddhadeb Dasgupta, representations of metareality serve a purpose similar to that in his poetry. There is an inherent absurdity in essentialising for the sake of metaphor, for the process necessarily involves the rejection of established rationality. The metareality that had long been a part of his poetry before it assumed significance in his cinema presents perceptions of life in which certain selected aspects of it are magnified, with the intense, economic effect of immediacy of meaning or, sometimes, even shock engendering a creative involvement of the reader. The metaphorical value of such distortions or recreations or extensions of reality that characterise Dasgupta's verse have, since *Bagh Bahadur*, become entrenched in his films.

Poetic cinema will always present difficulties of interpretation for many viewers, especially given the overwhelming preponderance of cinema that is far from poetic or in any way profound, and which all too often seems to set the norm for the art. When sound and, later, colour came into the dream world of early cinema, the fantasy was diluted and there emerged a desire for verisimilitude and credibility that made realism the hallmark of this most comprehensively realistic art form. In Indian cinema, particularly, a credible narrative in a readily intelligible setting has long been the stuff of most films, good, bad and indifferent. Very often, however, the point of poetic cinema is missed, as viewers dwelling in the actual may fail to appreciate the abstract. 'Plot' in poetic cinema is usually not an end but a means; it is merely the familiar context that is the vehicle for the greater meaning that the filmmaker wants to convey. Hence, *Tahader Katha*, for example, may be said to be not a film about Indian history, or even a man's return to his family after a period of imprisonment, but an examination of the effects on a man's dreams brought about by his falling out of time. *Charachar* is to an even greater extent a film about dreams, in which narrative preparation for the climactic manifestation of the ocean would be rather like providing footnotes for the imagery in a lyric poem. What is important about poetry and poetic cinema is not what is stated but what is suggested—not the answers to questions, but the questions themselves.

For the poet to take on filmmaking has been quite a simple step sideways rather than some heroic leap forward. To communicate in images aural, visual and intellectual is the work of the filmmaker every bit as much as it is the work of the poet. Indeed, rhythm, balance, form and composition are as essential to fine cinema as they are to the other arts. Thus, in seeking to appreciate the creativity of Buddhadeb Dasgupta, what is most significant is the overall artistic vision of the man. Added to this one must recognise the warmth of his humanity and his acute perception of the complexities and variety of life, especially his gift for seeing beyond the material exterior to the yearnings of the simplest human heart. Dasgupta's films are clearly enhanced by a compassionate understanding of people, their needs and their feelings, and above all, by the clarity with which he sees the stream of time on which their lives advance, along with the dreams that buoy them on their passage.

Filmography

Duratwa ('Distance')
1978, Bengali, B & W, 98 mins.
Based on a story by Sirshendu Mukhopadhyay

Photography: Ranjit Roy
Music: Ain Rashid Khan, Mehmood Mirza
Editor: Mrinmoy Chakraborty
Produced by: Buddhadeb Dasgupta Productions
Script and Direction: Buddhadeb Dasgupta
Cast includes: Mamata Shankar, Pradip Mukherjee, Bijon Bhattacharya, Snighdha Banerjee, Niranjan Roy, Ajoy Banerjee, Provas Sarkar.

Neem Annapurna ('Biter Morsel')
1979, Bengali, B & W, 98 mins.
Based on a story by Kamalkumar Majumdar

Photography: Kamal Nayak
Music: Debashish Dasgupta
Editor: Gangadhar Naskar
Produced by: Buddhadeb Dasgupta Productions
Script and Direction: Buddhadeb Dasgupta
Cast includes: Monidipa Roy, Sunil Mukhopadhyay, Jayita Sarkar, Bhaswati Dasgupta, Monijit Lahiri, Nihar Roy, Shyamal Sengupta, Gopa Sengupta, Jayati Ghosh, Dulal Roy, Pradip Sen.

***Grihayuddha* ('Crossroads')**
1982, Bengali, Colour, 98 mins.
Based on a story by Dibyendu Palit

Photography : Sambit Bose
Music : Buddhadeb Dasgupta
Editor : Ujjal Nandi
Produced by : Government of West Bengal, Department of Information and Culture
Script and Direction : Buddhadeb Dasgupta
Cast includes : Anjan Dutt, Mamata Shankar, Goutam Ghosh, Shashanka Bhattacharya, Monoj Mitra, Probir Guha, Sunil Mukhopadhyay, Monidipa Roy.

***Seet Grismer Smriti* ('Season's Memoir')**
1982, Bengali, Colour, 58 mins.
Based on a story by Dibyendu Palit

Photography : Kamal Nayak
Music : Buddhadeb Dasgupta
Editor : Ujjal Nandi
Produced by : Doordorshan
Script and Direction : Buddhadeb Dasgupta
Cast includes : Anjan Dutt, Srila Majumder, Labanyamoy Bhaduri, Pritam Mukhopadhyay, Pradip Saha, Chanchal Gose, Pradip Sen, Dulal Roy, Kajal Chakraborty, Uttam Guha, Raja Sen, Nirmalya Sengupta, Mukul Chattopadhyay, Arun Guha Thakurta, Ramanath Naskar.

***Andhi Gali* ('Blind Alley')**
1984, Hindi, Colour, 140 mins.
Based on a story by Dibyendu Palit

Photography : Kamal Nayak
Music : Buddhadeb Dasgupta
Editor : Ujjal Nandi
Produced by : K. Bikram Singh
Script and Direction : Buddhadeb Dasgupta

Cast includes: Kulbhushan Kharbanda, Deepti Naval, M.K. Raina, K.K. Raina, Shyamanand Jalan, Satya Banerjee, Mahesh Bhatt, Anil Chatterjee.

Phera ('The Return')

1986, Bengali, Colour, 90 mins.
Based on a story by Narendranath Mitra

Photography: Dhrubajyoti Bose
Music: Jyotishka Dasgupta
Editor: Ujjal Nandi
Produced by: Buddhadeb Dasgupta
Script and Direction: Buddhadeb Dasgupta
Cast includes: Subrata Nandy, Alokananda Dutta, Aniket Sengupta, Sunil Mukhopadhyay, Chanda Dutta, Debika Mukherjee, Biplab Chatterjee, Kamu Mukherjee, Samit Bhanja.

Bagh Bahadur ('The Tiger Man')

1989, Hindi, Colour, 90 mins.
Based on a story by Prafulla Roy

Photography: Venu
Music: Santanu Mahapatra
Editor: Ujjal Nandi
Produced by: Dulal Roy
Script and Direction: Buddhadeb Dasgupta
Cast includes: Pavan Malhotra, Archana, Vasudev Rao, Biplab Chatterjee, Rajeswari Roy Chowdhury, Masood Akhtar.

Tahader Katha ('Their Story')

1992, Bengali, Colour, 93 mins.
Based on a story by Kamalkumar Majumdar

Photography: Venu
Music: Bishwadeb Dasgupta
Editor: Ujjal Nandi
Produced by: National Film Development Corporation
Script and Direction: Buddhadeb Dasgupta

Cast includes: Mithun Chakraborty, Anasuya Majumdar, Dipankar Dey, Subrata Nandi, Ashok Mukhopadhyay, Bidisha Bhattacharya, Debarshi Chakraborty.

Charachar ('The Shelter of the Wings')

1993, Bengali, Colour, 90 mins.
Based on a story by Prafulla Roy

Photography: Soumendu Roy
Music: Bishwadeb Dasgupta
Editor: Ujjal Nandi
Produced by: Shankar Gope
Script and Direction: Buddhadeb Dasgupta
Cast includes: Rajit Kapoor, Labani Sarkar, Sadhu Meher, Indrani Haldar, Monoj Mitra, Shankar Chakraborty.

Lal Darja ('The Red Doors')

1996, Bengali, Colour, 100 mins.

Photography: Venu
Music: Bapi Lahiri
Art direction: Ashok Bose
Editor: Ujjal Nandi
Produced by: Chitrani Lahiri
Script and Direction: Buddhadeb Dasgupta
Cast includes: Champa, Shubhendu Chatterji, Asad, Indrani Haldar, Nandini Malia, Soma Chakraborty, Sadhana Roy Chowdhury, Payal Guha Thakurta, Haradhan Banerjee, Biplab Chatterjee, Barun Chanda, Sudip Majumdar.

Uttara ('The Wrestlers')

2000, Bengali, Colour, 95 mins.
Based on a short story by Samaresh Basu

Photography: Asim Bose
Music: Bishwadeb Dasgupta
Art direction: Ashok Bose
Editor: Rabi Ranjan Maitra

Produced by : Dulal Roy
Script and Direction : Buddhadeb Dasgupta
Cast includes : Jaya Seal, Tapas Pal, Shankar Chakraborty, Asad, Tapas Adhikari, Saurav Das, Gautam Warshi, Masud Akhtar, Subrata Dutta.

Manda Meyer Upakhyan ('A Tale of a Naughty Girl')
2002, Bengali, Colour, 90 mins.
Based on a short story by Prafulla Roy

Photography : Venu
Music : Bishwadeb Dasgupta
Art direction : Kaushik Sarkar
Editor : Rabiranjan Maitra
Produced by : Arya Bhattacharya
Script and Direction : Buddhadeb Dasgupta
Cast includes : Samata Das, Rituparna Sengupta, Arpan Basar, Ramgopal Bajaj, Pradeep Mukherjee, June Malia, Sudipta Chakraborty, Shreelekha Mitra.

Swapner Din ('Chased by a Dream')
2004, Bengali, Colour, 90 mins.

Photography : Venu
Music : Bishwadeb Dasgupta
Art direction : Satadal Mitra
Editor : Rabiranjan Maitra
Sound : Aloke De
Produced by : Jhamu Sughand Productions
Story, Screenplay and Direction : Buddhadeb Dasgupta
Cast includes : Prasenjit, Rima Sen, Rajesh Sharma, Raima Sen.

Bibliography

Writings of Buddhadeb Dasgupta

Poetry

Gabhir Ariel ('Deep Ariel'), 1963
Kaphin kingba Sutkes ('A Coffin or a Suitcase'), 1972
Hinyug ('Ice Age'), 1977
Chhatakahini ('Stories of Umbrellas'), 1982
Roboter Gaan ('Robot Songs'), 1985
Shrestha Kabita ('Selected Poems'), 1990
Bhambaler Ashcharya Kahini o Anyanya Kabita ('The Amazing Story of Bhambal and Other Poems'), 1993
Love and Other Forms of Death: The Poems of Buddhadeb Dasgupta, 1997.

Novels

Nikhiler Beche Thaka ('The Way Nikhil Lives'), 1994
America, America, 1995
Rahasyamay ('Mysterious'), 1996
Yasiner Ashcharya Kahini ('The Strange Story of Yasin'), 1996

Essays

Swapna, Samay o Sinema ('Dreams, Time and Cinema'), 1993